TAKEN BY STORM

CONTENTS

Taken by Storm

RANDALL J.
BREWER

INTRODUCTION

F aith is not merely a concept to be admired; it is a life to be lived, a journey to be walked, and a fight to be won. From the moment a believer says "yes" to Jesus Christ, he or she is enlisted into a spiritual journey that demands both courage and conviction. The Bible makes it clear that "the just shall live by faith" (Romans 1:17). Faith, therefore, is not an accessory to the Christian life; it *is* the very essence of it.

Yet faith is not a passive thing. It does not sit idly by, waiting for circumstances to change. True faith stands, speaks, acts, and endures. It is the firm assurance that what God has promised, He is also able to perform. It is the unseen anchor that holds us steady when the winds of doubt and fear beat violently against the soul. Faith is what turns ordinary believers into extraordinary warriors. It is what transforms trials into testimonies and obstacles into opportunities for God's glory to be revealed.

The Christian walk is both a pilgrimage and a battleground. On one hand, we are called to "walk by faith and not by sight" (2 Corinthians 5:7)—to trust in God's leading even when the path ahead is dark or uncertain. On the other hand, we are commanded to "fight the good fight of faith" (1 Timothy 6:12)—to resist the forces of unbelief, temptation, and discouragement that seek to pull us off course. To walk in faith requires intimacy with God; to fight the good fight requires perseverance and spiritual strength. Together, these two dimensions—*walk-*

ing and *fighting*—form the heartbeat of the victorious Christian life.

This book is written to help you understand and master both. It will teach you how to walk in faith when life doesn't make sense, and how to fight in faith when everything seems to be against you. You will learn that faith is not an emotion, nor is it blind optimism. Faith is rooted in the unshakable character of God. It is born from His Word, nurtured through obedience, and strengthened in adversity. The trials that come against you are not meant to destroy your faith, but to refine it—proving its authenticity and producing perseverance in you.

Every believer will face moments when faith feels tested beyond measure. There will be times when you must choose to believe God even when every natural sign points in the opposite direction. You will have to walk by faith when you cannot yet see the fulfillment of God's promises. You will have to fight the good fight of faith when the enemy whispers lies, when the flesh grows weak, and when circumstances appear impossible. It is in those moments that faith becomes your greatest weapon and your deepest treasure.

The Apostle Paul understood this well. Near the end of his life, he declared, "I have fought the good fight, I have finished the race, I have kept the faith" (2 Timothy 4:7). Notice that faith was not just something Paul *believed in*; it was something he *kept*. He guarded it like a precious jewel, because he knew that faith was the currency of heaven and the key to victory in every spiritual battle. You cannot finish the race of life successfully without faith, and you cannot win the battles of life apart from it. Faith is both your compass and your sword—your direction and your defense.

Walking in faith means living each day with an unwavering confidence that God's Word is true, no matter what you see or feel. It means stepping out when God calls, even if the water beneath your feet has not yet solidified. It means choosing to trust God's promises rather than your own understanding. The fight of faith, on the other hand, is the daily warfare that takes place in the heart and mind of every believer—the battle to stay in faith when fear and doubt press in. It is the fight to keep believing, keep standing, and keep speaking God's Word until the victory manifests.

Throughout this book, we will explore how to build unshakable faith that endures every storm, how to guard your heart from unbelief, and how to use the Word of God as your spiritual weapon. You will learn how to resist the enemy, how to persevere through trials, and how to see the unseen hand of God moving in your life.

Faith is not just about believing for miracles; it is about trusting the Miracle Worker. It is not about having confidence in yourself; it is about having confidence in the God who cannot fail. The faith life is not an escape from hardship—it is the power to overcome hardship. It is not the absence of struggle—it is the strength to stand in the struggle and come out victorious. As you read, may your faith be stirred, your spirit strengthened, and your confidence in God renewed.

Because when you learn to walk in faith, you will discover peace in every storm. And when you learn to fight the good fight of faith, you will learn what it means to live in triumph—no matter what comes your way. Faith is not for the faint of heart, but for those who dare to believe that with God, all things are possible.

So let this be your declaration: *I will walk by faith. I will fight the good fight. I will not quit, I will not retreat, and I will not be moved. My faith is in the One who never fails.*

Welcome to the journey—and to the battle—of faith.

| 1 |

"THE MEASURE OF FAITH"

Faith is the most important subject in all of scripture. It is a spiritual force given to you by God when you got born again. You are saved by faith and you are to live by faith (Rom. 1:17). The Christian life is a walk of faith and Gal. 6:10 says that all believers "are of the household of faith." Faith is a journey and not a destination. It is a lifestyle that began in eternity past and will continue through the present age and into the eternal future. The Greek word for faith is "pistas" and it means to have 'a firm persuasion or a conviction based on hearing.' Faith is the conviction of the reality of things not seen and is the title deed to all the promises of God recorded in His Word (Heb. 11:1). Faith calls those things that be not as though they were (Rom. 4:17) and continues to call them until they are. Faith is a "knowing that you know" and says "It is finished" before it sees the manifestation. Faith is the evidence of things not seen and has the same value as the thing hoped for and desired.

Faith stands in the place of the things you're believing for until it is manifested. Until then your faith is the only evidence you have. If other evidence is needed besides the Word of God then it's not faith. Faith is the substance of things hoped for. It's the spiritual energy needed to bring the promise into manifestation. Faith is not blind, it always sees through the storm. It always sees the end result. Paul said "the things which are seen are temporary, but the things which are not seen are eternal" (2 Cor. 4:18). God's method is to take eternal forces and change things that are temporal. That is good news because all evil is temporary. There is no such thing as an eternal evil. Faith is the ability to conceive into the human spirit what God has promised and then acting on it. It's a spiritual conception and it comes when you hear yourself speak the Word of God. Problems come to everybody but God has given you a measure of faith as a way to walk victorious through the trials of life. God is a faith God and it takes faith to please Him (Heb. 11:6).

Faith in action is God's personality in manifestation. Heb. 1:3 says Jesus is "the brightness of His glory and the express image of His person." The word "person" in this verse is the same Greek word for "substance" in Heb. 11:1, "Now faith is the substance of things hoped for, the evidence of things not seen." Jesus, who is the Word manifested in the flesh, is the exact expression of God's substance. He said, "If you've seen me, you've seen the Father" (John 14:9). Words are expressions of thoughts and desires so God's Word is the express image of His person and substance. Heb. 11:1 can therefore be rendered, "Now faith is the person of things hoped for, the personification of things not seen." Everything God has ever done was done by faith and so it is to be with you. Faith is the currency of the kingdom of heaven and it comes by hearing the anointed

Word of God and is released with words and actions. Faith is how you function and operate in the kingdom of God and if you ignore faith you do so at your own loss and harm.

Rom. 12:3 says, "For I say, through the grace given to me, to everyone who is among you, not to think of himself more highly than he ought to think, but to think soberly as God has dealt to each one a measure of faith." The NLT says, "Be honest in your evaluation of yourselves, measuring yourselves by the faith God has given us." Your estimation of yourself should be connected to your faith. God didn't say not to think highly of yourself. He said don't think more highly than what's true. You are to have a sober and realistic assessment of who you are and what your value is in life according to your measure of faith. Pride is not believing good things about yourself for even Paul said in Philemon 6, "that the sharing of your faith may become effective by the acknowledgement of every good thing which is in you in Christ Jesus." Pride is believing lies about yourself. It's when you take credit for something God did. James 1:17 says, "Every good gift and every perfect gift is from above, and comes down from the Father of lights."

People who walk in faith act and talk a certain way. They respond to the trials in life that are different from others. Victory resides on the inside of them and it radiates out of them. They are overcomers and more than conquerors through the Greater One who lives inside of them. They act like it and talk like it. They don't give place to the devil by wearing all their problems on their sleeves. They don't walk around telling others what's wrong in their life. No, they glorify God and openly confess how good He is and how He supplies all their need according to His riches in glory by Christ Jesus (Phil. 4:19). They tell how He is able to do exceedingly, abundantly above all they could ask or think (Eph. 3:20). Those who walk in faith are "strong in the Lord, and in the power of His might" (Eph. 6:10). This is a rest and a ceasing from your own labor. Faith is a rest which means you don't have to be strong enough to deal with all of life's problems in your own strength and might. You are not strong in yourself but in the Lord and His might.

With your measure of faith you are to "put on the whole armor of God, that you may be able to stand against the wiles of the devil" (Eph. 6:11). You don't fight against the symptoms of sickness, poverty, and what other people say about you. No, you fight against the subtlety and craftiness of the devil. You resist and stand against the trickery and strategies of the evil one in his attempt to get you to fear and doubt. When you fight the pain and discomfort, and all the negative reports, you are fighting the wrong thing and it will wear you out and make you vulnerable to other attacks. The Lord never told you to fight these things. To walk in faith is to be not moved by all that but rather to fight against the temptation to grow weary and faint. Having symptoms is the devil's way of distracting you from the real battle. He is pleased when you spend all your time rebuking the pain in your body instead of calling those things that be not as though they were.

Rebuking pain all day puts it front and center in your mind and you can't fight the good fight of faith if you've got "pain on the brain." When you fight the symptoms you are fighting a losing battle. You are fighting in the flesh and not in the spirit. The challenge is to not pay any attention to the pain and to resist any thought of fear that you may not finish your course. By rebuking the pain you are in essence trying to obtain with human effort what Jesus already bought and paid for on the cross. You are trying to get what you already have. The devil knows this and he is laughing in your face when you waste your time and energy rebuking pain all day. He is sly and cunning and when the pain doesn't go away he'll whisper in your ear that this pain is your own personal cross that you have to carry all the days of your life. Don't listen to him. The fight is not in the arena of reasoning but in the arena of faith. If you will fight where the battle is supposed to be fought then the devil doesn't stand a chance. You will have victory every time.

Jesus took your pain and carried your diseases (Is. 53:4) and you've got to stop fighting the symptoms. Use your weaponry against the crafty wiles of the enemy. Rom. 4:17 says God "gives life to the dead and calls those things which do not exist as though they did." Don't go around saying "I have no pain" but instead say "I am healed." What some people call faith, God calls lying. To say you're not sick when you are sick is a lie. But to say you are healed when the symptoms are still there is faith in action. When you say "I am healed" you are calling those things that do not exist as though they did and are operating in the God-kind of faith. This is what happened when God called Abraham "the father of many nations" when he and Sarah were still childless. This is what is meant in Joel 3;10 which says, "Let the weak say 'I am strong.'" You call those things that be not as though they were because "faith comes by hearing, and hearing by the word of God" (Rom. 10:17).

Faith can be discerned and is measurable in each individual. What you receive and how much you receive is based solely on the measure of your faith. If you're not believing for or receiving the big things of life it's because the measure of your faith is not at that level yet. Many people pray and confess for big things when all they have is little faith. When they don't get what they want they turn around and blame God and say the faith message doesn't work. They are disillusioned because faith always works. Jesus said, "Be it unto you according to your faith," not according to faith you don't currently have. There is no such thing as faith failures. Faith is evident because it works every time so if people don't get what they think they're believing for then it wasn't real faith. God and His Word do not fail. He is faithful to His people and is forever ready to perform His Word. Abraham never wavered in believing God's promise. Rom. 4:21 (NLT) says, "He was fully convinced that God is able to do whatever he promises."

To grow in faith you need a deeper and greater reverence for the things of God. Jesus said in Matt. 7:6, "Do not give what is holy to the dogs; nor cast your pearls before swine, lest they trample them under their feet, and turn and tear you in pieces." You can't give precious things to people who don't value them. In order to get greater things from the Lord, your reverence and respect for Him and the things of God has to come up to a higher level. Heb. 2:1 says, "Therefore we must give the more earnest heed to the things we have heard, lest we drift away."

The degree of the respect and reverence you give to the Word of God is the degree to which the anointing and revelation will flow, thus allowing your faith to grow to a higher measure. Job 23;12 says, "I have treasured the words of His mouth more than my necessary food." Jer. 15:16 says, "Your words were found and I ate them, and Your word was to me the joy and rejoicing of my heart." When the Word is precious to you, you will learn more and grow more and receive more.

God is a faith God and you need to be as interested in faith as He is. Faith is not knowledge nor is it desire. Wanting something and needing something is not faith, and neither is knowing what's in the Bible from cover to cover. Faith is real and is developed through nourishment and exercise. When you feed on the anointed Word, you are nourished in the word of faith. You need to read and meditate on the Word of God morning, noon, and night. Jesus said, "With the same measure you use, it will be measured back to you" (Matt. 7:2). You must also exercise your faith. You must use your faith and walk in it daily. The just shall live by faith (Heb. 10:38) and only by exercising it will you begin to develop your faith and grow stronger in it. Paul said in 2 Thess. 1:3, "We are bound to thank God always for you, brethren, as it is fitting, because your faith grows exceedingly, and the love of every one of you abounds toward one another." Faith can grow. It is tangible and on any given day it can be at a different level than it was the day before.

Your faith is growing and your love is abounding. That means you're not sitting still and you're not losing ground. As you consistently exercise your faith day after day, year after year, what was once hard and almost impossible for you to believe for now becomes easy. Your measure of faith is now at a high level where you are well able to believe for the bigger and better things in life. Great faith turns the impossible into the possible. Nothing can hold you back and no devil and no man can stop you from accomplishing what you set out to do. Faith never fails and always does the work you call for it to do. Knowing how to live a victorious life is not a great mystery. You've got to walk in faith every day of your life. If you're sad and complain all the time you are not walking in faith but rather are yielding to unbelief. Faith rejoices and gives thinks and is glad every waking moment. Job 5:22 says, "You shall laugh at destruction and famine, and you shall not be afraid of the beasts of the field."

Faith is the way. Always has been, always will be. You laugh because you walk by faith and not by sight. You look not at that which is seen but at the eternal things that are unseen. You are believing for something that is different from what you're seeing and experiencing. You don't talk about what you see, you talk about what you believe. If you'll believe in your heart and doubt not, you will have what you say (Mark 11:23). Walking in faith is the most powerful thing you can do to change your life and your circumstances around. When you laugh at the devil and resist him, he will flee from you. You don't get more faith by asking for more faith. God will increase what you have when you start using what He's already given you. Be faithful with what you have for he who is faithful over a little will be made ruler over much (Matt. 25:21). When you use the faith, you already have, God will add another measure to you, and then another, and another, and in time you will be well developed and will walk in great faith.

Faith is measurable from one individual to another. Jesus talked about people who had little faith and people who had great faith and those who had no faith. The proportion and measure of your faith determines the limits of your ministry. No power is manifested until the faith you have is acted upon. You need to get out of the boat and take a step of faith. The enemy is afraid of the power of God. He fears it. No demon ever wants to tangle with the power of God. The devil did not tempt Jesus until after the anointing power came on Him at His baptism. He knew that if the Lord's anointing ever got released that his yoke of bondage on people would be broken forever. Strongholds that took generations to be put in place would be destroyed in an instant of time. This power is released by faith and this is why your faith is the number one target of the enemy. He tries to get you to doubt and fear for this is what causes your faith to be null and void.

The point where you begin to fear is how you measure how much faith you have. If little things scare you, you have little faith. If nothing scares you, you have great faith. Fear is everywhere and you need to train yourself to discern fear so that you won't fall prey to its deadly snare. When you yield to fear any power that was manifested in your life because of faith stops. Peter walked on the water until he feared the wind and the waves. His faith got measured at that moment and because of the fear he began to sink. You need to cut off everything in your life that causes fear, be it the news or the people you associate with. You need to starve your fear and feed your faith. Don't talk about your problems, talk about the solution instead. Talk about the goodness of God and how He always leads you in triumph in Christ Jesus. Before long, your faith will grow and as you step out the power will be manifested in your life. You are stronger now and you'll go farther than you did before. Great is your faith for there is nothing you fear.

Paul wrote in 1 Cor. 2:4,5, "And my speech and my preaching were not with persuasive words of human wisdom, but in demonstration of the Spirit and of power, that your faith should not be in the wisdom of men but in the power of God." The Message Bible says "your life of faith is a response to God's power." Heb. 6:5 talks about those who "have tasted the good word of God and the powers of the age to come." This same power is going forth and happening right now. You can taste and experience today the powers of the world to come. Faith is eternal and the way you'll operate in faith in heaven is how you should walk in faith in the here and now. Jesus walking on the water and passing through walls is a foretaste of the powers to come. It supersedes and goes beyond the laws of science that govern the world in which we now live. Not only are you to hunger and thirst for righteousness but you are to also crave and hunger for the power that goes along with the good word of God and the operation of your faith.

Ps. 34:8 says, "Oh, taste and see that the Lord is good; Blessed is the man who trusts in Him!" God's Word is good and His power is good also. You don't want to have a form of godliness that has no power (2 Tim. 3:5). You want what Jesus had when He walked the earth. You want the power that was displayed at the beginning of the church age. Acts 8:39,40 tells how Philip was preaching one moment and the next moment he was translated to another city. A similar thing happened in John 6:21. Jesus walked on the water out to His disciples in the middle of the sea and after telling them to not be afraid the verse says, "Then they willingly received Him into the boat, and immediately the boat was at the land where they were going." They were supernaturally transported to the other shore. This is not science fiction. This is the power of the world to come. One moment you're here, the next moment you're somewhere else.

People getting miraculously healed and raised from the dead are demonstrations of the powers of the world to come. Peter walked by people and his shadow caused people to get healed. Acts 19:11,12 says, "Now God worked unusual miracles by the hands of Paul, so that even handkerchiefs or aprons were brought from his body to the sick, and the diseases left them and the evil spirits went out of them." These stories are in the Bible and their reality cannot be denied. These same types of manifestations should be happening in the church today. Jesus operated in this power because He was filled with the Holy Spirit and anointed to do so (Acts 10:38). He did this as a man and not as God. God does not have to be anointed. He is the anointing. Everything He does and says is anointed. Jesus lived and functioned as a man to be your example and to show you how you are supposed to live. He always walked in faith and He flowed in the powers of the world to come.

These miracles didn't stop happening when Jesus went back to heaven. Rom. 8:29 says, "For whom He foreknew, He also predestined to be conformed to the image of His son, that He might be the firstborn among many brethren." The Holy Spirit is still here today and so is the power to walk on water, heal the sick, and raise the dead. The power is available for you to speak to a raging storm and say, "Peace, be still" and it will obey you. You are anointed by God (2 Cor. 1:21) and you can speak to a fever, cancer, diabetes and any other sickness and it will obey your command. You have the power to confess the things that be not as though they were. With faith the impossible becomes the possible. The power of God is real and it is manifested in you and on you and through you when you use your faith to please Him. Faith is used to show that you are available to be used for His purposes and glory. Isaiah said, "Here I am. Send me" (Is. 6:8). You say the same thing when you walk in faith.

Faith comes by hearing the anointed Word of God and is released by action. Before Jesus turned water into wine His mother told the servants, "Whatever He says to you, do it" (John 2:5). Jesus told Peter "Come" and he got out of the boat and began to walk on the water. Notice there is an order here. First God speaks, then you respond with action. People who are passive hear the Word but don't act on it or else they walk in presumption and act before they hear from God. Both are wrong and this is why you need to be led by the Spirit daily so you'll know what to do. Many people learn the principles of faith in their head but fail to grasp the spirit of faith in their heart. You must have a living relationship with the one, true God and faith begins when you hear Him speaking to you personally. Open your heart and your mind and ask God to reveal to you His perfect will for your life. Ask Him to show you what steps of faith you are to take and then do what He tells you to do.

God knows where your faith is and the Holy Spirit will lead you based on where you're now at. Your faith can grow and your faith will grow but never despise the day of small beginnings. Job 8:7 says, "Though your beginning was small, yet your latter end would increase abundantly." If you don't start where you're now at, you will stay at the level you're currently at. People who are passive are waiting all the time and never get out of the boat. You've got to do something! Faith needs actions to grow, actions based solely on what God specifically told you to do. Don't give away your car because God told somebody else to. Only do what God tells you to do. Keep feeding your faith, take corresponding actions, enjoy your life in the process, and before you know it your faith has grown to the next level. You are an earthen vessel, a clay pot, but inside of you is something amazing. Inside of you is the power of God that gets activated when you walk in faith. Faith is the fuse that sets off the power.

Growing in faith is not a hundred yard dash, it's a marathon. It took years for Abraham to get to the level where he had enough faith to sacrifice his son on the altar believing God would resurrect him from the dead. It didn't happen overnight so don't despise taking small steps of faith. In time Abraham was called "the father of our faith" and became an example to all who desire to walk by faith. What worked for Abraham will work for you and this is why you should "contend earnestly for the faith which was once for all delivered to the saints" (Jude 3). Do not be tricked by the wiles of the devil. He is a liar and a deceiver and he will try to tell you that faith doesn't work and that God is to blame for all the hurt and pain you're going through. Don't listen to him. Not only is he the accuser of the brethren (Rev. 12:10), he is also the accuser of God. He is looking for every opportunity to get you to question the goodness and faithfulness of God. Never for one moment entertain any thought that says God is not a good God.

Mary told the servants, "Whatever He says to you, do it." This is the key to miracles. This is so simple yet so powerful. A three year old can understand it. People get disillusioned about faith and how it works and it's not because it's hard to understand. The problem is that the enemy is putting darkness between them and the revelation of God's Word and their eyes are blinded to what's being said. There is resistance to light in this earthly realm and this is why you always have to be persistent and never back away and quit. Keep reading the Bible over and over again and eventually divine revelation will come. When it does come you will scratch your head in wonderment for you can now see how simple and profound the Word of God actually is. 2 Cor. 4:6,7 says, "For it is the God who commanded light to shine out of darkness who has shone in our hearts to give the light of the knowledge of the glory of God in the face of Jesus Christ. But we have this treasure in earthen vessels, that the excellence of the power may be of God and not of us."

You can't be passive when it comes to faith. You must get out of the boat and start taking steps of faith. Ps. 37:23 says, "The steps of a good man are ordered by the Lord, and He delights in his way." People get in trouble when they don't acknowledge the steps God is telling them to take. They think it's enough to pray and confess scriptures all day but a parked car never went anywhere. Their eyes are so focused on the final destination that they lose sight of the steps they have to take to get there. Some steps will be so small and so natural that if you don't pay attention to what God is saying you'll ignore them. Don't get in pride and think that these small steps are too insignificant for you to take. Understand that small steps of faith lead to the big things of God. David killed the lion and the bear before he killed Goliath. If the truth be told, most people don't have the faith for the things they're believing for. They're believing for big things with little or no faith and when they don't receive what they want they get mad and frustrated at God.

God knows what you should do better than you so listen to Him and seek His counsel. Prov. 3:5,6 says, "Trust in the Lord with all your heart and lean not on your own understanding. In all your ways acknowledge Him, and He will direct your paths." David said in Ps. 23:3, "He leads me in the paths of righteousness for His name's sake." Obey God and do what He tells you to do. You walk by faith and this means you take one step at a time. To reach your final destination you must trust God to lead you with every step you take. Abraham left his family not knowing where he was going but had faith that God would lead and guide him as he went. Turn your brain off and with laser sharpness listen for that still, small voice down on the inside of you. You are hearing from God and the voice of a stranger you will not follow (John 10:5). Trust God and believe he will get you to your final destination. Just as a puzzle gets put together one piece at a time, so do journeys of faith get fulfilled one step at a time.

Unless the Lord tells you to do something you will never have the faith to do it. You've got to humble yourself like Jesus and acknowledge you can do nothing without the Father. Don't get in pride and decide for yourself what you want to believe for. This is what the devil did just before he fell from grace and was cast out of heaven. He wanted what he wanted with no regard for the will of the Father. Presumption is when you try to believe for something God didn't tell you to believe for (Deut. 18:20). It's when you step outside the boundaries of faith and take liberties for yourself that are not given. People who do this are walking in unwarranted boldness and confidence that has no foundation. Always seek God's will and be totally dependent on Him. Don't do anything or believe for anything until you first hear from Him. No matter how bold you may be, and how many verses you confess, if the Lord did not speak to you there will be no power in what you try to do.

Faith grows when you continually do what God tells you to do. Faith that is true and authentic will catapult you to the higher things of God. There is so much more available to you than you've ever seen or known. You were not created to live small. You serve a big God and it is not His will for you to have small dreams and set little goals. You were created to live an abundant, wholesome life where each day is better than the day before. God is a God of increase and He has something bigger and better planned for your life than what you're experiencing today. Never say where you're at today is as good as it's ever going to get. Limited thinking will cause you to live a limited life. Your life is full of possibilities so start thinking bigger, living bigger, and expecting bigger. You have been dealt from God a measure of faith and it's your responsibility to exercise and use the faith you've been given. Your faith can grow exceedingly and, the greater your faith, the greater the grace will be poured out and manifested in your life.

God has a big life planned for you. When His plans become your plans, He will amaze you with the things He will do for your life. He wants to take you to places you've never been and show you things you've never seen. Your destiny is calling out to you. There are new horizons to explore, bigger mountains to climb. There is a wide, spacious life prepared for you. Enlarge your vision because God's plan for your life will supersede anything you've ever imagined before. Faith believes and then gets ready to receive. Little faith gets ready for little things to happen and big faith gets ready for big things. What are you getting ready for? What are you stirred up and excited about? You have a measure of faith and daily that faith can get bigger and stronger. Jesus said "according to your faith be it done unto you." Not a day goes by where God is not ready and willing to do something good for you. Ps. 68:19 says He is the God "who daily loads us with benefits." The question is, are you getting ready to receive what He is willing to give?

| 2 |

"THE AUTHENTICITY OF FAITH"

The apostle Paul knew that his days on planet earth were quickly drawing to a close and one day he sat down and penned his final epistle to his young associate, Timothy. Timothy became a convert of Paul when the apostle was in Lystra on his first missionary journey. He later was ordained to the ministry and served as a devoted companion and assistant to Paul in several of his travels. He often dealt with frequent infirmities, was timid and youthful, but still he was a gifted teacher who was trustworthy and diligent. During Paul's third missionary journey Timothy labored with him in Ephesus, Macedonia, and Corinth. Paul later left him in Ephesus to supervise the work there and to become the pastor of the church that gathered within its' borders.

This was not an easy assignment for the young man and when Paul wrote his two final letters to him, he sought to exhort and encourage Timothy in his efforts to solidify the Ephesian church. Paul wrote to challenge Timothy to fulfill the task before him and to combat false teachings with sound doctrine. What Paul had learned so thoroughly himself he was now passing on as he endeavored to show Timothy how to develop a leadership style that would be a benefit to him and the local church. Paul's final letter before his death is really a combat manual for spiritual warfare and as he was about to relinquish his heavy burdens the godly apostle labored to challenge and strengthen his faithful friend.

After much prayer and careful pondering the apostle Paul sat down to pen his final words and as the anointing flowed through his fingertips he began to write, "Paul, an apostle of Jesus Christ by the will of God, according to the promise of life which is in Christ Jesus. To Timothy, my beloved son: Grace, mercy, and peace from God the Father and Christ Jesus our Lord. I thank God, whom I serve with a pure conscience, as my forefathers did, as without ceasing I remember you in my prayers night and day, greatly desiring to see you, being mindful of your tears, that I may be filled with joy, when I call to remembrance the genuine faith that is in you, which dwelt first in your grandmother Lois and your mother Eunice, and I am convinced is in you also" (2 Tim. 1:1-5).

It was no accident that at the beginning of his final epistle that the foremost thought in the mind of Paul was the genuine faith of his young protege. The Message Bible translation calls it "your honest faith - and what a rich faith it is." It stands to reason that if there is a true, genuine faith then there must also be a pretend faith, a faith that is false and does not bring into manifestation that which one is believing for. It is the responsibility of all believers to thoroughly study the subject of faith and find out for themselves if they truly are walking in faith. This is what Paul told the Corinthian church to do in 2 Cor. 13:5, "Examine yourselves as to whether you are in the faith." The Message Bible states, "Test yourselves to make sure you are solid in the faith. Don't drift along taking everything for granted. Give yourself regular checkups."

As divine truths radiate off the pages of God's Word it will be revealed that the major difference between a true faith and a false faith is that a genuine faith always gets results. There are no faith failures and a true faith gets results every time. If your faith fails then it wasn't a true, genuine faith. The Bible teaches us that an authentic faith is a "hearing" faith. Faith does not exist unless there is a message to be heard and believed. Paul told the church in Rome, "But they have not all obeyed the gospel. For Isaiah says, 'Lord, who has believed our report?' So then faith comes by hearing, and hearing by the Word of God' (Rom. 10:16,17). The Message Bible says, "before you trust, you have to listen." The message to be believed comes by the Word of God and is sent by the command of God. It is His Word, sent by His direction, and if heard attentively a genuine faith will be produced.

There are different ways to hear from God. The Holy Bible is God's voice speaking to you in written form. Too many people, unfortunately, teach that this is the only way to hear from God without mentioning how to hear God's voice inside of you. Many answers to the trials we face are not found in scripture but only come as we become more sensitive to God's still, small voice spoken in our heart. David always inquired of the Lord and when by faith he obeyed the Lord's command the victory was won. Even Jesus said He only did and spoke what He was told by the Father and this is why He had great faith. Your faith will never rise above your ability to hear from God. Begin to be still before Him and listen to the voice of God and become more sensitive to the leading of His Spirit directing you what to have faith for.

Faith failures happen when people step out of the realm of hearing from God and attempt to believe for something at their own discretion. They go to the funeral home and try to raise their grandmother from the dead when God didn't tell them to. Their ignorance will cause the things of God to appear foolish and will bring confusion and reproach to those who witness their ill-advised behavior. A mockery is made unto God and later less effort will be made by those who are not saved to draw close unto God for themselves. Miracles start with hearing from God and a person desirous to have a genuine faith should never believe for things on their own. Real faith is not based on need or desire but on the solid foundation of hearing from God. Once you know you've heard from Him you can then be bold and have the confident expectation that you will see the results you were believing for.

The result of hearing from God is that you will know God and when you know God you will experience God. Never trust a person you don't know. When Paul mentioned the faith of Timothy's mother and grandmother, he was saying it's important who you associate with. He even wrote in 1 Cor. 11:1, "Imitate me, just as I also imitate Christ." You become like the people you hang around so spend quality time with those who will feed you the Word of God and help you come to know Him in a more deep, personal way. Faith comes as a result of knowing Him and is not based on what you heard about Him. Abraham knew that a genuine faith is a "knowing" faith and for this reason he staggered not at the promise of God. He knew God in such a personal way that he was called the friend of God and this is why he was "fully convinced that what He had promised He was also able to perform" (Rom. 4:21).

Having a genuine faith is so important that God even made the stipulation that it's impossible to please Him without it (Heb. 11:6). So vital is the need for faith that God has even given Himself a name that reveals to us the value of this dynamic, spiritual force. In Heb. 3:1 Jesus is called "the Apostle and High Priest of our confession." An authentic faith a "speaking" faith and when we confess out loud what we believe it becomes the responsibility of our High Priest to bring it to pass. A person with an unfeigned faith is an artist who creates manifested realities with the power of his words. David boldly told Goliath that God would deliver him into his hands and moments later the giant lay dead. Not long before this happened Goliath also made a confession but his faith was not in God but in himself. Paul once said "I know Whom I believed" (2 Tim. 1:12) and this solidifies the fact that a speaking faith is based on how well you know God. David was a man after God's own heart whereas the god of the prideful giant was himself. The winner revealed to all Who the one, true God really was.

Ps. 116:10 says, "I believed, therefore I spoke." One of the greatest miracles recorded in scripture happened because a man believed and therefore spoke. Joshua and his army were fighting a battle and night time was fast approaching. More daylight was needed and we read in Josh. 10:12,13, "Then Joshua spoke to the Lord in the day when the Lord delivered up the Amorites before the children of Israel, and he said in the sight of Israel: 'Sun, stand still over Gibeon; and Moon, in the valley of Aijalon.' So the sun stood still, and the moon stopped, till the people had revenge upon their enemies." Pay close attention to what is said in vs. 14, "And there had been no day like that, before it or after it, that the Lord heeded the voice of a man; for the Lord fought for Israel." Faith is precious (2 Peter 1:1) and when you're in faith you can say what God will do. What Joshua said came to pass because the Lord heeded his voice. Joshua believed it, he said it, and God did it. This is how a true, genuine faith operates.

Everybody has the ability to believe and people should always be creating something with their words. Always strive to keep your mouth connected to your heart because in order for faith to work you have to believe what you hear yourself say. Still, a lot of people think they have faith when in reality they don't. Faith failures happen when people say things they don't really believe. Some people make a lot of noise to cover up for the faith that isn't there and this is when pride and arrogance enter in. Pride always wants to impress and for this reason some people foolishly try to raise the dead or believe for large sums of money before the sun goes down. Desire and want, mixed with confessing an abundance of empty words, is no sign that a person is walking in faith. Big talk is not a sign of big faith and the sooner these people put a muzzle over their mouths (Ps. 39:1) the better off they'll be.

A person should never say they're believing for something without knowing what they're basing their faith on. You must hear from God! If faith isn't there then you must hear, and hear, and hear some more. To help us know that we've actually heard from God we've been given a Helper and Comforter to indwell us, the Holy Spirit. 1 John 5:6a states, "And it is the Spirit Who bears witness, because the Spirit is truth." Once you believe in your heart and faith comes the Spirit will bear witness with your spirit (Rom. 8:16) that faith is there. You'll have a divine confirmation down on the inside of you that you've actually heard from God thus giving you a solid foundation on which to base your faith. This will prevent you from making vain confessions that is void of the power needed to bring to pass that which you say.

Always strive to be led by the witness of the Holy Spirit for this is where your confidence comes from. There is somebody on the inside of you besides yourself and He is forever ready to lead you and guide you as you travel down the path of life. 1 John 5:9 says, "If we receive the witness of men, the witness of God is greater." Look for the witness down on the inside of you and don't act until you know it's there. A supernatural "knowing" will rise up inside of you and you'll "know that you know" you are doing the right thing. The witness is not a voice so don't go off and start listening for voices. It's a "knowing" and with it comes a divine assurance that tells you you're in the perfect will of God. At the same time, don't ignore the lack of a witness. Many times, you can be led by what God doesn't say as much as by what He does say. If you don't have a witness to raise grandma from the dead, then by all means don't do it. The Holy Spirit bearing witness with your spirit is a sure way to prevent faith failures from happening in your life.

Just as there is natural and spiritual hearing, so also is there natural and spiritual seeing. Peter wrote in 2 Cor. 4:18, "While we do not look at the things which are seen, but at the things which are not seen. For the things which are seen are temporary, but the things which are not seen are eternal." The things that are seen is the unbiblical condition we are currently in and that which is not seen is the rich fulfillment of what we are believing for. As one continues to examine themselves, they will find that a genuine faith is a "seeing" faith. Walking in faith will give you the supernatural vision to look at things that are not seen and this is a major key to fighting the good fight of faith. Faith comes by hearing and when you hear it you will see it. A spiritual artist is somebody who used their words so well that they are able to paint pictures that can be seen with the eyes of faith.

God is one such artist. We read in Ps. 89:19, "Then You spoke in a vision to Your holy one." God speaks in visions because He wants His people to see what they're believing for. God told Abraham to look at the stars in the sky and the sand on the seashore and so shall his descendants be. God painted a picture for Abraham because he couldn't receive it by faith until he first saw it. Another time God told Abraham to look to the north, south, east, and west and all that he saw God would give him. Faith and vision go together and this is why Jesus spoke in parables when He taught the people. He said in Matt. 13:13, "Therefore I speak to them in parables, because seeing they do not see, and hearing they do not hear, nor do they understand." The people could not see or understand until Jesus painted a picture for them.

Prov. 29:18 says, "Where there is no revelation, the people cast off restraint..." Without a vision people run wild and perish and this is why you have to see in the spirit what you're believing for. This will cause your vision to become real to you and will give your faith the foundation it needs to stand on. David saw the giant beheaded and Joseph had his two God-given dreams telling him he would one day be in a position of authority. In the New Testament the woman with the issue of blood had a vision that if she touched the hem of Jesus' garment she would be healed. Her vision became the blueprint of what she wanted and her faith produced for her what she saw in the spirit. Likewise, you can have the assurance that God has committed Himself to respond to your faith in the same way. You can have bold confidence that what you see in the spirit you can have in the natural.

The reason it is so important to verbalize where you see your vision taking you is found in 2 Cor. 3:18, "But we all, with unveiled face, beholding as in a mirror the glory of the Lord, are being transformed into the same image from glory to glory..." What Paul is telling us is that you become what you behold. If you want victory in your life, then you must have a vision of

victory down on the inside of you. You must see yourself being more than a conqueror in Christ. Don't base tomorrow on
what you see today. Instead, look with spirit eyes into the unseen realm and speak out what you see. When you see your
future filled with the blessings of God the bad things you see
happening today won't matter anymore. You don't look at
what is seen but at those things that are unseen. Before you
build a house, you need a blueprint and a plan and this is what
your vision is. Your faith will do what your vision has pro-
grammed it to do. Your faith will produce what you see and
this is what it means that you become what you behold. You
will never rise above your vision and as your faith increases so
also will the size of your vision.

One person who understood this was Jacob. For fourteen long
years he had worked for his deceitful uncle Laban and the time
came when Jacob was ready to return to his homeland. But first
he wanted to be compensated for his many years of toil and
hard work. Given the choice to name his wages Jacob asked for
all the speckled and spotted goats and sheep as well as all the
brown lambs. Thinking only the pure white and unblemished
livestock was worth anything financially Laban heartily agreed.
Unbeknown to him Jacob had a vision that would cause him
to surpass all the wealth of his rich uncle. And along with that
blueprint was a genuine faith that would bring to pass the plan
he had down in his heart.

Hab. 2:2 tells us to "Write the vision and make it plain on
tablets that he may run who reads it." The Hebrew word for
"tablets" is 'billboards' and this Jacob must have had on his

mind as we read in Gen. 30:37-39, "Now Jacob took for himself rods of green poplar and of the almond and chestnut trees, peeled white strips in them, and exposed the white which was in the rods. And the rods which he had peeled, he set before the flocks in the gutters, in the watering troughs where the flocks came to drink, so that they should conceive when they came to drink. So, the flocks conceived before the rods, and the flocks brought forth streaked, speckled, and spotted." Jacob put up a series of spotted billboards and an image was planted in both the mind of Jacob and the minds of the animals. And it was this image, this faith imagination, that caused Jacob's faith to grow and eventually the flock became what they beheld. A herd of spotted livestock was produced causing Jacob to become very prosperous and this allowed him to return to his homeland.

Down in the hearts of all believers should be a God-given vision for which we are continually striving to fulfill. The Lord is forever faithful to reveal to each of us His specific plan and purpose for our individual lives. When He does it then becomes our responsibility to develop in our hearts a strong, genuine faith that has the power to defeat the enemy and cause our vision to come to pass. God gave Joshua a vision of victory over every obstacle and enemy and he was told to keep the Word in his mouth and meditate on it day and night (Josh. 1:1-8). This is the key to success for it reveals how to have a faith that is authentic. Paul wrote in 2 Cor. 5:7, "For we walk by faith, not by sight." The Message Bible says, "It's what we trust in but don't yet see that keeps us going." This is how the good fight of faith is fought and won. You trust in God and always keep going forward. Joshua had a genuine faith that caused him to never give up and brought him victory over all his enemies. His life proves that there are no faith failures when one has a faith that is true and genuine.

| 3 |

"THE PURSUIT OF FAITH"

P aul taught Timothy many valuable things in the two letters he wrote to his young and faithful friend just prior to his own death. Knowing the abundance of trials and persecutions that he himself had been through, Paul encouraged Timothy with these now famous words found in 1 Tim. 6:12, "Fight the good fight of faith, lay hold of eternal life, to which you were also called and have confessed the good confession in the presence of many witnesses." The Message Bible says it like this, "Run hard and fast in the faith. Seize the eternal life, the life you were called to, the life you so fervently embraced in the presence of so many witnesses." An abundance of books and teachings have been written on the subject of this verse and Christians everywhere should take heed to these important words from the great apostle Paul. However, equally important are the words in the verse written just prior to this one.

To prepare Timothy to fight the good fight of faith Paul listed the many sinful trappings he would one day encounter and then wrote in 1 Tim. 6:11, "But you, O man of God, flee these things and pursue righteousness, godliness, faith, love, patience, gentleness." A similar verse is written to Timothy in Paul's second letter to his young protégé. "Flee also youthful lusts; but pursue righteousness, faith, love, peace with those who call on the Lord out of a pure heart" (2 Tim. 2:22). How does one aim at and pursue faith? First, you must have a pure heart which comes as a result of pursuing righteousness and godliness. 1 Peter 3:11,12 says, "Let him turn away from evil and do good; Let him seek peace and pursue it. For the eyes of the Lord are on the righteous, and His ears are open to their prayers; But the face of the Lord is against those who do evil."

The Message Bible puts it this way, "Whoever wants to embrace life and see the day fill up with good, here's what you do: Say nothing evil or hurtful; Snub evil and cultivate good; run after peace for all you're worth. God looks on all this with approval, listening and responding well to what He's asked; But He turns His back on those who do evil things." It is a given truth that those who tolerate sin in their lives will not be successful in their walk of faith. Num. 15:30 (AMP) says, "But the person who does anything wrong willfully and openly shall be cut off from among the people that the atonement made for them may not include him." This verse precedes a story where God commanded a man to be stoned to death because he picked up a few sticks to build a fire on the Sabbath day. God hates sin - any sin, whether big or small - and so should you.

Sin separates, destroys, and is the author of death. Paul continually told Timothy to flee the youthful lusts and sinful snares of this world. 1 John 2:15 instructs us, "Do not love the world or the things in the world. If anyone loves the world, the love of the Father is not in him." A holy and just God cannot be expected to perform His Word (Jer. 1:12) for those where sin runs rampant in their lives. Ps.66:18 confirms this, "If I regard iniquity in my heart, the Lord will not hear." A blind man healed by Jesus testified, "Now we know that God does not hear sinners, but if anyone is a worshipper of God and does His will, He hears him" (John 9:31). Consider Prov. 15:29, "The Lord is far from the wicked, but He hears the prayer of the righteous." Our God is a just God but He is also a merciful God. A price that we could not pay had to be ransomed for sin and for that purpose the Heavenly Father sent His only begotten Son into the world. "For He made Him Who knew no sin to be sin for us, that we might become the righteousness of God in Him" (2 Cor. 5:21).

Called "the great exchange," Jesus became what we were so that we might become what He is. Because of what Jesus did we can consider ourselves to be "dead indeed to sin, but alive to God in Christ Jesus our Lord. Therefore, do not let sin reign in your mortal body, that you should obey it in its' lusts" (Rom. 6:11,12). Although the penalty for sin has been paid for nearly two thousand years, the temptation and opportunity to sin still exists. So, what must one do? The same thing Paul told Timothy to do. Flee from sin! 2 Tim. 2:19 says, "Let everyone who names the Name of Christ depart from iniquity." Paul told the Roman church to "Hate what is evil (loathe all ungodliness, turn in horror from wickedness), but hold fast to that which is good" (Rom. 12:9b AMP). When was the last time you turned in horror from sin and wickedness? Prov. 28:13 says, "He who covers his sin will not prosper, but whoever confesses and forsakes them will have mercy." God said through the prophet Isaiah, "Wash yourselves, make yourselves clean; Put away the evil of your doings from before My eyes. Cease to do evil" (Is. 1:16). We are told to flee and forsake all sin because in reality we are the ones responsible for the sin we do and not the devil.

James 1:14 (AMP) says, "But every person is tempted when he is drawn away, enticed and baited by his own evil desire (lust, passions)." To prevent this from happening James goes on to tell us, "Therefore submit to God. Resist the devil and he will flee from you. Draw near to God and He will draw near to you. Cleanse your hands, you sinners, and purify your hearts you double minded. Humble yourselves in the sight of the Lord and He will lift you up" (James 4:7,8,10). Did you notice that when you flee from sin the devil will flee from you? On the other hand, when you draw near to God, He will draw near to you. Both God and the devil will respond to whatever you choose to do. One draws near to God by drawing near to his Word, and it is His Word that will make your heart pure. Ps. 12:6 tells us, "The words of the Lord are pure words, like silver tried in a furnace of earth, purified seven times." Ps. 119:9 also says, "How can a young man cleanse his way? By taking heed according to Your Word."

Paul told the Ephesian church that we are cleansed and made pure by "the washing of water by the Word" (Eph. 5:26). Jesus Himself said, "You are already clean because of the word which I have spoken to you" (John 15:3). Wrong thoughts, words, and actions will keep you from Gods' Word but Gods' Word will keep you from having wrong thoughts, words, and actions. Ps. 119:11 says, "Your Word I have hidden in my heart that I might not sin against you." If you will make a quality decision to make the Word of God the "apple of your eye" and the desire of your heart, then the darkness of sin and its' fleshly desires will flee from the presence of the light of God's Word that is within you. Once the cancer of sin has been dealt with, you must also develop the proper motive for the pursuit of faith. There is a divine calling on the life of each born-again believer and faith is to be used for the fulfillment of that call. Performing and completing the will of God for your life should be your top priority and the driving force that propels you forward in life.

Paul wrote in Col. 4:17, "And say to Archippus, 'Take heed to the ministry which you have received in the Lord, that you may fulfill it.'" He told Timothy, "Do not neglect the gift which is in you, that special inward endowment which was directly imparted to you by the Holy Spirit" (1 Tim. 4:14 AMP). Notice what Paul says next, "Practice and cultivate and meditate upon these duties, throw yourself wholly into them (your ministry)" (1 Tim. 4:15 AMP). It will not take long to realize that those things which God calls us to do will be impossible to accomplish by mere human effort. Walls and barriers will arise before you in an effort to block your forward motion. But through each wall there is a door - the door of faith. It is of paramount importance that you understand that faith is not some "get rich" formula that you selfishly use for your own personal advancement. Instead, it is a tool to be used to bring forward into your lives those things which are necessary for the fulfillment and completion of that which God called you to do.

Col. 3:2 (AMP) instructs us to "set your minds and keep them set on what is above - the higher things - not on the things that are on the earth." Worldly and fleshly lusts will not bring you true contentment or satisfaction and that is why we must only seek those things with which we can serve God. The fourth chapter of James speaks of a lust people have for worldly things and a setting too high a value on worldly pleasures and friendships. James 4:3 (AMP) says, "Or you do ask God for them and yet fail to receive because you ask with wrong purpose and evil, selfish motives. Your intention is, when you get what you desire, to spend it in sensual pleasures." These people ask God to give them success in their undertakings not that they can glorify their Heavenly Father and do good with what they have but that they may consume it upon their own selfish lusts. They pray for a raise at work not so they can help support a foreign missionary but so they can buy a new set of golf clubs. God cannot and will not bless such selfish motives. Prov. 15:27 says, "He who is greedy for gain troubles his own house."

The matter of your prayer of faith must be agreeable with the declared will of God and you are not to petition Him for things with wrong intentions brought about by a covetous heart. God is not against you having and enjoying the luxuries of life as long as He has first place in your heart. This is why He said, "You shall have no other gods before Me" (Ex. 20:3). Jesus said, "But seek first the kingdom of God and His righteousness and all these things will be added unto you" (Matt. 6:33). When you put God and the advancement of His glorious kingdom first, then all the blessings of the Lord will be yours to richly enjoy. Paul said in 1 Tim. 6:17 (NIV), "Command those who are rich in this present world not to be arrogant nor to put their hope in wealth, which is so uncertain, but to put their hope in God, Who richly provides us with everything for our enjoyment." When your hope is in God and not money, then Prov. 10:22 can be applied to our lives, "The blessing of the Lord makes one rich, and He adds no sorrow with it."

David said in Ps. 37:4, "Delight yourself in the Lord, and He shall give you the desires of your heart." What God will do when your delight is in Him is bless you with enough money to support that foreign missionary with plenty left over to buy that set of golf clubs, What a loving and generous Heavenly Father we have! He is indeed a "rewarder of those who diligently seek Him" (Heb. 11:6). John 1:16(NIV) tells us, "From the fullness of His grace we have all received one blessing after another." God's will is always what's best for His children and the believer who is in continual fellowship with the Heavenly Father will not ask anything contrary to His will. It is with this attitude of giving God first place in your life that you can begin the pursuit of faith. One does not go from "a measure of faith" (Rom. 12:3) to "great faith" (Matt. 8:10) simply because they are a born-again believer. Once faith is planted in your heart at the new birth it must be pursued in order to grow. The word "pursue" means 'to follow in order to overtake; capture.' You must crave the increase of your faith with everything that is inside you because you will never possess what you're not willing to pursue.

Ps. 119:10 says, "With my whole heart I have sought You; Oh let me not wander from Your commandments." To pursue faith means to do whatever it takes to get the Word of God into your heart and back out your mouth. We are instructed in James 1:21 to receive the "implanted Word." Accomplishing this will take more than a simple glancing at or casual reading of a verse or two from time to time. It will take diligent effort to read, study, and meditate upon the Word on a consistent, daily basis. To do this you must develop within yourself the attitude of the prophet Jeremiah who said, "Your Words were found and I ate them, and Your Word was to me the joy and rejoicing of my heart" (Jer. 15:16). Compare this with Ezek. 3:1-3, "Moreover He said to me, 'Son of man, eat what you find; eat this scroll, and go, speak to the house of Israel.' So I opened my mouth, and He caused me to eat that scroll. And He said to me, 'Son of man, feed your belly and fill your stomach with the scroll that I give you.' So I ate it, and it was in my mouth like honey in sweetness."

Heb. 6:5 speaks of those who "have tasted the good Word of God." The more of God's Word you put into your "belly" the more your seed of faith will be watered thus causing it to grow. Feeding on the Word of God will bring joy to your heart as you put your trust in the Heavenly Father to bring the manifestation of all His promises into your life. Trusting God will bring you as much if not more joy and blessed fulfillment as you would get receiving from Him. There is an unsurpassed joy that comes on the journey of faith. This is a lesson David richly learned as evidenced in the words of Ps. 34:8, "Oh, taste and see that the Lord is good. Blessed is the man who trusts in Him." Prov. 2:1,4,5 says, "My son, if you will receive my words, and treasure my command within you, if you seek her as silver and search for her as for hidden treasure; then you will understand the fear of the Lord and find the knowledge of God." You will never experience an increase to your faith until you develop a strong passion for God's Word. The word "passion" is defined as 'intense, extreme, ardent affection for, strong desire, fanaticism.'

The reason so many Christians are not enjoying God's best is simply because they have not become a fanatic for the uncompromised Word of God. This is so vital because "faith comes by hearing and hearing by the Word of God" (Rom. 10:17). Luke 10:38-42 tells the story about a young woman who had a "passion" for Gods' Word. These verses tell about a time of refreshing Jesus spent in Bethany at the home of Lazarus and his sisters, Mary and Martha. This was not a home where Jesus was treated as a stranger but rather as a member of the family. It seems that Martha was the owner of the house and being the older sister was the dominate figure as well. While Martha busied herself with the distracting details of serving her guests, Mary instead chose to sit at the feet of Jesus in the recognized posture of a disciple and listened to every precious word that her Lord had to say. She had a "passion" for the Word and her actions depict the attitude of an eager learner not wanting one morsel of truth spoken from the lips of Jesus to slip past her.

Troubled by her sister's reluctance to help with the serving, Martha was filled with an inward anxiety thus causing an outward response. Without thinking she boldly and bluntly confronted Jesus and said, "'Lord, do You not care that my sister has left me to serve alone? Therefore, tell her to help me.' And

Jesus answered and said to her, 'Martha, Martha, you are worried and troubled about many things.'" Notice that worry and trouble always go together and that you can never worry about just one thing. It was not Martha's service that Jesus rebuked. Her preoccupation with the preparation of an elaborate meal for Jesus and His disciples was a praise worthy desire born out of a deep regard for her honored guest. What Jesus rebuked was her over occupation with the material side of her duties which caused her to have anxiety and a nervous distraction which eventually led to her jealous outburst of temper.

Jesus continued, "'But one thing is needed, and Mary has chosen that good part which will not be taken from her.'" The lesson that is being taught here is that to be occupied "with" Jesus is more important than being occupied "for" Him. To devote oneself to the Word of God is more important than to be busy for Him. Jesus said that one good thing was needed. Not two. Not three. One!! And that good thing is to receive His Word and to treasure them in the deepest caverns of your heart. Nobody has more faith than another. We all have the same amount of faith the same way we all have the same number of muscles as a body-builder. Faith has no limits but, like the body-builder with his muscles, it too must be developed. Great faith is developed faith and what you do with the measure of faith you receive at the new birth will determine its ability and activity in your life.

We are given by Peter a divine order in which to pursue and develop great faith. He tells us in 2 Peter 1:5, "But also for this very reason, giving all diligence, add to your faith virtue, to virtue knowledge." Virtue, or moral excellence, must be added to your measure of faith. This means that when you get born-again you must with all diligence make a conscious effort to get rid of all habitual sin from your life. At the same time and with the same diligence you must also strive to obtain a thorough knowledge of God's Word. This is so vitally important and necessary because we need knowledge of the Word so our faith will know what to believe and confess. For example, how will we know that we can believe for healing and divine health unless we first know that "by His stripes you were healed" (1 Peter 2:24)? It is a sad but undeniable truth that the majority of believers in the body of Christ today are not living in the fullness of all that God has for them because of a lack of knowledge pertaining to His Word.

God said through the prophet Hosea, "My people are destroyed for lack of knowledge" (Hos. 4:6). Notice that this verse does not say that a lack of knowledge will cause you to have a little inconvenience in life. No, it says you will be destroyed! A lack of knowledge is more than simply the result of neglect but in the eyes of God is considered to be a criminal action. This is true because when you reject the knowledge of the Word you are in fact rejecting God. We need to seriously think about these words from the book of Isaiah, "Therefore my people have gone into captivity, because they have no knowledge; Their honorable men are famished and their multitude dried up with thirst. Therefore, Sheol has enlarged itself and opened its mouth beyond measure" (Is. 5:13,14). This is what it means to be destroyed for a lack of knowledge. This only happens because most people are not willing to make the same sacrifices to increase their knowledge of Gods' Word as the body-builder makes to develop and increase the size of his muscles.

Jesus once told a parable about a man who had a fanatical passion for the Word of God and was willing to make the ultimate sacrifice. He said, "the kingdom of heaven is like treasure hidden in a field, which a man found and hid; and for the joy over it he goes and sells all that he has and buys the field" (Matt. 13:44). This verse reveals the diligence it takes to get the Word planted within you. Because the Word and the joy it brings was first place in this man's life, he went and sold all he had in order to obtain it. Nothing should come between you and the time you spend in the Word. Notice also that the treasure is buried in the field. People who do not study the Word but only skim over it maybe once a week are only looking at the surface of the field. The richest mines are often in grounds that appear most barren.

Prov. 15:28a says, "The heart of the righteous studies how to answer." The word "study" means 'to apply the mind in acquiring knowledge, to examine and search into, to memorize, to follow a regular course of instruction.' Interestingly, the Greek word for "study" means 'to make an effort, to labor.' Know for certain that time and effort will be required in order to obtain the true riches that are buried in Gods' Word. Don't just read the Word, study it! Prov. 4:20-22 says, "My son, give attention to my words; Incline your ear to my sayings. Do not let them depart from your eyes; Keep them in the midst of your heart; For they are life to those who find them and health to all their flesh." Notice that the words of God are life to those who "find" them. You find the words of God by seeking them out in a consistent and diligent study of the holy scriptures.

Ps. 119:2 tells us, "Blessed are those who keep His testimonies, who seek Him with the whole heart!" God gave His all to us in the person of Jesus Christ and it is now your responsibility, your obligation, and your privilege to give your all to Him. You cannot seek God half-heartedly and expect to receive in return all the blessings that He has prepared for you. No, the verse says to seek Him with your whole heart and when you diligently do that you will develop within yourself a deep, fanatical passion for God's Word. Great faith will come when you can say with conviction the words of Ps. 119:127, "Therefore I love Your commandments more than gold, yes, than fine gold." Deut. 11:18 gives us these important instructions, "Therefore you shall lay up these Words of Mine in your heart and in your soul, and bind them as a sign on your hand, and they shall be as frontlets between your eyes." For this to happen you must not only read and study the Words of God but you must also learn to meditate on them.

Ps. 119:15,16 says, "I will meditate on Your precepts and contemplate Your ways. I will delight myself in Your statutes; I will not forget Your Word." Ps. 1:2 also says, "But his delight is in the law of the Lord, and in His law he meditates day and night." The word "meditate" means 'to ponder by talking to oneself.' God told Joshua, "This Book of the Law shall not depart from your mouth, but you shall meditate in it day and night" (Josh. 1:8). Meditation is a spiritual exercise and it means 'to speak in a low tone with compressed lips, to murmur.' If you say something often enough it will get planted down in your heart and as a result your faith will grow. As you go through the normal routines of the day begin to quote the Word over and over again to yourself. Say out loud, "The Lord is my shepherd; I shall not want. The Lord is my shepherd; I shall not want." This is what it means to meditate on God's Word.

Meditation, therefore, will build your faith and will increase your ability to receive. Jesus said in Mark 4:23,24, "If anyone has ears to hear, let him hear. Take heed what you hear. With the same measure you use, it will be measured to you; and to him who hears, more will be given." To develop great faith, you must learn to listen because hearing the Word governs receiving from God. Remember, "faith comes by hearing, and hearing by the Word of God" (Rom. 10:17). Listening to yourself speak God's Word produces knowledge and knowledge produces faith. Therefore, the reward you receive will always be in direct proportion to the amount of time you spend hearing yourself speak God's Word. It's that simple. For those who find studying the Word of God a burden then the first thing they should do is read all of Ps. 119. This is the longest chapter in the Bible and rightfully it should be because in it the author does nothing but give praise to the holy scriptures and the value they have in one's life.

Consider for example these verses: "My soul clings to the dust; Revive me according to Your Word" (vs. 25). "My soul melts from heaviness; Strengthen me according to Your Word" (vs. 28). "Make me walk in the path of Your commandments, for I delight in it" (vs. 35). "And I will delight myself in Your commandments, which I love" (vs. 47). "I thought about my ways and turned my feet to Your testimonies. I made haste, and did not delay to keep Your commandments" (vs. 59,60). "Teach me good judgment and knowledge for I believe Your commandments" (vs. 66). "Forever, O Lord, Your Word is settled in heaven" (vs. 89). "I will never forget Your precepts for by them You have given me life" (vs. 93). "I have more understanding than all my teachers for Your testimonies are my meditation" (vs. 99). "You are my hiding place and my shield; I hope in Your Word" (vs. 114).

"Your testimonies are wonderful; Therefore, my soul keeps them" (vs. 129). "Direct my steps by Your Word and let no iniquity have dominion over me" (vs. 133). "Your Word is very pure, therefore Your servant loves it" (vs. 140). "I rejoice at Your Word as one who finds great treasure" (vs. 162). And finally, "Great peace have those who love Your law, and nothing causes them to stumble" (vs. 165). To be led by the Word of God is the only guarantee we'll ever have for a victorious and prosperous life. The writer of Ps. 119 got hold of this message when he penned these words, "Your Word is a lamp to my feet and a light to my path" (vs. 105) and "The entrance of Your Words gives light; It gives understanding to the simple" (vs. 130).

The pursuit of faith is a result of having a hunger and thirst for the Word of God. Prov. 4:5,6 says, "Get wisdom! Get understanding! Do not forget, nor turn away from the words of my mouth. Do not forsake her and she will preserve you; Love her and she will keep you." Ps. 63:1 describes a thirst David had for

God when he was in the wilderness of Judah. "Oh God, You are my God; Early will I seek you; My soul thirsts for You; My flesh longs for You in a dry and thirsty land where there is no water." He goes on to say, "When I remember You on my bed, I meditate on You in the night watches" (Ps. 63:6). Ps. 119:148 says, "My eyes are awake through the night watches that I may meditate on Your Word." Vs. 97 reveals the attitude of the heart which we should all strive to obtain, "Oh, how I love Your law! It is my meditation all the day." How often should we study and meditate on Gods' Word? Early in the day! Late in the evening! In the middle of the night! All day long!

| 4 |

"THE JOURNEY OF FAITH"

There is nothing mysterious about the journey of faith. True Biblical faith is simply believing God and acting on what you believe. Although people may fail you, faith in God is a sure thing but in the natural it does involve taking a risk because faith deals with the unseen. In fact, faith is "the evidence of things not seen" (Heb. 11:1). The problem many people have is that they live in a type of comfort zone and, like doubting Thomas, only believe and feel secure in what they can see, taste, smell, hear and touch. To walk by faith, however, one must be willing to let go of what looks like security to them and take what appears to be a risk. People who walk by faith must be willing to burn the bridges they cross over because in the good fight of faith there is no turning back. Julius Caesar once sent explorers to a foreign land and to assure the mission's success he gave the command for the ships to be burned once hiss men arrived at the destination. For him, there was no turning back.

The farmer Elisha, when called to follow Elijah, went back to his farm and slaughtered his oxen and burned his plowing equipment (1 Kings 19:21). He destroyed his means of income because he was not willing to start something for God that he was not willing to finish. For him, there was no turning back. Mark 10:50 tells how blind Bartimaeus threw aside his garment when called by Jesus to Whom he had cried out for mercy. This piece of cloth signified that he was legitimately blind and was his license to be a legal beggar. Bartimaeus, however, had faith in his Lord and he knew he would no longer need his garment so he threw it aside. This blind beggar stepped out in faith and for him there was no turning back. God has put in the hearts of all His children a burning desire to do something in and for the kingdom of God. As one grows in their walk with the Lord they will find that the things God tells them to do will more than likely be impossible by human standards. This is so because if it were possible in the natural realm then it wouldn't require any faith.

The worst thing a person can do is sit back and do nothing for this gives the enemy free reign to wreak havoc in your life. No, to win the battle of life and the good fight of faith you must forever be moving forward. In order to please God you must be willing to face the impossible and take a risk. Even a farmer who has faith in his crop must take a risk and hire laborers to reap his fields before he receives payment for his harvest. A risk taker is a person who doesn't consider the circumstances surrounding them but instead is able to use their faith to hook up with the supernatural power of God. They are the ones willing to burn the bridges behind them and put their trust in God and His Word even when the odds seem to be against them. Jesus said in Mark 9:23, "If you can believe, all things are possible to him who believes." The question is, do you believe and do you trust God? Down in your heart do you really, truly trust Him? If so, then take that match and turn around and set fire to that bridge you just crossed over because, in the journey of faith, there is no turning back.

The trials of life are often compared to storms. Many times people encounter hurricane-type conditions such as what was described by the apostle Paul in 2 Cor. 1:8 when he said he was "burdened beyond measure, above strength, so that we despaired even of life." One thing to learn in the midst of all these trials is that life goes on. The clock is always ticking and any meteorologist will tell you that all storms move forward as well. In the center of all hurricanes is a peaceful, calm harbor of rest known as the "eye of the hurricane" and this is where you will find the throne room of God. As long as you are here in this earth-suit you will have problems that will not go away on their own but thankfully you can go to God who is your "refuge and strength, a very present help in trouble" (Ps. 46:1). And where do you find Him? In the eye of the hurricane. You will always find Him in the center of your storm. The problem many people have is once they've taken refuge they want to strip themselves of their armor and rest awhile.

This is not bad in and of itself because you will need a season of rest from time to time. The Bible does say in Ps. 46:10, "Be still, and know that I am God." However, you cannot set up camp here and discontinue the good fight of faith because the enemy does not know what the word "rest" means. That storm is always moving and with it so is its peaceful center. If you remain still in your comfort zone and don't move forward also, then the eye of the hurricane will pass over you and the turbulent winds of the violent storm will hit you from behind when you least expect it. If you would take inventory of those times when you've been wounded in battle you would realize that it happened when your shield of faith was so full of arrows that you just had to lay it down and you rested longer than you should have. Resting too long brings with it the temptation to fall asleep on your watch and this you cannot do. To remain in the center of the eye of the hurricane you must continue to confess God's Word and always keep going forward.

In World War II the great General George S. Patton was known for his relentless drive to keep going forward even in the heat of battle. "No retreat, no surrender" was his motto and this must be yours as well. There is, of course, a reason for this. Shortly after Paul wrote of his hardships at the beginning of his second letter to the Corinthian church, he went on to write these encouraging words, "Now thanks be to God who always leads us in triumph in Christ" (2 Cor. 2:14). This verse doesn't say that God will take a victory and instantly drop it in your lap. No, it says that God will lead you to that victory. The reason you must keep going forward is because that's where your victory is. It's out there in front of you. Even while Jesus was hanging on the cross He was looking forward to the victory that would be His and yours at the resurrection. Therefore, don't look at what you're going "through" but focus on where you're going "to." Don't look at what is, look at what is going to become.

Being led to victory can be compared to when you ask a taxi driver to take you someplace. There are many routes he can take to get you to the proper destination but you don't concern yourself with that. You know where you want to go and you trust the driver to get you there. This is how it is when God leads you in triumph. Like you do with that taxi driver, you must put your total trust in Him to get you where you want to go. If a trial comes your way and you find yourself in "the valley of the shadow of death" then you must trust God and realize that this valley is on the route that leads to your victory. Sometimes you may feel like you're on a rugged obstacle course going through a maze of difficulties and the end to your problem is nowhere in sight. Once again, the only thing you can do is put your total trust in the One who is leading you. This may seem confusing at times but, thankfully, you don't have to understand it in your mind in order to believe it in your heart. Prov. 20:24 says, "A man's steps are of the Lord; how then can a man understand his own way?"

Nobody said this journey was easy. It's not. You are in a war and even Jesus said to "count the cost." What He also said is that He would never leave you or forsake you. A valley is not a bad place to be if you and Jesus are going through it together. Ps. 37:23,24 says, "The steps of a good man are ordered by the Lord and he delights in his way. Though he fall, he shall not be utterly cast down for the Lord upholds him with His hand. At all times you must believe that you are on the road to victory and are being led every step of the way by the One you call your Lord. Remember, the only way out of the valley is to march forward and go through the valley. Someone once said that great people are ordinary people with extraordinary amounts of determination. Obey the Lord's command to "Rise up!" and never allow that trial to keep you idle. Doing nothing only increases the opportunity for you to feel sorry for yourself and you know that will get you nowhere. Keep going forward and take hold of that victory that rightfully belongs to you.

Where is you victory at? It's on the path you're already on so keep your head held high knowing that trials and hardship are on the road to your miracle. And, by all means, never look back but always keep your eyes in front of you because that is where your victory is. When you've had a setback, don't take a step back, get ready for a comeback. Though the wind may blow and the rain will fall, you find comfort in the eye of the hurricane by putting your confidence in the words spoken in Nahum 1:3, "But the Lord has His way in the whirlwind and in the storm." Rest assured, the victory is there but you must march forward to get it. Put one foot in front of the other and go after it. Shout aloud the battle cry of the overcomer, "Onward!" The Word of God is powerful. It is sharper than any two-edged sword and will turn you into the type of person who believes that whatever you do will prosper and succeed. The Bible says you can do all things in Christ but first you must adjust your thinking to line up and agree with the thoughts of God.

Rom. 12:2 says, "And do not be conformed to this world but be transformed by the renewing of your mind." The way you think can either cause you to press forward in the midst of a trial or it can become a roadblock that prevents your advancement in life. Thomas Edison once performed ten thousand experiments in his quest to invent the light bulb and none produced the results he wanted. "I have not failed," he said. "I have successfully found ten thousand ways that will not work." When you think like that there is no way the enemy can stop you from accomplishing what you set out to do. Paul said in 2 Cor. 4:8,9, "We are hard pressed on every side yet not crushed; we are perplexed but not in despair; persecuted but not forsaken; struck down but not destroyed." The Message Bible puts it this way, "We've been surrounded and battered by troubles, but we're not demoralized; we're not sure what to do, but we know that God knows what to do; we've been spiritually terrorized, but God hasn't left our side; we've been thrown down, but we haven't broken."

A winner is not a person who has never suffered a setback. A winner is someone who knows that when the setback comes, he or she must rise to the occasion and continue forward. The thoughts, words, and actions of a winner will always be in agreement with the Word of God. This, in turn, will determine whether you will be a success or failure because what happens "in" you is more important than what happens "to" you. You can have the attitude that God is bigger than any obstacle you face or you can believe that He's not. The former will allow you to release the power of God into your situation through faith, whereas the latter will confine you to a life of fear and failure. This truth is illustrated in Num. 13 which tells the story of when Moses sent twelve people to spy out the Promised Land. After being gone for several weeks, the spies came back and told of seeing huge fortified cities there and strong giants dwelling in the land. Everything the spies said about the land was true, the difference being Joshua and Caleb came back with a good report while the remaining ten returned bearing a bad report.

Num. 13:30,31 says, "Then Caleb quieted the people before Moses and said, 'Let us go up at once and take possession for we are well able to overcome it.' But the men who had gone up with him said, 'We are not able to go up against the people for they are stronger than we are.'" You need to understand that faith is not a denial of the circumstances. Joshua and Caleb saw the same giants as the other spies but they knew God had given them the land and refused to allow the circumstances to dictate to them how things were going to be. This is called faith and faith always has a good report. To walk victorious, you need to feed on the Word of God continually and maintain a good report on the evil day when circumstantial giants block your path. Num. 14:36-38 says that because the ten spies brought back a bad report they immediately died by the plaque before the Lord whereas Joshua and Caleb were the only members of their evil generation who entered into the Promised Land. This reward was given to Joshua and Caleb because they believed God in spite of the circumstances and as a result brought back to the people a good report.

There is another story in the Bible where under grave circumstances a woman overlooked a tragic event in her life and won a major victory by confessing a good report and going forward on her journey of faith. Her story is found in 2 Kings 4:8-37. One day Elisha traveled to the city of Shunem where he met a woman who constrained him to come into her home and eat some food. This happened regularly and this same woman persuaded her husband to build an upper bedroom onto their house so that the prophet of God could have a comfortable dwelling place whenever he traveled to that region. During one of his visits, Elisha decided to bless the family for their kindness and upon hearing that the woman and her elderly husband had no children he foretold that in about a year's time they would have and embrace a baby son. In time the child grew and one day he ran out into the field to be with his father and immediately complained of a pain in his head. The boy was taken to his mother where he sat on her lap and eventually died.

Now was the moment of truth for this woman who longed to be in the presence of the man of God. A person's faith is most tested when all they have is taken away. Oftentimes a person is required to use their faith when they are drained emotionally, mentally, and physically. The young boy's mother did this by not preparing her son for burial but instead went and laid him on the bed of the prophet. She immediately got ready to run to the man of God and when asked why she was going all she said was "It is well." She made a good report in spite of the loss a mother is sure to feel at the death of one of her children. For this mother there was no turning back and without delay she departed and went to Mount Carmel to see the man of God. Elisha instructed his servant when he saw her approaching, "Please run now to meet her, and say to her, 'Is it well with you? Is it well with your husband? Is it well with the child?' And she answered, 'It is well.'" For the second time this woman gave a good report and confessed "It is well."

It is interesting to compare what this mother said to Elisha to what Martha said to Jesus at the death of her brother, Lazarus. Jesus was not present when Lazarus passed away and the first thing Martha said was, "Lord, if You had been here my brother would not have died." When Jesus responded that her brother would rise again Martha said, "I know that he will rise again in the resurrection at the last day." Martha had faith for the past and for the future whereas the dead boy's mother displayed a "now" faith by twice saying "It is well." The timing of faith is vitally important to those who desire to live a victorious life that is pleasing to God. To walk by faith, you must forget about yesterday and look beyond tomorrow in order to focus on today. Faith is a present tense reality and the first three words of Heb. 11:1 say, "Now faith is." When Moses asked God what His Name was, He said "I Am Who I Am." God is a "now" God and so also is His faith which He gives to you when you confess and believe His Word.

Knowing that faith is the firm foundation under everything that makes life worth living is what compelled the young boy's mother to confess "It is well" and as a result of her "now" faith the prophet went and ministered the miracle-working power of God into the body of her lifeless son. The lad was raised up and went on to live a rich full life and it all began when his mother gave a good report in the face of adversity. The ten spies who brought back the evil report and Martha walked by sight while the young boy's mother was able to walk by faith because of the commitment she made to be in the presence of the man of God. On the other hand, it was Martha's younger sister, Mary, who sat at the feet of Jesus and listened to everything He said while Martha chose instead to busy herself with the task of serving her guests. It is this commitment to the Word of God what will enable you to give a good report on the evil day and will cause you to rise up and boldly proclaim, "It is well!"

When God told Moses to lift up his rod and split the Red Sea, He first told him to "tell the children of Israel to go forward" (Ex. 14:15). God demands participation! Faith without works is dead (James 2:17). The Message Bible says "God-talk without God-acts is outrageous nonsense." Moses had to lift up the rod but the people had to go forward. Faith never backs up; it only goes forward. When the time came to enter the Promised Land, the people refused to go forward and cross over the Jordan River. The result of their disobedience is that with the exception of Joshua and Caleb that entire generation died off in the wilderness. They refused to fight the good fight of faith and take the land by storm and did not enter in because of unbelief (Heb. 3:19). On the contrary, if your faith is genuine then you must persistently heed the words of Heb. 10:39 (NIV), "But we are not of those who shrink back and are destroyed but of those who believe and are saved." The Message Bible says, "But we're not quitters who lose out. Oh, no! We'll stay with it and survive, trusting all the way."

| 5 |

"THE AUDACITY OF FAITH"

Is faith common or is it rare? Jesus asked in Luke 18:8, "When the Son of Man comes, will He really find faith on the earth?" Why would Jesus ask this? A lot of people believe that everybody has faith to one degree or another. They quote Rom. 12:3 that says God has dealt to each man a measure of faith. What this verse is actually saying is that everybody has been given the opportunity to have faith. Everybody has the ability to have faith but not everybody does. 2 Thess. 3:2 says pray "that we may be delivered from unreasonable and wicked men; for not all have faith." In the parable of the talents two servants took what the master gave them and used it and it grew and became more. Another servant didn't use it at all but went out and buried it. It is possible for God to give you something but you don't use it, and if you don't use it, you don't have it. It's available to you but it's not developed or producing anything in your life.

When Jesus walked the earth, He emphasized faith wherever He went. He was always talking to people about faith or the lack of it. He asked many people, "Where is your faith? Why don't you believe?" To others He said, "Your faith has made you whole. Great is your faith." Those who walked in faith and demonstrated it openly greatly impressed Him. God honors those who know that faith is the determining factor as to whether or not they please God and live a victorious life. 1 John 5:4 says, "For whatever is born of God overcomes the world. And this is the victory that has overcome the world - our faith." You have something in you from God that makes you an overcomer. If you will let what's inside you be fed so that it becomes strong and rises up, if it dominates your thinking and guides your life, you will be able to do all things through Christ who strengthens you. All things are possible to them that believe. When you choose to believe audaciously you become an overcomer and will do great exploits in and for the kingdom of God.

Jesus is the same today as He was then and so are the condition of the people. Why would people today think that everybody is full of faith? It would be nice if it was true but that is not reality. People are believing and assuming wrong things and are blaming God for all their failures. They say faith don't work when in reality they didn't have any faith to begin with. Real faith works and there is no such thing as a faith failure. If you failed then faith was not involved in the situation. Faith in God is real and it is powerful and it works every time for every person who uses it. Why did Jesus ask if He would find faith on the earth when He returns? Because it is rare and precious. 1 Peter 1:7 says faith is "much more precious than gold" and 2 Peter 1:1 again calls faith "precious." Faith is precious and it is a treasure to God. Faith pleases God so much so that Jesus marveled and showed amazement when He saw those around Him walking in faith (Matt. 8:10). God calls faith "precious" and you need a fresh revelation of how precious your faith is to God.

Living by faith does not mean you won't have any more challenges. What it does mean is that you will overcome every one that does come. David wrote in Ps. 56:11, "In God I have put my trust; I will not be afraid. What can man do to me?" Faith is a choice you make to trust God and when you do trust Him you relax. Trust is the cure for doubt and unbelief and is the remedy for panic and fear. No more will you panic or become frantic when the storms of life blow your way. You don't pace the floor at night and call your friends telling them how bad your situation is. Your sleep will be sweet and you have peace because you have the faith and confidence that somehow, some way, everything will turn out good for you and in your favor. Ps. 34:8 says, "Oh, taste and see that the Lord is good; Blessed is the man who trusts in Him!" Your trust is in God and it makes no difference what the enemy may try to do to you. You are more than a conqueror in Christ Jesus (Rom. 8:37) and you will win, win, win, and then win some more.

You can do all things through Christ and can overcome anything with the Greater One living inside of you. Still, faith is not automatic. You have to choose to believe and you have to choose to resist fear. It's a choice you make in your heart and not your head. It's also a choice you have to make every single day of your life. You can be in faith one day and in doubt the next. Faith is a lifestyle that you walk in with every breath you take. When bad situations come your way, you can be like Paul who said "none of these things move me" (Acts 20:24). Never do you feel sorry for yourself and never do you feel hopeless and quit. You can choose to have faith and this will put a twinkle in your eye and a spring in your step. It will put a song in your heart and a shout on your lips. Your faith is in Jesus and He will never leave you or forsake you. He is in you and He communes with you day and night. 2 Tim. 1:12 says, "For I know whom I have believed and am persuaded that He is able to keep what I have committed to Him until that day."

God has you in the palm of His hand and you will be victorious no matter what the devil throws your way. Acts 17:28 says "in Him you live and move and have your being." When you live in a dark world it is easy to slip into unbelief and doubt. This earth is filled with darkness, fear, and confusion and faith is not everywhere. When you do find faith, it is a bright light, a beacon of hope and confidence in a dark world. Faith is a rarity and when you find it and walk in it all of heaven rejoices. It will cause you to run your race and finish your course with joy. Ps.100:2 says, "Serve the Lord with gladness; Come before His presence with singing." Faith is to be used for a whole lot more than just getting your needs met and possessing the finer things in life. Faith is primarily to be used to help you overcome the trials of life while at the same time remaining stable and strong no matter what is happening, thus enabling you to be a blessing to someone else.

Hab. 2:4 says, "The just shall live by faith." This is how those who walk with God live. There is no other way because without faith it is impossible to please God. Rom. 1:17 says the righteousness of God is revealed from faith to faith. The Amplified Bible says, "Both spring from faith and leading to faith." As your faith develops you can do more and better things for the Lord. You can receive more, you can minister more, and you can know with more clarity what His vision for your life is. Everything you do is done according to where your faith is. Rom. 12:6 says, "Having then gifts differing according to the grace that is given to us, let us use them; if prophecy, let us prophecy in proportion to our faith." God will not show you some things until your faith is at a level where you will receive it. If He did show it to you and you weren't ready it would overwhelm you to the point of you getting discouraged and possibly giving up. There is no reason for God to say "you can" if you're going to turn around and say "you can't."

God has an amazing plan for your life, an impossible dream for you to pursue. If your dreams are possible then you're not dreaming big enough. God wants you to be an impossibility thinker. He wants you to dream beyond the realm of possibility where without His help and you using your faith it will not come to pass. God will show you His plan on how to fulfill your dream little by little as your faith is able to receive it. His plan is revealed to you from faith to faith. The more your faith is developed, the more He will show you what His plan is. He will reveal His plan to you and bring you into it as your faith is able to lay hold of it. As you walk in newness of life you will find that His plan for you will be exceedingly, abundantly, above what you could ask or think (Eph. 3:20). When it does get revealed, you can respond like Mary did and say, "Let it be done to me according to Your word" (Luke 1:38). Faith says "I can" and unbelief says "I can't." You are able to say "I can" if you would only believe.

Prov. 29:18 says, "Where there is no vision, the people perish." If you don't have a vision you're dying on the inside. Most people when they retire die within three years because they stopped dreaming. Accept by faith that God has a glorious, good plan for your life no matter what age you are. God has you on His mind and He has a plan for your life, a plan He had before the creation of the world. Jer. 1:5 says, "Before I formed you in the womb I knew you; before you were born I sanctified you; and I ordained you a prophet to the nations." God later said in Jer. 29:11, "For I know the thoughts that I think toward you, says the Lord, thoughts of peace and not of evil, to give you a future and a hope." The Amplified Bible says God wants "to give you hope in your final outcome." Paul says in Eph. 2:10, "For we are His workmanship, created in Christ Jesus for good works, which God prepared beforehand that we should walk in them." The Message Bible says, "He creates each of us by Christ Jesus to join Him in the work He does, the good work He has gotten ready for us to do, work we had better be doing."

God has a specific mission that He wants you to accomplish in your lifetime. 2 Tim. 1:9 says that God "has saved us and called us with a holy calling, not according to our works, but according to His own purpose and grace which was given to us in Christ Jesus before time began." Before God created the heavens and the earth, He had a specific mission for your life which you will one day be held accountable for. Far too many Christians are lazy and live as though they will never have to give an account for their lives. They think getting born again is the end of their obligation to God instead of the beginning of a lifetime of being a faithful servant to Him. They don't realize that there is rank and file in heaven and there are no promotions there. Once you leave this life your eternal destiny is forever sealed and where you go and what happens to you is all based on what you do in the here and now. The parable of the talents give stark details about what happens to believers who fulfill their heavenly calling and those who ignore what God wants them to do with their lives. Indeed, it is a fearful thing to fall into the hands of the living God (Heb. 10:31).

It is of utmost importance that you conform your will to God's calling on your life. You need to make His interests the top priority in your life instead of trying to shape and mold Him into your own. The secret to doing this is hidden in your daily routine. What you do on a daily basis will either take you closer to your dream or farther from it. If you change your habits, you can change your future. Success is something you attract by the person you become. If you want more, you must become more. Luke 12:48 says, "For everyone to whom much is given, from him much will be required." Turn these words around and you will find that much is required in order for much to be given. Matt. 5:6 says, "Blessed are they which do hunger and thirst after righteousness; for they shall be filled." God alone deserves the throne of your heart and He is more than willing to reveal His plan to anyone who hungers and thirsts for it. The Message Bible says, "You're blessed when you've worked up a good appetite for God. He's food and drink in the best meal you'll ever eat."

Discipline is a decision you make and if done consistently there are things you can do daily that will change your life and help bring your dream into manifestation. Start off in prayer and by spending quality time with the Lord every day. Talk to Him and, equally important, listen to Him. When you draw near to God, He will draw near to you. Matt. 7:7 says, "Ask, and it shall be given you; seek, and you shall find; knock, and it shall be opened unto you." Col. 1:9 says to pray "that you might be filled with the knowledge of His will in all wisdom and spiritual understanding." Discovering your mission in life will require time and effort on your part. Even Jesus had to spend time seeking the will of the Father. He fasted and prayed for forty days (Luke 4:1-15). He studied the Word and based His ministry on scripture (Luke 4:18). He developed a habit of praying for long hours on end (Luke 6:12). Jesus was not born with the knowledge of what He was supposed to do, He discovered it. He did so by spending quality time with the Father. You, also, must do the same.

While you are seeking God and waiting for His will to be revealed you need to turn off the television and read your Bible and other books related to successful Christian living. Listen to motivational messages that will build your faith and begin to speak positive declarations over your life. What you repeatedly hear you eventually believe. Use the words you speak to prophecy your future. Prov. 18:21 says, "Life and death are in the power of the tongue." God responds to the words you speak. Your tongue controls the direction of your life the same way a small rudder controls the direction of a ship (James 3:4,5). What's coming out of your mouth has everything to do with what happens in your future. 1 Sam. 17:44 says, "And the Philistine said to David..." The devil will talk to you and tell you that you're a failure. What should you do when he does? Vs. 45 tells us. "Then David said to the Philistine..." Talk back to the devil and do it out loud. You need to declare openly what you are believing for. That's exactly how God spoke the entire world into existence.

Your future begins with a dream and if your vision is impaired, you'll stay right where you are. You have to see where you're going before you move in the direction you have to go. This is why Hab. 2:2 says, "Write the vision and make it plain on tablets, that he may run who reads it." Dreams not written down are just wishes. Imagine building a house without blue-prints. Write down everything God tells you to do and read it out loud every day. "Habakkak" is an unusual Hebrew word derived from the verb "habaq" which means 'embrace.' His name means 'one who embraces or clings.' This is precisely what God wants you to do. Cling to the call that is on your life. If you don't have a call on your life then you are merely existing. When you stop dreaming, you stop living. Nobody stumbles upon success and you must dream and think about what God wants you to do. Dreaming precedes achievement and the greater your thinking, the greater your potential will be. Henry Ford once said, "Thinking is the hardest work there is, which is probably the reason so few engage in it."

You are the one who decides what you will do with the rest of your life and your thoughts are the pathway to your destiny. You succeed or fail based on what's going on in your thought life. Prov. 23:7 says, "For as he thinks in his heart, so is he." The world says "don't just sit there, do something" but God says "don't just do something, sit there." God wants to awaken the dream that's on the inside of you for He knows that whatever you think about, you bring about. It's called "the law of attraction" and your life will go in the direction of your most dominate thought, whether it be good or bad. Paul understood this and wrote in Rom. 12:2, "And do not be conformed to this world, but be transformed by the renewing of your mind, that you may prove what is that good and acceptable and perfect will of God." This you must do every day of your life. The word "transform" means 'to make a thorough and dramatic change' and this begins in your thought life. It's not a one-time thing you do but is a daily "washing of water by the Word" (Eph. 5:6).

You have a call on your life and Satan wants to deceive you into thinking you can't fulfill it by dropping little thoughts of fear and doubt into your head. He is seeking whom he can devour and you open the door to him when you meditate on and speak out of your mouth the thoughts he gives you. Don't do it. 1 Peter 1:13 says you are to "gird up the loins of your mind." That is a battle term and the Message Bible says, "Prepare your minds for action." You can't be passive when bad thoughts come. You must prepare for war! If the devil can deceive you, he can defeat you. A deception is a lie that becomes truth to you when you believe it. You live and behave according to the way you see yourself. You prepare for action by filling your thoughts with what God says about you. He says you are a success. He says you are more than a conqueror. Confessing God's Word is how you bring every thought captive to the obedience of Christ (2 Cor. 10:5). You don't capture those thoughts with other thoughts, you capture them with the words you speak.

General Douglas MacArthur said that the first rule of war is to know your enemy. The devil comes in like a roaring lion seeking whom he can devour and you must stay in the Word of God so you'll be ready when he does come. Rev. 12:11 (NIV) says "they triumphed over him by the blood of the Lamb and by the word of their testimony." The Message Bible says "they defeated him through the blood of the Lamb and the bold word of their witness." Use bold words and get loud when you confess God's Word over your life. It's time to get fighting mad at the devil and it's time to speak against him. Tell him "greater is He who is in me than he who is in the world." The sword of the Spirit is the Word of God and each time you confess what God says you are stabbing the devil. God's Word torments the devil and this is what will force him to back off and leave you alone. Stay in the Word for Matt. 12:34 (AMP) says, "For out of the fullness (the overflow, the superabundance) of the heart the mouth speaks."

You will never live a victorious Christian life if you don't take control of your thoughts. It's an ongoing daily process where you must always be on guard filtering every thought through the Word of God. He has so much more in store for you than you're currently experiencing but you've got to get your thoughts in agreement with Him. God gave Jeremiah an assignment and he responded, "Ah, Lord God! Behold, I cannot speak, for I am a youth" (Jer. 1:6). God said back to him, "Do not say, 'I am a youth'" (vs. 7). God knew if Jeremiah kept saying he couldn't fulfill his assignment that he would ruin God's plan for his life. The same thing happened in Luke 1:18-20. Zacharias spoke against the plan of God and was made dumb until after the plan was fulfilled. Don't hinder the plan of God for your life by saying you can't do it. Stop making excuses. You limit what God can do with small thinking and He gets angry when you say you can't do something when He says you can (Ex. 4:14). It insults Him because you are saying you know more than He does.

In spite of your shortcomings God has chosen you anyway and your only response is to submit your will to His. It's true, you can't do it on your own but you are not on your own. God will never leave you or forsake you (Heb. 13:5). He is in the business of making champions out of failures. He will take a person who is flawed and make them mighty. He'll give you beauty for ashes (is. 61:3). God hand-picked you for a special work to do and He is fully expecting you to fulfill that call. God can use anybody and that includes you. You are not too old to serve God. Moses was eighty when God called him. Neither are you too young. Jesus fed the multitude with the loaves and fishes of a young boy. God used murderers, prostitutes, and smelly fishermen to do His work on planet Earth. Consider the lustful Samson and the ever-impulsive Peter. Who was more flawed than they? Saul of Tarsus, Abraham, Moses, Gideon, Elijah, and David all made mistakes but God used each of them in a powerful way. And if He used them, He most certainly can use you.

People need to stop making excuses for why they are not serving the Lord. Too many people are waiting for God to do something when in fact it is God who is waiting on them to do something. Stop telling God how flawed and unworthy you are and begin to put your hand to the plow and do the job that is available to you now. God is not looking for qualifications or a person with great skills in a certain area. Above all else He is looking for faithfulness. Jesus said, "He who is faithful in what is least is faithful also in much" (Luke 16:10a). God usually speaks to those who are faithfully doing something. Elisha was plowing a field, Gideon was thrashing wheat, David was taking care of his father's sheep, and Peter was fishing when the Lord spoke to them of their upcoming ministries. It is time for you to begin doing faithfully whatever your hand finds to do. God does not look for the many, He looks for the few. He is looking for a few good men and women who have hearts to serve Him no matter what the cost. Always remember, the door of tomorrow won't open until you do something today.

To those who are flawed in character but mighty in spirit the Lord gives a powerful command in Luke 17:32, "Remember Lot's wife." When God delivered Lot and his family out of Sodom and Gomorrah He told them, "Do not look behind you" (Gen. 19:17). God was telling them that everything they needed to live a good life was ahead of them. Lot's wife ignored this command, looked back, and instantly was turned into a pillar of salt. Lot's wife lost her future because she looked back.

There is a reason the windshield of your car is bigger than the rear-view mirror. God wants you focused so much on what's ahead of you that you don't even notice what's going on behind you. Is. 43:18,19a says, "Do not remember the former things, nor consider the things of old. Behold, I will do a new thing, now it shall spring forth, shall you not know it?" Satan is a thief and he is after your dream. He wants you stuck in the past so you'll never move forward. He's hoping that you'll lose your future by looking back. God says remember Lot's wife. Don't look back, always look forward.

Your faith will overcome every attack from the enemy, including negative thoughts and memories from your past. You need to have audacious faith if you are going to achieve the dream God put in your heart. You need the audacity to believe God will do what He said He would do and that you can do all things through Christ who strengthens you. The word "audacity" means 'nerve, grit, fearlessness, courage, and daring.' Have the audacity to believe in yourself, to forget he past, and to believe that what happened yesterday does not define who you are today. Your identity is in Jesus and He made you the head and not the tail, above and not beneath. On the road to success, you have to believe that every day matters. What you are doing today prepares you for tomorrow. John Wooden said, "Prepare now for when opportunities come it will be too late to prepare." Heb. 11:7 says by faith Noah prepared an ark. Faith gets ready. Prepare now for what God is calling you to do. Smith Wigglesworth said, "It's better to live ready, than to get ready."

The will to succeed is important but what's even more important is the will to prepare. You have to invest in your future. Preparation takes effort and you must make time to learn, to grow, and to expand your thinking. Expose yourself to new things, new people, new books, new places. Your calling won't just happen by itself, you have to go after it. Many people don't hear the call on their lives because they've ignored it for so long. Other people may see the gifts you possess and the potential in you but you don't see it anymore. Pick up the call and put one foot in front of the other. Your days are numbered and your life is fleeing away. It's time to pursue God's calling with everything you've got. It's time to prioritize your life. Make time with God your number one priority. When you pursue God, you are pursuing your dream. Spending time with God will cause you to get closer to Him, more comfortable with Him, and more sensitive to His voice. Divine direction will come because very rarely will God allow you to see beyond the horizon that is ever before you. Don't prioritize your schedule, schedule your priorities.

The deciding factor in having a bright future is based on whether or not you step forward and do that which you were born to do. Jesus said in Mark 10:46, "Even the Son of Man did not come to be served, but to serve, and to give His life as a ransom for many." Since Jesus gave His life to serve others, you also need to devote your life to doing the same thing. You need to make up your mind and decide once and for all that you are going on with God no matter what. Decisions are like earthquakes. They have tremors and they last on and on and affect other people's lives. Your destiny is calling out to you and it's time to step out of your comfort zone and into the unknown. Stepping out definitely requires overcoming fear and insecurities, doing what may not come natural to you, and flat out trusting God with everything you've got. Be so determined to go after God's plan for your life that turning back is not an option. Your decisions today affect your life tomorrow.

Have the audacity to visualize your future. You will never leave where you are until you see where you'd rather be. If you can conceive it, you can receive it. Have the audacity to believe that God can use you in a powerful way. Believe in yourself. Dream big and take the limits off your life. There is no limit as to how high you can go with God but you have to get in line with what He wants. Never settle where you are. In Gen. 11:31 Abraham's father Terah set out with his son to go to the land of Canaan but stopped along the way and settled in Haran. God never meant for you to settle where you are. He wants you to go all the way with Him to your own personal promised land. Jesus hung on the cross with His head down so yours could be lifted up. Throw your shoulders back and dig your heels in and begin to walk out God's plan for your life. Fulfilling your call is one big exciting adventure and it begins right here, right now.

| 6 |

"THE ATMOSPHERE OF FAITH"

The glory of God is the manifestation of God's presence, His power, and His goodness. Now is the time for you to see these manifestations to a greater degree than you've ever seen before. You are to let nothing stop you from running your race and finishing your course. For this to happen you must create an atmosphere for God to move. He is not going to show up where He's not welcome. The proper atmosphere where God always shows up is the atmosphere of faith. Be determined to put the Word in you on a continual basis because that is the foundation faith is built on. Be inspired by hearing sermons on the subject of faith. Listen to them on your way to work or when you're cooking a meal. Build up your inner man for out of your heart spring forth the issues of life (Prov. 4:23). As you do all that continually an atmosphere of faith is created and this is when God shows up. Wherever you go this atmosphere follows you and others will sense that there is something different about you. They'll want what you have and doors will be opened for you to tell them about how good God is.

It is God's will for Him to manifest His glory in your life. In Ex. 33:18 Moses pleaded with God saying, "Please, show me your glory." Without any hesitation or deliberation God said back to him, "I will make My goodness pass before you, and I will proclaim the name of the Lord before you. I will be gracious to whom I will be gracious, and I will have compassion on whom I will have compassion." Moses asked to see God's glory and the first two words God said was "I will." This proves that it is God's will that you see in your life the manifestation of His presence, His power, and His goodness. God wants to show you His glory today and tomorrow and every day thereafter for the rest of your life. It is, however, your responsibility to create an atmosphere for this to happen. God does not respond to your needs, He responds to your faith. Faith makes a demand on God's ability to save, heal, and restore. It's what gives God access to your life.

2 Chron. 16:9 says, "For the eyes of the Lord run to and from throughout the whole earth, to show Himself strong on behalf of those whose heart is loyal to Him." God is looking for people who trust Him, people who believe in Him. At the tomb of Lazarus Jesus told Martha, "Did I not say to you that if you would believe you would see the glory of God?" (John 11:40). Believing is an act of faith. Jesus is saying that if you will create an atmosphere of faith, you will see the glory of God. God is famous for unexpected acts and surprises. If you diligently try to live a life of faith and obedience before God then you can be

going about your daily routine when suddenly you'll be over-taken with a blessing from above. Ps. 23:6 says, "Surely good-ness and mercy shall follow me all the days of my life." Believe that the blessings of God will come on you so often that they'll overtake you. Strive to get to the point where this becomes the norm. You can live your life where you don't have to consume all your effort asking God to bless you all the time. No, seek God, obey Him, and then stand back and watch the blessings come on you suddenly. God wants to bless you but first it's up to you to expect the unexpected.

Creating an atmosphere of faith also creates an atmosphere of expectancy. When you are in faith your head is held high be-cause you are looking for God to move at any moment. Faith is required because as Heb.11:6 says, "But without faith it is impossible to please God." Another word for "please" is "sat-isfy" and this word means 'to provide what is needed.' This verse can therefore be translated, "It is impossible to satisfy God without providing that which is required." That which is required is faith. When you provide the faith God promises that you will see the glory of God. He has obligated Himself to show up in your life when an atmosphere of faith is created. Your faith-filled words will open the door for the Lord to come in and bless you exceedingly, abundantly, above what you could ask or think (Eph. 3:20). God is listening to what you say and is eagerly waiting for the atmosphere of faith to be created. Jesus said in Luke 12:32, "Do not fear, little flock, for it is your Fa-ther's good pleasure to give you the kingdom."

If you want to become the winner in life that God wants you to be, then you must develop your faith. 1 John 5:4 (NLT) says, "For every child of God defeats this evil world, and we achieve this victory through our faith." Faith works so if you are not enjoying your life then your faith is not fully developed. Without faith you will not live a victorious Christian life. The Message Bible says, "Every God-begotten person conquers the world's ways. The conquering power that brings the world to its knees is our faith." It's only consistently exercising and releasing your faith that you're able to lay hold upon everything that God has promised you in the Word. If you have faith nothing will be impossible to you (Matt. 17:20). Faith removes all limitations. It changes the impossible into the possible. It's the victory that overcomes the world. Everybody should want what God has promised but it all comes down to what you're doing with your faith. God has dealt to each person the measure of faith (Rom. 12:3) and what you do with it is up to you.

To create an atmosphere of faith you must look on the inside how body builders look on the outside. You need to continually feel your spirit man. There are no shortcuts. The Bible says the just shall live by faith (Rom. 1:17). It should be second nature to you to get in the Word several times a day. Faith is a lifestyle. It's how you live. It is possible, through faith, for you to be victorious and abundantly blessed every single day of your life. No more will you feel hopeless when things don't go the way they should. No more will you walk in fear, doubt, and unbelief. No more will you dread waking up in the morning. You can get to a point in your life where nothing will be impossible. You will have breakthrough in every area of your life. David was one of the greatest warriors to ever walk the planet. A great call was placed on his life when Samuel poured the anointing oil on his head and from that day forward, he went out to defend the honor of his God. Throughout his ministry the storms of life raged against him but he was able to stand strong in the heat of battle because he knew the Lord was always with him.

2 Samuel 5:17-20 says, "Now when the Philistines heard that they had anointed David king over Israel, all the Philistines went up to search for David. And David heard of it and went down to the stronghold. The Philistines also went and deployed themselves in the Valley of Rephaim. And David inquired of the Lord, saying, 'Shall I go up against the Philistines? Will You deliver them into my hand?' And the Lord said to David, 'Go up, for I will doubtless deliver the Philistines into your hand.' So, David went to Baal Perazim, and David defeated them there; and he said, 'The Lord has broken through my enemies before me, like a breakthrough of water.' Therefore, he called the name of that place Baal Perazim." God delivered David and He will "doubtless" deliver you also. He is the captain of your salvation and if things don't happen in the time frame, you'd like then wait on Him with patience and eager anticipation. Stay strong regardless of the circumstances and how long it takes. Always be consistent with your believing and boldly proclaim that giving up is not an option.

The term "Baal Perazim" literally means 'Master of Breakthroughs.' To David his God would always be the 'Lord of the Breakthrough.' This is why he could write in Ps. 23:4,5, "Yes, though I walk through the valley of the shadow of death, I will fear no evil; For You are with me; Your rod and Your staff, they comfort me. You prepare a table before me in the presence of my enemies; You anoint my head with oil; My cup runs over." What David discovered is that in order to defeat your enemies you need supernatural food from a supernatural God on a supernatural table. He knew you had to eat supernatural bread in the time of your storm. Jesus said in John 6:47,48,51, "Most assuredly, I say to you, he who believes in Me has everlasting life. I am the bread of life. I am the living bread which came down from heaven. If anyone eats this bread, he will live forever." Yes, Jesus is the "bread of life" and in Matt. 6:11 He taught us to pray, "Give us this day our daily bread." Every day we need a heavy dose of Jesus. He is "the way, the truth, and the life" (John 14:6).

Faith is based on the truth of God's Word and if this truth is in you then you will shine as a beacon of light in this dark world in spite of all the bad things that are happening. You are to walk in love, joy, and peace every day of your life and it's by faith that you are able to do this. Do not allow unbelievers to intimidate you no matter what position they hold or how much money they have. Do not argue with them or debate theological issues with them. They're not interested in what you have to say and no matter how sound your beliefs are they still won't believe it. You will have a greater impact if you stay above, it all and don't get pulled into some silly debate. In your heart you know in whom you have believed and that He is faithful to keep and sustain all that you have committed to Him. God justifies those who believe in Jesus because they have an unshakable confidence that He will do what He said He would do. God honors and rewards the committed faith of people who believe He is on their side no matter what they go through and that He will bring them out to rich fulfillment.

David was a man after God's own heart and this was his greatest strength. He wrote in Ps. 34:4, "I sought the Lord, and He heard me, and delivered me from all my fears." David ate supernatural bread in the time of storm and this is why he could write in vs. 8, "Oh, taste and see that the Lord is good; Blessed is the man who trusts in Him." If God is for you then nobody can successfully be your enemy. You must have a deeply help belief that no weapon formed against you will prosper (Is. 54:17). The world needs more Christians with true grit, those who will run the race and stay the course with determination and refuse to give up and quit. Heb. 6:12 (MSG) says, "Don't drag your feet. Be like those who stay the course with committed faith and then get everything promised to them." Draw a line in the sand and tell the devil if it's a fight he wants, it's a fight he's going to get. Be like Abraham who had unwavering faith. Rom. 4:20,21 says, "He did not waver at the promise of God through unbelief, but was strengthened in faith, giving glory to God, and being fully convinced that what He promised He was also able to perform."

In the New Testament the book of Acts tells of a major storm that burst upon the life of the apostle Paul. He and other prisoners were on a ship heading for Italy and all during their trip strong winds blew hard against their ship. Acts 27:7 says, "And when we had sailed slowly many days, and arrived with difficulty off Cnidus, the wind not permitting us to proceed." Many stops were made along the way but still the storm raged on. Paul advised against the continuance of this journey but the head centurion listened to the helmsman instead and sailed on (Vs. 10,11). Then disaster struck. "But not long after a tempestuous wind arose" (vs. 14). This storm came upon them suddenly and was so strong, so dense, and so difficult that the situation seemed hopeless. "And because we were exceedingly tempest-tossed, the next day we threw the ship's tackle overboard with our own hands. Now when neither sun nor stars appeared for many days, and no small tempest beat on us, all hope that we would be saved was finally given up" (vs. 18-20). The loss of hope is the peak of spiritual bankruptcy. When you lose hope, you doubt your beliefs and believe your doubts.

Hope deferred makes the heart sick (Prov. 13:12) and causes nothing but fear and sorrow. It is in those times when all hope seems to be lost that you need to tie a knot in the end of your rope and hang on for dear life. "But after long abstinence from food, then Paul stood in the midst of them and said, 'Men, you should have listened to me, and not have sailed from Crete and incurred this disaster and loss'" (vs. 21). Paul was his usually bold self and said they brought this situation on themselves. Problems begin when you refuse to hear and obey the Word of the Lord. "And now I urge you to take heart, for there will be no loss of life among you, but only of the ship. For there stood by me this night an angel of the God to Whom I belong and Whom I serve, saying, 'Do not be afraid, Paul; you must be brought before Caesar; and indeed, God has granted you all those who sail with you.' Therefore, take heart, men, for I believe God that it will be just as it was told me" (vs. 22-25). Paul was telling them to take heart and be of good cheer for every life has a purpose. God has a destination for you but you must stay in the boat on your way to see Caesar. If you don't jump ship and lose hope, you'll fulfill the call of God on your life.

Paul was telling those who sailed with him to take heart and trust God. He knew that your expectations are more powerful than any negative thing that Satan can put before you. They'll override any negative circumstances no matter how frequently they come in your life. The psalmist writes in Ps. 42:5,6, "Why are you cast down, O my soul? And why are you disquieted within me? Hope in God, for I shall yet praise Him for the help of His countenance." Jesus said in John 14:1, "Let not your heart be troubled; you believe in God, believe also in Me." In the midst of your storm "do not cast away your confidence which has great reward. For you have need of endurance, so that after you have done the will of God, you may receive the promise" (Heb. 10:35,36). The Message Bible says, "But you need to stick it out, staying with God's plan so you'll be there for the promised completion." Paul told his comrades to "take heart" for he knew much endurance was needed to ride out this storm of demonic proportions. He knew also that something else was needed to assure the survival of all those on board the ship.

"And as day was about to dawn, Paul implored them all to take food, saying, 'Today is the fourteenth day you have waited and continued without food, and eaten nothing. Therefore, I urge you to take nourishment, for this is for your survival, since not a hair will fall from the head of any of you'" (Acts 27:33,34). It is a sad reality that in times of storm many people lay down the sword of God's Word and enter into a state of depression. Job said, "May the day perish on which I was born. Why did I not die at birth? Why did I not perish when I came from the womb?" (Job 3:1,11). Likewise, when chased by Jezebel Elijah said, "It is enough! Now, Lord, take my life, for I am no better than my father!" (1 Kings 19:4). Depression comes from many avenues. Extreme disappointment can cause depression as well as low self-esteem and a feeling of being trapped in a hopeless situation. The truth is that you are only limited by your ability to limit yourselves. The person who stays depressed is the one who chooses to believe that their storm is permanent. Paul knew this and he encouraged those with him to eat bread in the time of storm.

He prayed in Eph. 3:16 that God "would grant you, according to the riches of His glory, to be strengthened with might through His Spirit in the inner man." Ps. 118:5 says, "I called on the Lord in distress; The Lord answered me and set me on a broad place." From the belly of the fish Jonah prayed, "I cried out to the Lord because of my affliction, and He answered me" (Jonah 2:2). Vs. 7 says, "When my soul fainted within me, I remembered the Lord; And my prayer went up to You, into Your holy temple." Jonah ate bread in the time of storm. While in prison "at midnight Paul and Silas were praying and singing hymns to God, and the other prisoners were listening to them" (Acts 16:25). They, too, ate supernatural bread in the time of storm. This was the message Paul was saying in Acts 27. Vs. 36,36 says, "And when he had said these things, he took bread and gave thanks to God in the presence of them all; and when he had broken it, he began to eat. Then they were all encouraged, and also took food themselves."

Don't ignore God when you are attacked for the anointing's sake. Don't run from Him, run to Him. Eat bread in the time of storm. Don't sit around doing nothing as you wait for some "deep" revelation to come to you. No, open up your Bible and read! Go back and major in the basic, fundamental doctrines of God's Holy Word. Legendary football coach Vince Lombardi once said that champions are people who major in the basics. At the start of each training camp, he would stand before the players on his team, veterans and rookies alike, hold a football up in his hand and say, "Gentlemen, this is a football." His philosophy of majoring in the basics led his team to back-to-back Superbowl victories in the 1960's. Likewise, champions for God should also major in the basics. What are some of the basics of abiding in Jesus? The Lord said in John 15:7, "If you abide in Me, and My word abide in you, you will ask what you desire and it shall be done for you." Jesus said that God's holy Word must abide in our hearts. This is the first step of getting back to the basics of Christian life.

As born-again believers we must all develop a huge appetite for the Word of God. We must crave Spiritual food like we crave natural food and that craving should be so great that it is impossible to satisfy. We need to become so addicted to the Word of God that it seems like we can't get enough of It. The more we get the more we'll want. Jer. 15:6 says, "Your words were found, and I ate them, and Your Word was to me the joy and rejoicing of my heart; For I am called by Your Name, O Lord of hosts." Ezekiel says the same thing, "Moreover He said to me, 'Son of man, eat what you find, eat this scroll, and go, speak to the house of Israel.' So I opened my mouth and He caused me to eat that scroll. And He said to me, 'Son of man, feed your belly, and fill your stomach with this scroll that I give you.' So I ate it, and it was in my mouth like honey in sweetness" (Ezek. 3:1-3). God says to "fill" your stomach with His Word. Don't nibble on it a little bit. Don't be content reading one verse on some "promise card" you have stored on some dusty shelf off in the back bedroom.

To become addicted to the Word of God a person should read no less than ten chapters a day. No less! This may seem like a lot but remember, we're talking about an addiction here. The more you grow in the Word, the more the Word will grow in you. Make a quality decision to give yourself completely to the Word of God. Focus your time and attention to it. Carry a pocket Bible with you in your purse and in your lunch box. Put a Bible in the glove compartment of your car. Have one on the coffee table in your living room and on the night stand in your bedroom. And, by all means, don't let those Bibles just sit there and collect dust. Read them, chew on them, meditate on them. The more you give yourself to God's Word the more your desire for it will grow. Come to a place where you can't get enough of it. Let it consume your spiritual, mental, and physical life. Get addicted to the Word. Even Job said, "I have treasured the words of His mouth more than my necessary food" (Job 23:12). Oh people, taste and see that the Lord is good,

Another basic element we need to major in is prayer. How many times do we read in the gospels that Jesus went off by Himself to pray? Many people shake and tremble when faced with this important necessity to abiding in the Lord. That's because they don't really understand what prayer is. They think God is in some far off place and if you kneel on some hardwood floor long enough until your knees become raw then maybe, just maybe, He might listen to you. Prayer to them is burdensome, it makes a demand on their time, and they develop a contentment of praying at bedtime a prayer that begins, "Now I lay me down to sleep." People like that don't really know God at all and they definitely don't know what prayer really is. All prayer means is to talk with God. We talk and communicate with people every day of our lives, and how we talk to them is determined by the type of relationship we have with those to whom we are directing our words. You will say more to a spouse whom you are deeply in love with than some stranger standing on a street corner.

If you go to some department store there will probably be hundreds of other customers there whom you have never met before. How many of those strangers will you go up to and begin to share your most intimate and personal thoughts with? Probably none. But if you go into that same store and meet your best friend whom you've known for over twenty years, you will probably share with him or her every detail of what's gone on in your life since the last time the two of you talked. See the difference? How you talk to someone and what you say to them is determined by the quality of relationship you have with them. So, the question is, "What type of relationship do you have with God?" Do you know Him? Is He your best friend or some stranger you've never met? Jesus made it clear that He wants to be your friend. In John 15:15 He says, "No longer do I call you servants, for a servant does not know what his master is doing; but I have called you friends, for all things that I heard from My Father I have made known to you."

Jesus said that you were His friend and now you must decide if you want Him to become your friend. Just how does a person become a friend with God? Jesus tells us in the preceding verse. "You are My friends if you do whatever I command you" (John 15:14). The degree to which you are obedient to God is the degree to which you become His friend. Abraham was called the friend of God (James 2:23; Is. 41:8) and he was obedient to the point where he was willing to offer up his only son as a burnt offering to his Lord. Nothing will bring you closer to God than your obedience to His Word. Exodus 33:11 says, "So the Lord spoke to Moses' face to face, as a man speaks to his friend." Begin today talking to God as if He were your friend. When you get out of bed each day begin by saying, "Good morning, Lord, how are You today?" Get personal with Him. Talk to Him about anything and everything. He cares about the smallest details of your life. He really does.

God wants to get involved in every area of your life. He loves you so much that you can talk to Him about anything and everything. What makes all of this so meaningful is that He wants you to. In the garden of Eden He walked side-by-side with Adam in the cool of the evening. Can the imagine all the things they talked about? Equally important is to learn to listen when spending time with God. The Bible says, "Be still and know I am God" (Ps. 46:10). Before long you will develop a special bond with Him where He'll be able to talk to you as a man speaks to his friend. God resides on the inside of you, and as you get quiet before Him "a small, still voice" will rise up out of your innermost being. Instantly you will know that this is the voice of God. He is talking to you. He is telling you what's on His heart. He is your friend and He wants to get intimate with you. This is the ultimate reward of majoring in the basics of Christian life. What could be better than that? Nothing, nothing at all.

| 7 |

"THE VOICE OF FAITH"

Faith has a voice and it is the voice of victory. You can tell who is an overcomer by the way they talk. Their words are filled with hope and confidence believing that all things will work out for their good. You will see victory in their eyes and hear it in their voice. Their faith in God shines brightest when darkness is everywhere and all hope seems lost. There is a gleam in their eye and a bounce in their step no matter what's going on around them. They're so joyful that you could never guess what's going on behind the scenes. They testify what God is doing and never talk about what the devil is doing. 2 Cor. 4:13 says, "But since we have the same spirit of faith, according to what is written, 'I believed and therefore I spoke,' we also believe and therefore speak." The only thing coming out of their mouth is the sound of victory. Faith is precious and it is powerful. In all of God's creation it is the one thing that gives you the right and the ability to choose your own words and to release power into those words.

A person who is spiritually mature is able to control their mouth. James 3:2 says, "For we all stumble in many things. If anyone does not stumble in word, he is a perfect man, able also to bridle the whole body." One of the greatest things you can do to control and improve every area of your life instantly is to begin to monitor the words that come out of your mouth. Most people think the primary purpose of talking is to tell people how they feel and to make known what they want. They think words are nothing more than an expression of thoughts and feelings. But you are different. You are made in the image of God and He never speaks words that are without meaning and void of power. He never says things for the sake of saying them and He doesn't say things He doesn't mean or believe. There is faith in every word He speaks to cause whatever He says to come to pass. This is why it is impossible for God to lie. When He says something, it happens. When He decrees it, it comes to pass. He expects the same thing to happen to you. This is what walking in faith is all about.

If you want to change the direction of your life, you must change the words you speak. Don't say things you don't mean, words that will bind you up and stop you from living a wholesome life. When you control your mouth, you control your destiny. Knowing this will energize your inner man and you'll be led by the Spirit and not your flesh. You'll know what to do and what to say when things happen contrary to what they should be. You'll bind and you'll lose. You'll steer your life in the direction it should be going. Joel 3:10 says, "Let the weak say, 'I am strong.'" If symptoms of sickness and disease plague your body rise up and say, "By Jesus' stripes I am healed." If you are having financial difficulty, say, "I am rich. My God shall supply all my need according to His riches in glory by Christ Jesus. I come behind in no good thing." There is power in the spoken word. You are taking control of your destiny and now God can step in and do mighty things in your life.

Jesus has made you a king and a priest unto God (Rev. 1:6) and Eccl. 8:4 says, "Where the word of a king is, there is power." You are an overcomer and you reign in life with your words fully submitted to the lordship of Jesus Christ. The power of speech is one of the greatest powers God has given to man. A person can choose their own destiny by the words they speak. Prov. 18:21 says, "Death and life are in the power of the tongue, and those who love it will eat its fruit." Words are containers of faith. They paint pictures the same way an artist uses paint to express what's on the inside of him. Words can locate where a person stands "for out of the abundance of the heart the mouth speaks" (Matt. 12:34). When Jesus walked the earth, He was constantly measuring the faith of those around Him. He did so by listening to the words they spoke. He did it then and He is doing it today. This being so, it only stands to reason that the words you commit to hearing yourself speak is the Word of God. You are an artist with words and the image inside of you gets turned into reality by the words you speak.

God created the heavens and the earth by speaking words. Ps. 33:6 says, "By the word of the Lord the heavens were made, and all the host of them by the breath of His mouth." Vs. 9 says, "For He spoke, and it was done; He commanded, and it stood fast." Heb. 11:3 says the worlds were framed by the spoken word of

God. Faith is creative power and God puts a high emphasis on faith-filled words because they are the most powerful things on the planet. People will believe whatever they hear themselves say so never minimize the action of speaking. God told Abram that one day his descendants would outnumber the stars in the sky. Years later the promised son still was not born so God changed his name to Abraham which means "father of many nations." Each time he spoke his new name he was openly declaring the Word of God and a year later his son was born. In another story the Angel of the Lord called Gideon a "mighty man of valor" (Judges 6:12) and as a result of this confession of faith he later went on to defeat the Midianite army with only three hundred faithful men.

Faith always has something to say. It calls those things that be not as though they were. God did not see the world when He created it except through the eye of faith. God took His words and filled them with a spiritual force called faith. He spoke what He wanted and used His words as containers to transport that force into the spiritual darkness. This is how light was created out of darkness. God never does anything without saying it first and you are to do the same thing. At the time of creation, the words God spoke were the guidelines through which His faith went to work. Jesus said in Mark 11:23 that you are to release your faith the same way God releases His faith. "For assuredly I say to you, whoever says to this mountain, 'Be removed and be cast into the sea,' and does not doubt in his heart but believes that those things he says will come to pass, he will have whatever he says." Words released out of your mouth are powerful. They carry spiritual forces and faith-filled words will overcome the law of sin and death (Rom. 8:2).

When the creation of the heavens and the earth was completed, God next created man in His own image and gave him the job of having dominion over all the earth (Gen. 1:26-28). Since God rules the universe with words, so also did Adam use words to rule and have dominion over that which was entrusted to him. He did not have to hoe a garden or use hay to get a horse to come to him. All he had to do was speak to them. Adam patterned himself after God and until the time of the fall he used words to perform the calling on his life. Jesus is called "the second Adam" (1 Cor. 14:15) and He also ruled with words. When tempted in the wilderness by Satan He quoted the Word and did what the original Adam should have done in the same situation. Jesus understood the power of words and throughout His earthly ministry He spoke words into people, the wind and the waves, and He even spoke to a fever and a tree. Jesus used words to release His faith and so also must you. Eph. 5:1 (AMP) says, "Therefore be imitators of God - copy Him and follow His example as well-beloved children imitate their father."

The good fight of faith is a fight fought with words. Paul said in 1 Tim. 6:12, "Fight the good fight of faith, lay hold on eternal life, to which you were also called and confessed the good confession in the presence of many witnesses." Christianity is a confession and Christ Jesus is the Apostle and High priest of what you confess (Heb. 3:1). Your confessions rule you and your faith and life is measured by the words you speak. To make a confession means "to declare openly by way of speaking freely, such confession being the result and effect of deep conviction of facts." For the born-again believer confession was made unto salvation (Rom. 10:9,10) and the same principle is to be used throughout your walk of faith. Your confession is to your faith what thrust is to an airplane. Without thrust there will be no lift and without confession there will be no faith. Your confession is the ceiling for your faith for you will never rise any higher than your confession. The more you develop your confession of God's Word, the higher you'll get developed in your faith.

In the creation story nothing happened until words were spoken. Words are transmitters and they can transmit faith and they can transmit fear. Do not speak anything you don't desire to come to pass and that which is against your will. God's Word is His will for man and because you are created in His image your words should be your will for Him. You have the ability to conceive God's Word in your heart and it brings with it a spiritual force called faith. You then take that faith, fill your words with it, and use those words as containers to transport your faith into your present situation. Faith confessions create realities and is able to transform your current circumstance until it lines up with the Word of God. The gospel is the good news and is the power of God unto preservation, healing and soundness, and deliverance from temporary evils. Jesus said in John 6:63, "The words that I speak to you are spirit, and they are life." A faith confession means "to agree with God" and this is why you should always say the same words Jesus said.

Jesus said nothing would be impossible to them that believe. You can be assured that the fullness of God's faith is available to you because He lives in your heart. The secret to getting faith to work is to understand what Jesus said in Mark 4:26, "The kingdom of God is as if a man should scatter seed on the ground." Seedtime and harvest is God's way of doing things (Gen. 1:11,12) and it will be that way for as long as this planet is in existence (Gen. 8:22). In the parable of the growing seed Jesus is saying that you are the one who plants the seed. You take God's Word and you speak it out of your mouth. It then goes into your heart where it becomes a seed and begins to grow and produce. The power of words is the power of the seed. The life of what you're believing for is in the seed you plant. You plant seed by saying what God would say and you water it by doing what God would do. You have dominion through the power of words and if you are willing to plant faith as a seed then nothing will be impossible to you.

Jesus said in Mark 4:28, "For the earth yields crops by itself: first the blade, then the head, after that the full grain in the head." Sometimes people do silly things before the seed has time to grow. They think they can confess that they'll get a new car and it will appear in their garage the next morning. They work the faith formula but true faith has not yet been developed in their heart. Just because a promise is in the Bible does not mean it will work for you whenever you want it to. You must develop yourself in that specific area. You won't be able to believe for a new car if you can't first believe for a loaf of bread. The problem many people have is that they plant the seed and then go off and leave it. It takes time for the seed to sprout and grow so you have to take care of it until the manifestation comes. Keep the promise ever before you. Meditate on it day and night and speak it out of your mouth. Praise God and thank Him for the manifestation soon to be revealed.

Don't overload your faith. Don't go beyond the point where you're developed. Some people try to believe for a new house when they can't believe for a new pair of shoes. Operate in the faith you're currently developed in and go from there. You always have to start from where you're at. Don't throw away common sense just because your faith worked a time or two. Don't quit your job thinking God will supply all your needs and don't give away your car thinking you'll get a new one by the end of the day. You must draw a line between faith and presumption. Don't believe for a big house if you're not able to pay for its upkeep. Develop your faith to the point where you can take care of what you're believing for. People assume that if they can believe it in then they can believe for its upkeep. They are trying to operate in faith that has not yet been developed. They abuse the use of credit cards believing God will supply the monthly payments when they couldn't believe Him for the money to pay cash in the first place.

You've got to have good common sense to walk in faith. You can work the faith formula to get material possessions but you also need to have common sense where you sit down and count the cost for what happens once you receive it. You may want a big house but are you also able to believe for the finances to pay the huge tax bill that goes along with it? You can't throw away common sense and good business knowledge when you get turned on to faith. Walking in faith does not mean you don't have to put gas in the car anymore. It takes time to develop faith. It takes time to turn things around. Faith won't work overnight when you've walked in doubt and unbelief for the past thirty years. You've got to set things in motion and this takes time. Heb. 6:12 says that it is through faith and patience that you inherit the promises of God. The more highly developed you are in your faith the quicker the manifestation will come. This won't happen overnight but you can grow in faith and develop it day by day.

Jesus had great faith because He only said what He heard the Father say (John 12:49,50). When He did that, the faith of the Father came into Him. He told Satan, "Man shall not live by bread alone, but by every word that proceeds from the mouth of God" (Matt. 4:4). Just as Jesus always put the words of the Father in His mouth, so must you also do the same. Is. 59:21 (MSG) says, "'As for Me,' God says, 'this is My covenant with them: My Spirit that I've placed upon you and the words that I've given you to speak, they're not going to leave your mouths nor the mouths of your children nor the mouths of your grandchildren. You will keep repeating these words and won't ever stop.' God's orders." There is spirit life in every word of God and, when you speak His words, spiritual life and the God-kind of faith is directed to and birthed within your own spirit. This is how you follow Paul's instructions to "lay hold on eternal life" (1 Tim. 6:12). Faith don't come by reading the Word, it comes by you hearing it being spoken out of your own mouth.

Rom. 10:17 says, "So then, faith comes by hearing, and hearing by the Word of God." You cannot hear something that is not spoken and the child of God must realize that they will have more faith in what they hear themselves say than in what they hear someone else say. You were born with two sets of ears. You have the outer ears that are attached to your head and a bone structure inside your head called the inner ear. You hear other people speak with the outer ear but you hear yourself speak with the inner ear. It's the inner ear that takes what you say and delivers it into your heart. This is why the words you speak affect you more than what you hear somebody else say. Their words go into your brain but your words go into your heart. Ps. 45:1 says, "My heart is overflowing with a good theme; I recite my composition concerning the King; My tongue is the pen of a ready writer." This verse is saying that when you speak you are writing on the tablets of your heart.

Never underestimate the power of words to affect the human heart. James 1:26 says, "If anyone among you thinks he is religious, and does not bridle his tongue but deceives his own heart, this one's religion is useless." What your heart hears from your inner ear makes it believe that what you speak is what you want. The negative words you speak deceives your heart into believing that you want negative things to happen to you. Watch what you say because your inner ear is working to bring to pass that which it believes you want. In the parable of the growing seed the earth represents your heart where seed is sown. Mark 4:28 says, "For the earth yields crops by itself." In other words, your inner man will lead you in the direction it thinks you want it to go based on what it hears you say. The words inside your heart work the same way as seeds planted in the ground. Jesus said, "A good man out of the good treasure of his heart brings forth good things, and an evil man out of the evil treasure brings forth evil things" (Matt. 12:35). This is why words are the most powerful thing in the universe.

Train yourself to believe what you say. Learn to have faith in the words you hear yourself speak. An example of this is found in the story of David and Goliath. While standing in the presence of King Saul David said these faith-filled words, "The Lord, who delivered me from the paw of the lion and from the paw of the bear, He will deliver me from the hand of the Philistine" (1 Sam. 17:37), David then drew near to the giant and boldly proclaimed, "This day the Lord will deliver you into my hand, and I will strike you and take your head from you" (vs. 46). David spoke with a voice of victory and moments later the champion of the Philistine army lay dead just as David had proclaimed. Every person acts on what they believe in their heart and David won a great victory for the people of Israel because he had faith in the words he spoke. Faith is not moved by what it sees and David knew that you do not ignore the circumstances that confront you. Instead, you change them by the power of God's spoken word and not your own ability.

Num. 14:28 says, "Say to them, 'As I live,' says the Lord, 'just as you have spoken in My hearing, so I will do to you.'" God will do exactly as you say. This is why David confessed the outcome of the confrontation and then told Goliath "the battle is the Lord's" (1 Sam. 17:47). God will do exactly as you say and this is why you have to make sure that only faith-filled words proceed out of your mouth. A tongue that speaks doubt and fear "is a fire, a world of iniquity. It is an unruly evil, full of deadly poison" (James 3:6,8). Until the habit of making a good confession over your daily encounters becomes a manifested reality, until you are able to "call those things that be not as though they were," it is a good thing to develop in your life the vocabulary of silence. David said, "I will guard my ways lest I sin with my tongue; I will restrain my mouth with a muzzle" (Ps. 39:1). Sometimes what you don't say is just as important as what you do say.

The last thing you want is for your words to be your own worst enemy. They can work for you or against you so be careful what you say. People who murmur and complain all the time often wonder why they have no joy in their life and never walk in victory. Prov. 6:2 says, "You are snared by the words of your mouth." In other words, what you say, you allow. Challenge yourself to never say another negative word about yourself or the situation you are currently in. It is just as wrong to criticize yourself as it is to criticize someone else. When you criticize yourself, you are talking bad about God's very own personal creation. You are made in His image and when you say something bad about yourself you are in fact saying something bad about God. Don't talk about how things are but rather how you want them to be. Be like David who said in Ps. 139:14, "I will praise You, for I am fearfully and wonderfully made; Marvelous are your works, and that my soul knows very well." Confess those things that be not as though they were. This is what faith is all about.

Your words have the power to push you into your divine destiny. Don't allow your potential to lay dormant inside of you. Speak words of victory over your life and watch God take you from being a nobody to being a somebody who is great and powerful. There are seeds of greatness inside of you and faith-filled words causes those seeds to grow to full maturity. Allow your words to ignite the fire burning inside of you that will propel you to the next level of your destiny. Rise up with a new level of confidence and become all that God says you can become. Prov. 18:16 says, "A man's gift makes room for him, and brings him before great men." Believe this can happen to you. Believe that God can cause you to stand before kings and openly declare what you believe. God has given you the ability to see with eyes of faith what you can't see with the natural eye. Faith has a voice so speak out what you see on the inside of you. Speak words of victory into your future and move in the direction God is telling you to go.

Your words have creative power and have the ability to thrust you to where you'll be able to do great things in the kingdom of God. Live to be a blessing and help make somebody else great. One word of encouragement from you can change the direction of another person's life. Put their needs above your own then stand back and watch what God will do for you. Stir up the gift inside of you and rise up to the level of your expectations. There is no limit as to how high you can go when daily with the voice of faith you speak victory over your life. Say out loud, "I can do all things through Christ who strengthens me." Call out those seeds of greatness and your confidence will rise to a higher level. Soon you'll be doing things you could only dream about in times past. The chains that once put limits on your life are now broken and you'll be able to run your race and finish your course. You'll run toward the giant who is on your path to greatness and defeat him the same way David defeated Goliath. Shout the victory! Nothing can stop you now!

God is expecting you to leave your mark on this generation and it takes the voice of faith to do it. God has equipped you and given you creative power to do great things. Speak it out and call it into manifestation. Dream big and talk big. Be like Caleb who said, "Let us go up at once and take possession, for we are well able to overcome it" (Num. 13:30). You were born for such a time as this. You are not here by accident. In eternity past God planned for you to be alive right here, right now, for a specific purpose. God has plans to give you a future and a hope and you give life to them with the voice of faith. Look and see the vision inside of you and speak it out your mouth. Give life to it and water it and watch those seeds of greatness grow. Make plans to do something great with your life. Make plans to help change the direction this world is going. One person can change an entire generation and there is no reason that one person can't be you.

Words give life to whatever you're saying. Prov. 18:21 says you will eat the fruit of your words so be sure you always send your words in the direction you want your life to go. You cannot talk defeat and expect to have victory. You cannot talk sickness and poverty and expect to have health and prosperity. You are able to catch a glimpse of what your future will be like by listening to the words you're speaking today. Don't use your words to describe the situation you are in, use your words to change your situation. Don't talk about how things are, talk about how you want them to be. Instead of complaining, say openly that today is going to be the best day of your life and tomorrow will be even better. Declare health, favor, and abundance over your life and as you do that those seeds of greatness begin to grow. Soon you will see yourself and your circumstances in a whole new light. You will see what God sees and will believe that nothing can stop you or hold you back from fulfilling your destiny. That will give you something to shout about.

Ps. 47:1 says, "Oh, clap your hands, all you peoples! Shout to God with the voice of triumph!" Faith has a voice and it always makes a sound. The moving of the Spirit is like the blowing of the wind. Jesus said in John 3;8, "The wind blows where it wishes, and you hear the sound of it, but cannot tell where it comes from and where it goes. So is everyone who is born of the Spirit." Being born of the Spirit is like being born of the wind. Wind has a sound and on the day of Pentecost "suddenly there came a sound from heaven, as of a rushing mighty wind" (Acts 2:2). This was the Holy Spirit and He made a sound. This is how Jesus ministered on the earth. He made a sound with His words. He said "be cleansed" and they were. He said "be healed" and they were. He said "rise up and walk" and they did. He then said in John 14:12, "Most assuredly, I say to you, he who believes in Me, the works that I do he will do also, and greater works than these he will do, because I go to the Father."

How did Jesus do these works? He heard from the Father and said in faith what He heard the Father say. He spoke to the wind and waves and they obeyed Him. He spoke to a fever and it left and He cursed a fig tree and it withered and died. He called to dead Lazarus "come forth" and he came alive. All this is available to you if you would step up and rise to the fullness of what rightfully belongs to you. You are to walk in the Spirit and not in the flesh. In the flesh you are as limited as the unsaved world. But if you'll rise up and walk like Jesus did, if you'll walk in faith and in the Spirit, amazing things will happen and the impossible will be made possible. This is the type of life you will live when you walk by faith and not by sight. You don't talk about how you feel, you declare openly what you believe. You believe, therefore you speak. Words are containers and if there is no faith present then there is no life in them. To live a victorious life there has got to be more coming out of your mouth than hot air.

In the world of science, sound can pass through steel and change matter, and in the realm of the spirit faith sounds can change the impossible into the possible. When a trial comes you need to check your heart and decide what type of sounds, you're going to make. Are you going to make sounds of doubt and fear or are you going to make sounds of victory by saying what God's Word says about it? Do not speak until you're ready to release your faith. Paul talks about "idle talkers and deceivers" in Titus 1:10-16. The Message Bible says, "For there are a lot of rebels out there, full of loose, confusing, and deceiving talk. Those who were brought up religious and ought to know better are the worst. They've got to be shut up."

The word "idle" means 'unemployed' and describes people who stand around all day and don't do anything. Your words are not to be empty or idle but rather are supposed to accomplish something when you speak them out of your mouth. You are to use your words to change and frame your world just like God did.

Joshua 6 tells the story of the victory at Jericho and vs. 1,2 says, "Now Jericho was securely shut up because of the children of Israel; none went out, and none came in. And the Lord said to Joshua: 'See! I have given Jericho into your hand, its king, and the mighty men of valor.'" God calls those things that be not as though they were. Before anything happened, God gave the city to Joshua. Instructions were then given for the people to march around the city one time for six days. Vs. 4 says, "But the seventh day you shall march around the city seven times and the priests shall blow the trumpets." It is interesting to note that on the island of Patmos John wrote in Rev. 1:10, "I was in the Spirit on the Lord's Day, and I heard behind me a loud voice, as of a trumpet." The people did as the Lord instructed and when the priests blew their trumpets Joshua said to the people, "Shout, for the Lord has given you the city!" (vs. 16). Vs. 20 says the people shouted with a "great shout."

What are the people shouting about? They are not shouting to bring the wall down and neither are they shouting at the wall. They are shouting because God had already given them the city. It was a faith-filled victory shout. They're having a celebration and are shouting because it is now their city. They're on the outside looking in but as far as they're concerned the city is theirs. When they released their faith, power went forth and the wall fell down flat. People get angry and shout all the time trying to get their situation to change but it never happens. Many times, the situation gets worse. To change things, you've got to shout not an angry shout but a faith shout believing that your words will accomplish the assignment you assigned to them. Are there walls in your life? Are there symptoms of sickness in your body and bills to be paid? If so, then know there is a sound that can come out of your mouth that will change your situation around. The same spirit of faith that was in Joshua is in you so stand up and shout a faith-filled shout. That is the shout of victory.

| 8 |

"THE WORKS OF FAITH"

James 2:17 says, "Thus also faith by itself, if it does not have works, is dead." Faith can be discerned and it involves more than a private agreement between you and God. If it is a real, living faith there will be other evidence that you have it besides you confessing what you believe. Vs. 18 says, "Show me your faith without your works, and I will show you my faith by my works." There is no faith without corresponding actions and deeds. Real faith has action. Real faith does something. A person who makes confessions all day but doesn't do anything isn't walking in true faith. Vs. 26 says, "For as the body without the spirit is dead, so faith without works is dead also." Just saying you have faith is not enough to get you results. Real faith needs action produced by active zeal in contrast to being idle and doing nothing. It expresses itself by what it does. In order to get a manifestation of the power of God, what you believe in spirit must be expressed with deeds and action. Dead faith gets no answers.

God is not pleased with people who all they do is wait all the time. Some people have been waiting on God for years expecting Him to do something. Making a confession and waiting indefinitely is not living faith. You must initiate your own miracle by doing something. The woman with the issue of blood didn't stay at home like she was supposed to according to the law. No, she went out to where Jesus was. She pressed through the crowd, touched the hem of His garment, and received her miracle. Jesus said to her, "Daughter, your faith has made you well" (Mark 5:34). It took more than the will of God and the anointing to get this woman healed. It took her faith that was backed up and proven with corresponding actions. Faith without works is dead. You can't believe God for a job if you're not willing to go out and look for one. You can't move a parked car. Prov. 16:9 says, "A man's heart plans his way, but the Lord directs his steps." Taking steps of faith and doing something is faith in action and this is how you get results.

Faith in God is powerful and it works. There is no such thing as a faith failure. Faith that acts on what it believes always gets results. Always! If you are in faith, there will be action. There will be things you do because you believe. There are actions that will meet the power of God and will give Him a right to move in your life. Faith is a law and you act on what He told you and on what you believe. Many people justify their waiting on God by quoting the first half of Is. 40:31, "But those who wait on the Lord shall renew their strength." The problem is they didn't read the rest of the verse, "They shall mount up with wings like eagles, they shall run and not be weary, they shall walk and not faint." There is action here. You are to mount up, run, and walk. When you mount up you don't stay at home and do nothing. You rise up, you run, and you keep going. You need to seek the Lord and find out what you're supposed to do. You then mount up and do it with all your heart and soul. You keep doing it and doing it for that is how you get your miracle.

Faith is not passively waiting and making the occasional good confession. Faith is a walk, a way of life. You can't sit back and do nothing and say you're waiting on God to move when He's ready. That's just like a non-believer who says they're waiting on God to save them. No, Jesus already died for their sins on the cross and it's now up to them to respond to that finished work. The price has already been paid. They are not waiting on God to save them but they can initiate the new birth by what they say and by what they do. It takes action on their part and so it is with you when you are believing for God to move in your life. People say God is in control of everything but that's not true. He has left some things up to you. Matt. 6:33 says, "But seek first the kingdom of God and His righteousness, and all these things shall be added to you." Seeking first the kingdom is a continuous and repeated action and is a manifestation of faith. You don't look for something if you don't believe it's there. You don't search for it unless you believe you can find it.

Matt. 7:7 says, "Ask, and it will be given to you; seek, and you will find; knock, and it will be opened to you." Each one of these things is doing something. It's faith in action. Vs. 8 says, "For everyone who asks receives, and he who seeks finds, and to him who knocks it will be opened." Everybody knows that without faith it's impossible to please God (Heb. 11:6) but in the same verse it goes on to say "that He is a rewarder of those who diligently seek Him." This verse is saying that the action of seeking God must be added to your faith. You can't just wait all the time and do nothing. The blessings of God are not going to fall on you like ripe cherries off a tree. You've got to believe God and you've got to add action to your faith. You've got to do what He told you to do. You can't wait for the blessing to manifest itself if and when God gets ready to give it to you. The Bible says "that after you have done the will of God you may receive the promise" (Heb. 10:36).

You must take action and do the will of God before you receive the promise. Action comes first and this is what pleases God. Heb. 11:4 says, "By faith Abel offered to God a more excellent sacrifice than Cain." Abel did something. By faith Noah prepared an ark (vs. 7) and by faith Abraham went out not knowing where he was going (vs. 8). These are all action terms. They were in faith and they did something. People today are too result oriented. They think God will only be pleased when they get their bills paid. No, what pleases God is them standing in faith believing that they'll get their bills paid. Faith that doesn't give up and keeps pressing forward is what pleases God. Faith is the evidence of things not seen. Faith is what you do and say before the manifestation arrives. You've got to be willing to take a step, and then another step, and another one after that. If all you do is sit and wait, months are going to pass and even years. Nothing happens if all you do is sit and wait and this will make you greatly discouraged and want to give up.

God has a plan for your life and it's up to you to seek Him in order to find out what that plan is. You have to overcome the laziness of your flesh that wants to sit and do nothing but wait all the time. Jer. 29:13 says, "And you will seek Me and find Me, when you search for Me with all your heart." When you do seek the Lord, He will show you what to do but He won't tell you everything all at once. Rom. 4:12 says you are to "walk in the steps of faith which our father Abraham had while still uncircumcised." God will direct your steps. He'll tell you one thing to do and when you do it, He'll tell you what to do next. Little by little, step by step. You don't have to know the whole plan of God, you only have to know what the next step is. And don't go off and just do anything, only do what He tells you to do. God is expecting you to seek Him out because it is your responsibility to do so. It is not His responsibility to come to you first.

Paul said in Eph. 5:17, "Therefore do not be unwise, but understand what the will of the Lord is." The Message Bible says, "Don't live carelessly, unthinkingly. Make sure you understand what the Master wants." The Lord is standing on the outside knocking on the door of your heart. It's up to you to open the door and invite Him in. You've got to want to know what the will of the Lord is. If you could care less then you're not worthy of the call He has for your life. Your priorities must be in the proper place. You must be fully persuaded that God is a good God and that He's got an amazing plan for your life. You then take the first step and seek Him out. James 4:8 says, "Draw near to God and He will draw near to you." When you do that with a willing heart, the Lord will give you divine direction. He'll speak a word to you to get you started. It may not be a full sentence or a full paragraph. It may be only one word. But when you earnestly obey that word, you can be assured that further direction will come.

Some people wait for years and nothing ever happens. The problem is they're waiting for God to move when in reality He is waiting for them to take the first step. God told them to "Come" but they haven't gotten out of the boat yet. You need to stir yourself up and put one foot in front of the other. At the same time, get in the Word and build your faith up because God only gives big dreams and for sure it will take faith to fulfill it. The good news is that as you move forward, God will be by your side every step of the way. He will lead you step by little step. It takes faith to obey God and, as each step is taken, in time your faith will grow. When it does grow, little steps become big steps and, before you know it, the fulfillment of your call has come into manifestation. None of this would have happened if all you did was sit down and wait. No, you've got to get out of the boat. You've got to seek God and trust Him enough to believe that He will speak to you. Rest assured, He will speak to you and when He does, obey His voice and do what He tells you to do.

Always dream big but be prepared to take small steps at the beginning of your journey. Jesus said, "According to your faith be it done unto you." When you take the initiative and take that small step, God will be pleased with you and will soon tell you the next step to take, and the next step after that. You will be like a rocket that lifts slowly off the launch pad but soon gains momentum and before long is traveling at full speed. Job 8:7 says, "Though your beginning was small, yet your latter end would increase abundantly." To get to this point you can't be passive and do nothing. You must ask, seek, and knock. Some dreams take years to fulfill but if it wasn't worthwhile God wouldn't have given it to you in the first place. Caleb waited over forty years to receive his mountain and to him it was worth the wait. Gen. 29:20 says, "So Jacob served seven years for Rachel and they seemed but a few days to him because of the love he had for her." Time means nothing as long as you are faithfully doing what God told you to do.

James 1:25 says, "But he who looks into the perfect law of liberty and continues in it, and is not a forgetful hearer but a doer of the work, this one will be blessed in what He does." The NLT says "if you do what it says and don't forget what you heard, then God will bless you for doing it." The fulfillment of your dream begins with you earnestly seeking Him. He is your Father and He loves you. He knows what you need to do to reach your promised land. He knows what steps you need to take. You don't need to figure it all out but you do need to hear from Him. You need to pray and seek Him and, if necessary, fast a few days. Some people don't even try or else they try for a little while and give up. Jesus said in Luke 9:62, "No one, having put his hand to the plow, and looking back, is fit for the kingdom of God." God takes this very seriously and so should you. Don't cast away your confidence but take those steps of faith. Heb.10:38 says, "Now the just shall live by faith; But if anyone draws back, My soul has no pleasure in him."

Your mountain is waiting for you. Go after it and rest in the assurance that after you've done the will of God you will receive the promise. He will give you strength so you can run your race and finish your course. He will forever be by your side as He leads you to your miracle. He'll tell you what to do but you can't be a hearer only, you must be a doer of the Word (James 1:22). When you obey Him, you will be blessed in what you do. You'll see things happen that others say can't be done. God will open doors of opportunity for you that weren't there before. Miraculously you will be at the right place at the right time. He'll show you the way and in faith you step out and do it. One step here, one step there, and before you know it you've crossed over into your promised land. Millions of people are sitting home doing nothing but you are in the land flowing with milk and honey. The blessings of Abraham are yours because you took steps of faith just like he did. Ps. 84:11 says, "No good thing will He withhold from those who walk uprightly."

Faith that does nothing is worth nothing. James 2:14 (NLT) says, "What good is it, dear brothers and sisters, if you say you have faith but don't show it by your actions? Can that kind of faith save anyone?" You must go beyond saying what you believe if you're going to get results. You've got to do something. You've got to put action to your faith. The good news is that you don't have to figure out what to do on your own. God will tell you what to do. At the wedding in Cana of Galilee the mother of Jesus told the servants, "Whatever He says to you, do it" (John 2:5). That's the key to receiving your miracle. You do what God tells you to do and that gives Him the right to manifest His power in your life. Problems come when people do nothing. In 2 Kings 7 there was a famine in the land and four leprous men at the entrance of the gate said to one another, "Why are we sitting here until we die?" (vs. 3). This is a divine revelation because people are doing this all over the world. They sit and sit and sit and do nothing and then get mad at God when nothing good happens in their life.

All things are possible to them that believe but you've got to do something first. These four leprous men reasoned they were going to die anyway so they decided to do something. They rose up and went to the camp of the enemy to surrender themselves and when they arrived nobody was there (vs. 5). As they went, when they did something, the Lord performed a miracle for them. He amplified their footsteps and caused the Syrian army to hear the sound of a great army coming toward them. The added noise of chariots and horses caused them to flee the camp leaving behind all their livestock, food, clothing, and silver and gold (vs. 7,8). Back in the city the people were eating garbage but these four sick men were eating like kings, all because they did something. When they started moving, God started moving. When they did something, God did something. If you sit and do nothing, if you sit until you die, then nothing will happen no matter what you say you believe. Remember, faith that does nothing is worth nothing.

James 4:7 says, "Resist the devil and he will flee from you." One way to resist the devil is to put action to your faith. When you move, God moves. When God moves, the enemy flees. These four lepers resisted the Syrian army by marching into their camp and a great miracle happened. You've got to give

God something to work with. He can't lead you if you're sitting down until you die. Yes, He could have caused the Syrian army to flee on His own but He has chosen not to work that way. He chooses to use people who are walking by faith. These four lepers went and told the king what happened and before long the entire city was saved from the famine. God used the action of four lepers to feed a multitude of people. When Jesus fed the multitude He gave thanks, broke the bread and fish, "and the disciples gave to the multitude" (Matt. 15:36). The miracle happened when the disciples did something. The bread and fish were multiplied as the disciples went about giving the food to the people. Nothing would have happened if they stood there and did nothing.

Why did you get born again when you did? That's when you did something. When you drew near to God, He drew near to you. When you moved, He moved. Faith in action brings manifestation. In Luke 17 ten lepers asked Jesus to have mercy on them. Jesus said, "Go, show yourselves to the priests." Vs. 14 then says, "And so it was that as they went, they were cleansed." Jesus can't help you if you don't have enough faith to do as He says. It's faith and action that gives Him justification to do for you what He's not doing for everybody else. You did something and they didn't. Corresponding actions is proof to God that you believe Him. Lepers were not supposed to show themselves to the priests unless they were already cleansed but they went anyway. They did something and as they went a miracle occurred. They obeyed the instructions Jesus gave them. This goes right along with what Mary told the servants at the wedding feast, "Whatever He says to you, do it." A miracle happened then and a miracle happened now.

Faith is the answer to every problem, the solution to every need. But it only works when you step out and do what God tells you to do. People who do nothing has faith that is worth nothing. Faith is demonstrated in what you do. Acts 14:9 tells how Paul perceived that a certain lame man had faith to be healed. It is possible to have faith to be healed and not be healed. Just because you have faith doesn't mean a miracle is automatically going to manifest in your life. Faith must be released, it must be acted upon. You must step up and you must step out. Paul said to the lame man with a loud voice, "Stand up straight on your feet!" And he leaped and walked (vs. 10). The man did something. When he leaped up the miracle-working power of God came on him and he began to walk. This was not a case of God's timing for God wanted to heal this man all along. This man was not sitting there waiting for God to move, God was waiting for him to move. When he put action to his faith and leaped up, a miracle happened.

People who wait on God to move are blinded to reality. They are in error when they think everything is up to Him. They get haughty and combative when they say that God is in control of everything that happens. The enemy has worked non-stop to get people to believe this. It is a doctrine of demons that causes millions of people to get angry with God when their problems don't go away. Not everything that happens is His will and His plan. People try to have faith anyway but they're full of confusion and in truth don't know what to believe. They are believing the lies of the devil and this is why their faith doesn't work. Deut. 30:19 says God sets before you life and death, blessing and cursing. It's up to you to choose which one you will receive, not God. Yes, God is all powerful and all-knowing but He has chosen to give man a free will with which to choose the course of their life. It's up to you to decide where you'll spend eternity. It's up to you to receive your healing. It's up to you to receive your prosperity. It's up to you to fulfill your heavenly call. It's up to you to run your race and finish your course.

Speaking of the children of Israel, Heb. 11:29 says, "By faith they passed through the Red Sea as by dry land, whereas the Egyptians, attempting to do so, were drowned." With the Egyptian army behind them and the Red Sea before them, the people began to murmur and complain and they rebelled against God. The Lord said to Moses in Ex. 14:15, "Why do you cry to Me? Tell the children to go forward." The Message Bible says, "Order them to get moving." They did and the waters parted. Hebrews calls this act of going forward "faith." The people did what God told them to do and they passed through the midst of the sea on dry ground. The Egyptian army, on the other hand, did something God did not tell them to do. They followed the children of Israel into the midst of the Red Sea and the wall of water crashed down on top of them and they were all drowned. The children of Israel went forward by faith, the Egyptian army did it by experiment. Never do what other people are doing if the Lord didn't tell you to do it also. Only do what God tells you to do.

James 1:22 says, "But be doers of the word, and not hearers only, deceiving yourselves." If you believe something, you'll act on it. If you do nothing, you are deceived and God is warning you not to let that happen. Daniel 12:4 says that knowledge will increase in the last days. While this may be good in and of itself, one must be careful because in today's intellectual generation the devil can use increased knowledge to deceive you. He wants people so focused on learning new things that they fail to act on what they've learned. There are many people with a college education who are flipping hamburgers at the local fast food restaurant. They're not using and acting on the knowledge they've learned. This same type of scenario is happening in the church today. Believers have shelves filled with Christian books and recorded messages but still live a defeated life. They know this verse and that verse and are puffed up with how much knowledge they have of the Word. The problem is they're not acting on what they know and are thus deceived.

You can have an abundance of knowledge of the Word of God and not do anything with it. There is a danger in letting this happen. You can't read your Bible the same way you would a novel or the morning newspaper. A person can read a novel and never act on what they're read. They were entertained for a short period of time and when the book is finished, they put it down and soon forget what they've read. Many believers are doing the same thing with the Bible and are falling into the same trap of self-deception. They are deceived because they think if they know what the Bible says then everything will be all right in their lives. They read chapter after chapter and do nothing with it. Popular in the church today is the ritual of reading the entire Bible in a year. It doesn't matter to them if they act on it or not, as long as they maintain the daily reading schedule. When the year is finished, they pat themselves on the back thinking they've done some great deed. No, these people were deceived because they never acted on what they read.

Heb. 10:36 says, "For you have need of endurance, so that after you have done the will of God, you may receive the promise." When do you receive the promise? When you've done the will of God. It's not what you know that counts, it's what you do. Faith without works is dead. There comes a time when you have to stop reading, and stop talking, and start putting action to what you believe. It's when you get out of the boat that the power of God is manifested in your life. This is why it's better to learn and act on one verse of scripture than it is to read ten chapters a day and do nothing. Acts 6:7 says "a great many of the priests were obedient to the faith." Paul was commissioned "to tell Gentiles everywhere what God has done for them, so that they will believe and obey Him, bringing glory to His name" (Rom. 1:5 NLT). You believe and then you obey. If you're not getting out of the boat, then you're not trusting God. Walking in fear does not bring glory to your Heavenly Father. That right is reserved for those who believe and obey.

Miracles come through the obedience to a faith command. In John 5:8 Jesus told a lame man, "Rise, take up your bed and walk." The man obeyed and was healed. Jesus told Peter "Come" and he obeyed and began to walk on the water. This is what happens when you become a doer of the Word and not a hearer only. The action of you getting out of the boat is your way of telling God that you trust Him and this is what pleases Him the most. This is what gives Him the right to perform miracles in your life. Stop thinking that everything is all up to God. It's not, it's up to you and your willingness to act on what you believe. You must overcome all your fears and dread and obey Him anyway. It was fear that caused Peter to sink in the water, but it was his obedience to a faith command that caused the miracle to happen in the first place. God has an amazing plan for your life, and if that means getting out of the boat, then get out of the boat. By faith you can believe that the power of God will keep you afloat until the next step is ready to be taken.

| 9 |

"THE EYE OF FAITH"

You are sustained and controlled by your faith. Getting saved is not where faith ends, it's the starting point. Jesus said in Mark 11:22 (AMP), "Have faith in God constantly." After you've been saved from sin and condemnation you are to begin a journey where you live by faith every day of your life. Faith is a lifestyle and its consistency that brings about change. Rom. 1:17 says we go from "faith to faith." The Amplified Bible says, "For in the gospel the righteousness of God is revealed, both springing from faith and leading to faith, disclosed in a way that awakens more faith. As it is written and forever remain written, 'The just and upright shall live by faith.'" Trusting God with all your heart and soul will take you to a higher level of love, joy, and peace. There is no need you can't use your faith to get met, but at the same time, faith has to be released. The problem is many people are spiritually lazy and don't use their faith the way they're supposed to. Oftentimes it takes effort to sincerely walk by faith. It's one thing to have faith, it's another to use your faith and exercise it.

All things are not possible for everybody. The Bible says all things are possible for only a select few, them that believe. The just don't die early or go under when storms arise. They live on and they overcome by faith. 1 Tim. 6:17 says, "Fight the good fight of faith, lay hold on eternal life..." People who say "let go and let God" are saying God will do everything and they have to do nothing. This is not true. This is a deceptive fable for there is a part you have to play. The Bible says the just shall live by faith. Faith is not God's part, it's your part. You don't let go, you lay hold. Heb. 4:14 says, "Let us hold fast our confession." You don't back off and just leave everything up to God. Heb. 10:38,39 says, "Now the just shall live by faith; But if anyone draws back, My soul has no pleasure in him. But we are not of those who draw back to perdition, but of those who believe to the saving of the soul." Success is when you hang on when others have let go. Believe in the Word constantly. Faith in God always gets results. It's the victory that overcomes the world (1 John 5:4).

Real faith steps up and steps out. It is not passive but rises up and takes what rightfully belongs to it. It lays hold of something that has already been provided. John G. Lake once said, "The gospel is the strong man's religion." It is not for the faint of heart. It is up to you to enjoy the things God has already given you. Receiving by faith and resisting the devil is not up to God. That's the part you play. It takes faith to live a victorious life. The same way you got born again is how you live every day of your life. God will help you but He can't help if you're not doing anything. Yes, the Bible does say to come boldly to the throne of grace to obtain mercy and find grace to help in time of need (Heb. 4:16). Still, your actions and your involvement determine what God is going to help you with. A lot of people pray for God to do everything while they sit back and do nothing. Those prayers will not be answered. God will not help you until you are first willing to do something yourself. Faith without works is dead and the works you are doing are the works God will help you with.

Give God something to work with. When you do what you can do, having faith that He will help you, then when you reach the end of your ability you will find grace to help in time of need. Eph. 2;7 says "that in the ages to come He might show the exceeding riches of His grace in His kindness toward us in Christ Jesus." The Hebrew word for "grace" means 'to bend down or stoop down in kindness to.' Grace is when God reaches down to you when you can't reach up. Grace is freely given but it must be received by faith. Eph. 2:8 says "by grace you have been saved through faith." Knowing God will take care of you does not mean you don't have to release your faith. You still have to speak the Word and believe it will work for you. This is how you lay hold of what's been given to you. Trials will come but faith grows as you go through the bad experiences of life with God at your side. Get serious with God and exercise your faith so you will believe everything He says. Faith is a powerful force that can change you and the circumstances you are in.

Faith can grow but it only grows as you use it. It takes effort to grow in faith. The more you use it, the stronger it gets. Exercise and effort come in when the trial you're facing today is a little more severe than the trial you faced yesterday. A body builder develops his muscles by steadily increasing the amount of weight he endeavors to lift. Over time what was once hard for him will be no problem because his muscles have gotten stronger and better developed. To walk in faith, you can't be lazy. Doing the right thing does take effort. Faith has no power without works and spiritually lazy Christians will never stay protected from the plots and plans of the enemy. It takes effort to exercise your faith. 2 Peter 1:5 (AMP) says, "For this very reason, adding your diligence to the divine promises, employ every effort in exercising your faith to develop virtue (excellence, resolution, Christian energy) ..." You need to be motivated, get out of bed, and put forth some effort and be spiritually active by exercising your faith and be the person God wants you to be. The result of all this is that you will live a good life plus be a blessing to somebody else.

2 Cor. 4:18 says "we do not look at the things which are seen, but at the things which are not seen." Faith makes what you're believing for real to you in the spiritual realm even when you can't see it in the natural. Heb. 11:1 says, "Now faith is the substance of things hoped for, the evidence of things not seen." The Amplified Bible says, "Now faith is the assurance (the confirmation, the title deed) of the things we hope for, being the proof of things we do not see and the conviction of their reality, faith perceiving as real what is not revealed to the senses." Faith is the title deed to things not seen. It's the proof of existence of what you're believing for. You know it's there even though you don't see it. What you're believing for does exist whether you can see it or not. Abraham was called the father of many nations before he and Sarah had any children. Faith

starts with an image inside your head. God showed Abraham the stars and told him that's how many descendants he would have. God asked Jeremiah, "What do you see?" (Jer. 1:11). He is asking you the same thing.

Faith has an eye and you must see in the spirit what you're believing for. Faith creates an image and sees the end result before it actually happens. And when you see it in your heart, you will speak it out your mouth. "For out of the abundance of the heart, the mouth speaks" (Matt. 12:34). Your imagination is a powerful gift from God. It will take you to the life you've always wanted to have. Albert Einstein once said, "Your imagination is everything. It's a preview of life's coming attractions." Give yourself permission to dream and when you do always dream big. Let your faith arise and allow it to take you to the next level. God wants to speak to you. He wants to reveal to you His plan for your life. He wants you to dream big dreams and then with eyes of faith use your imagination to visualize those dreams coming to pass. Think about what God wants you to do. Dream outside the realm of possibility for as a man thinks in his heart, do does he become (Prov. 23:7). In order to get to the next level, you must be able to see the next level. To achieve big dreams, you have to imagine them first and then take the steps necessary to bring about their fulfillment.

In order to fulfill your God-given dreams, you must get serious and plan to succeed on purpose. Prov. 29:18 says, "Where there is no vision, the people perish." The major cause of failure is that most people wander aimlessly through life not knowing where they want to be five years from now. They have no vision and no goals. They don't get what they want because they don't know what they want. There are things God wants you to get serious about so get alone with Him and listen to what He has to say. Remember, this is a God-given dream and not your own. You need to know where you're going so you'll know which direction you should go. Stay focused on your God-given dreams and goals so you can start living instead of just existing. You become what you think about and your life will go in the direction of your most dominate thought. In order to achieve the impossible, you must first dream the impossible. Imagine what your future will look like for you must see it on the inside before it gets seen on the outside.

Your future begins with your ability to imagine your God-given dreams being fulfilled. God said concerning the people of Babel, "Nothing they have imagined they can do will be impossible for them" (Gen. 11:6). He also said in Ps. 46:10, "Be still, and know that I am God." Slow down from the bustling demands of life and take time to visualize your future. See beyond where you're at today. See yourself successful and fulfilling God's call on your life. You need to be able to identify what success means to you. Be specific because if you don't know where you're going you won't know how to believe God to get you there. You do not succeed by accident, you succeed on purpose and it all begins by seeing your future through the eyes of faith. Your faith imaginations precede achievement. The greater your thinking, the greater your potential. Every decision you make and every action you take begins first in your mind with a thought. If you think it, you'll believe it. If you saw a thought, you'll reap an action.

Your thoughts are the pathway to your destiny and is therefore the number one target of the enemy. Thoughts control your decisions and you will be successful when the thoughts you think are founded on the Word of God. Let God transform you into a new person by changing the way you think. Rom. 12:2 says, "And do not be conformed to this world, but be transformed by the renewing of your mind, that you may prove what is that good and acceptable and perfect will of God." The Message Bible says, "Fix your attention on God. You'll be changed from the inside out. Readily recognize what He wants from you, and quickly respond to it." The Bible is like a mirror where you see a reflection of yourself as God sees you. He sees you valuable, important, gifted and talented. He sees you achieving all your dreams and leaving your mark on this generation. He sees you being a blessing to the body of Christ. With eyes of faith, you can see what God sees and you will say what God tells you to say and do what He tells you to do.

To reach your full potential you must next give voice to what you visualize with your imagination. 2 Cor. 4:13 says, "But since we have the same spirit of faith, according to what is written, 'I believed and therefore I spoke,' we also believe and therefore speak." Faith is revealed in the words you speak. Words create images and the more you confess the Word of God, the clearer the image will become inside of you. The spoken word is what God used to create the heavens and the earth. Heb. 11:3a says, "By faith we understand that the worlds were framed by the word of God." God transported faith in the container of words and He called light out of darkness. He said "Light be" and light was. You frame your world daily by the words you speak. They are framing an image inside of you and you will live out the reality of that image. This is why it's so important to let the Word of God build an image in you and not the circumstances you are going through.

Mark 4:35-41 tells the story of when Jesus calmed the storm. He was asleep in the stern of the boat and the disciples woke Him up fearing for their lives. Vs. 39a says, "Then He arose and rebuked the wind, and said to the sea, 'Peace, be still!'" Notice that Jesus went to the cause of the problem first. If He stopped the waves before the wind quit blowing then the waves would come right back. When He rebuked the wind He was going to the root of the problem. Many problems go unsolved because people deal with the symptoms and not the root. Jesus said, "Peace, be still!" He called those things that be not as though they were. By doing that He was creating an image of what He wanted and this is how you calm the storms in your life. You say what you believe and you believe what you say. Keep your words spiritual. Never speak contrary to the Word of God. So many people talk about their problems instead of talking to their problems. The problem with that is the more you talk about the problem the bigger it gets and the more you believe in it.

Don't pray the problem, pray the solution. You magnify what you talk about and this is why David said in Ps. 141:3, "Set a guard, O Lord, over my mouth; Keep watch over the door of my lips." Jesus said "Peace, be still!" when there was no peace. The waves were still pounding against the side of the boat. When you pray the problem, you are in reality complaining and telling God what the devil said. The disciples said, "Teacher, do You not care that we are perishing?" (vs. 38). God does not want to hear what the devil said. The words you speak are like seeds and they will produce. Faith comes by hearing whether it's the words of God or the words of the devil. If you hear the words of the devil long enough, in time you'll have more faith in him than in the words of God. Heb. 11:3 says "by faith we understand..." People who don't have faith in the Word of God don't understand the things of life. This is why many believe people evolved from monkeys. They are looking for answers in the wrong places and are easily deceived and manipulated.

Heb. 11:1 says, "Now faith is the substance of things hoped for, the evidence of things not seen." You should be hoping for the things God has given you. The NLT says, "Faith is the confidence that what we hope for will actually happen; it gives us assurance about things we cannot see." In Heb. 1:3 it says Jesus was "the brightness of His glory and the express image of His person." The Greek word for "person" in this verse is the same Greek word for "substance" in Heb. 11:1. This means that Jesus is the exact expression of God's substance. He said, "If you've seen Me, you've seen the Father" (John 14:9). He was saying that He was the substance of God, therefore, faith is the personification of things hoped for. Jesus is the Word (John 1:14) and He said in John 15:7, "If you abide in Me, and My words abide in you, you will ask what you desire, and it shall be done for you." The Bible is the image of the will of God and the amount of faith you have is based on how much of the Word abides in you. God has given His Word to all of mankind and within the pages of the Bible is all the faith there ever will be.

The Word of God is filled with faith. The more you hear it, the more you believe it. The more you believe it, the more you say it. Faith comes more quickly when you hear your own voice proclaiming what God said. You are to stand on the Word but you can only stand on the Word that abides in you. How does the Word abide in you? Rom. 10:8 says, "The Word is near you, even in your mouth and in your heart." Your heart is the production center of your life. When you speak God's Word it gets down into your heart and makes a demand that forces production. The human spirit will then search the avenues of God's wisdom to find out how to cause what you're believing for to come to pass. It will cause you to be at the right place, at the right time, for the right situation. Your spirit captures the image of whatever you expose it to. When you confess the Word of God that image will grow in your heart and will allow you to live in the reality of what you're believing for.

Is. 55:10,11 says, "For as the rain comes down, and the snow from heaven, and do not return there, but water the earth, and make it bring forth and bud, that it may give seed to the sower, and bread to the eater, so shall My word be that goes forth from My mouth; It shall not return to Me void, but it will accomplish what I please, and it shall prosper in the thing for which I sent it." God's Word is like rain on the earth that will cause it to produce. Faith works! Jesus said you could have what you say if you believe in your heart and doubt not. Jesus is the Word manifested in the flesh and He is "the author

and finisher of our faith" (Heb. 12:2). Everything starts with the
Word and finishes with the Word. God upholds all things by
the word of His power (Heb. 1:3). The NLT says "He sustains
everything by the mighty power of His command." His power
is in the Word. When you put the Word in you the power also
gets in you. It's a spiritual force and it's called the law of faith
(Heb. 3:27). It comes by hearing and will come more quickly
when you hear yourself give an audible voice to the Word of
God.

Confessing the Word works because it causes faith to come. It
changes what's on the inside of you. If changes your heart and
keeps the answer before you. Never talk about your problems
but rather confess what the Word says the solution is. Don't
tell everybody how sick you are but confess by Jesus' stripes
you are healed (1 Peter 2:24). With eyes of faith, you see that
which is unseen and confess those things that be not as though
they were. The more you talk about your problems the more
problems you're going to have. You magnify what you talk
about. The more you say it, the more you'll believe it. A confession based on the Word will create in your heart and mind
an image of success and blessing and prosperity. These images
are created with the words you speak and your confession sets
the law of faith in motion (Mark. 11:23,24). You pray the answer, not the problem. Don't get caught telling God what the
devil said and that His Word does not work. You can do something about the situations and circumstances in your life. With
eyes of faith, you can see how life is supposed to be.

In the Bible Abraham is called the father of our faith and the father of us all (Rom. 4:16). God promised him in Gen. 13:16, "And I will make your descendants as the dust of the earth; so that if a man could number the dust of the earth, then your descendants also could be numbered." God promised Abram a son yet he asked in Gen. 15:2, "What will you give me, seeing I go childless?" At that time Abram did not yet see himself as the father of many nations. He's thinking naturally for the word God spoke to him had not yet been implanted in his heart. Abram knew and heard what God said but that was not enough to bring forth the promise. You've got to get the Word inside of you. To help Abram, God took him outside and showed him the stars and said to him, "So shall your descendants be" (Gen. 15:5). God was using the image of the stars to get Abram to come in agreement with the promise given to him and then to confess it with his mouth. There is no record that Abram ever did that. Twenty-four years after the promise was given the child still was not born. To fix this problem God then changed his name to Abraham which means "father of many nations."

To receive the promise Abram had to say what God said about him. Daily he would confess "I am Abraham." Abram did not believe God the way Abraham believed God and in less than three months his wife was pregnant with the promised child. Confessing the Word works. He only confessed one word and it changed the course of history. All he said was "I am Abraham." He was calling those things that be not as though they were (Rom. 4:17). He was saying he was the father of many nations before his son was even born. Abraham was the same man he was before, the only difference being the confession of

God's Word. He had to say what God said and when he did it changed the whole situation around. This principle of saying what God says can be used in every day life. God chose to do it this way. 1 Cor. 1:28 says God has chosen "the things which are not to bring to nothing the things that are." God has chosen things that are not seen in the natural realm to bring to nothing the things that are manifested that don't agree with the Word of God.

The "things which are not" are seen with the eyes of faith and this is how God created the heavens and the earth. Heb. 11:3b says "the things which are seen were not made of things which are visible." You could not see the things with which God created the world. It was the spiritual force of faith that He used to call light out of darkness. He reduced to nothing the darkness that was there and called light out of it. He then said in Gen. 1:26, "Let Us make man in Our image and let them have dominion." Man has dominion the same way God has dominion. He uses faith-filled words based on the authority of the Word of God. Six times in the creation story it says "Then God said...and God saw." God told Abraham that He would give him everything he saw but first he had to say it. This is what happened when Abram began to say "I am Abraham." He could not see the full and complete manifestation until he said what God told him to say. Why? Because words create images. Faith is the divine energy of God and you frame your world by the words you speak.

The power of believing is an awesome thing. Jesus said in Luke 17:6, "If you have faith as a mustard seed, you can say to this mulberry tree, 'Be pulled up by the roots and be planted in the sea,' and it would obey you." A mustard plant is a plant you can't hybrid. You cannot cross pollinate it with any other plant. It is going to be mustard no matter what type of pollen you put on it in the blooming stage. You cannot change it. Jesus was saying that if you had faith that won't change under any circumstances, faith that won't blend with anything else like doubt and unbelief, you could speak to the mulberry tree and it would obey you. He didn't say it would obey God, He said it would obey you because you have dominion over this planet. Notice also that the tree is planted in the sea. If you just throw it in the water, it will wash back on shore and you'll have to deal with it again. But if it's planted in the sea, it will stay there and not return.

God gave man dominion over this planet and you have the same authority and divine energy He has. You can tell that mountain to be plucked up and cast into the sea. You can re-buke the storm that's raging in your life and say to it, "Peace, be still!" There is power in knowing the authority of words and in being a child of God. You can have authority on this planet and you can bring to nothing those things that don't line up with the Word of God. You have a right to call what-ever you're believing for into existence. Learn to release faith in every word you speak. Believe what you say and say what you believe. When you confess the Word daily you can live a limitless life in Christ. Jesus said in John 17:16, "They are not of the world, just as I am not of the world." The Message Bible says, "They are no more defined by the world than I am de-fined by the world." The word "defined" means 'marked by its boundaries.' Those who see with eyes of faith do not have the same limitations that the world has. They don't have their restrictions and boundaries.

Ps. 119:130 says, "The entrance of Your words give light; It gives understanding to the simple." When the light goes on, you'll see things you couldn't see in the dark. When you get filled with the Word of God, you'll see things you never saw before. You'll come to realize that what the world says can't be done is not so with you. Phil. 4;13 says, "I can do all things through Christ who strengthens me." In Christ you have no limitations. The Amplified Bible says, "I am ready for anything and equal to anything through Him who infuses inner strength into me." If the world tells you there is something you can't do then be quick to do what Paul said in 2 Cor. 10:5a, "Casting down arguments and every high thing that exalts itself against the knowledge of God." The Message Bible says you are to fit "every loose thought and emotion and impulse into the structure of life shaped by Christ." Your imagination is God-given and He wants you to have an image of big things. He wants you to see what He sees.

God wants you to imagine the future that He has planned for your life. Truly it is a future with no limitations. You are made in the image of God and in Him there are no boundaries. Sarah laughed within herself when told she would have a child in her old age and God responded by saying, "Is anything too hard for the Lord?" (Gen. 18:14). God is the God of the impossible and when you walk in faith the limitations and confinements of life are no longer there. Jesus came to give you a life better than you ever dreamed possible so do not allow the world with all its boundaries to dictate what your life and destiny will be like. Let the Word of God be the final authority in your life and it will come to pass if you will believe and doubt not. You are highly favored and the blessings of God are on your life. Giving up is no longer an option. Prov. 4:22 says the words of God are life to those who find them. The Message Bible says, "Those who discover these words live, really live." You can live the high life and it all begins with you gaining a thorough knowledge of the Word of God and seeing with the eyes of faith. Don't waste another minute. Start today.

| 10 |

"THE EXPECTATION OF
FAITH"

There are many great and wonderful things God wants to do in the lives of all who profess to know Jesus but so many people have gotten satisfied way too early. Because of that, believers have stopped expecting God to move in their lives. They are satisfied with the small wage increase they received at their job so they don't believe to get their house and car paid off. They are satisfied to make the minimum monthly payment on their credit card bills without believing God for all their bills to be paid in full. People are not believing for enough of the right things. God is looking for an opportunity to be good to you and is not limited in what He can do. He is looking for people who will use their faith to activate His power and receive what He so graciously wants to give them. God has a plan and a purpose for your life. You are called to be a blessing to the body of Christ but you can't be good to other people unless you first let God be good to you.

God wants to bless you exceedingly, abundantly above what you could ask or think (Eph. 3:20). Wake up each morning believing that something good is going to happen to you. A good life is when you've always got something good to look forward to. Get excited about life and what each day can bring. You need to live like a little child who eagerly expects his parents to bless him with good things. With faith and confidence, you need to draw those blessings out of the spiritual realm and into manifestation in your everyday life. For this to happen you need to "see exactly what it is He is calling you to do, grasp the immensity of this glorious way of life He has for His followers, oh, the utter extravagance of His work in us who trust Him - endless energy, boundless strength" (Eph. 1:18,19 MSG). You need to have a positive attitude about everything that happens in life no matter what it is. With faith and the power of hope you can believe confidently that in the end all things will work out for your good (Rom. 8:28).

Ps. 23:6 says, "Surely goodness and mercy shall follow me all the days of my life; and I will dwell in the house of the Lord forever." If you will keep believing, God will keep working in your life. Heb. 11:1 says, "Now faith is the substance of things hoped for, the evidence of things not seen." The Message Bible says faith "is the firm foundation under everything that makes life worth living. It's our handle on what we can't see." Start expecting good things to happen to you. Don't go out looking for a job and not expect to find one. No, expect God to move in your life in a powerful way. Expect favor and blessing wherever you go. The blessings are available but you've got to be determined to stand strong and fight the good fight of faith.

You can't passively stand around all day waiting for something to happen. You've got to rise up and take charge of your life and destiny. Speak to those dry bones and prophecy good over your life. Ezek. 37:7 says, "As I prophesied, there was a noise, and suddenly a rattling; and the bones came together, bone to bone."

A good God can only do good things. You need to make up your mind once and for all that, as you walk with God, good things will happen to you. Be consistent in what you believe. If you're double-minded you can't suppose that you'll receive anything from the Lord (James 1:7), plus it will make your life miserable. The key to victory is to put your hand to the plow and never look back. Abraham "did not waver at the promise of God through unbelief, but was strengthened in faith, giving glory to God" (Rom. 4:20). Learn to praise God continually. There is more to praise than singing upbeat songs. More than anything it has to do with your attitude. Praise is "a narration, a tale, telling forth what God has done for you." If you are in a trial, the best thing you can do for yourself is talk about all the good things God has done for you in the past. Before facing Goliath, David talked about how God delivered him from the lion and the bear. Don't talk about your current problems but rather speak of God's faithfulness in times past. That's what praise does.

Like the woman with the issue of blood, you need to press through the obstacles that stand between you and the victory you so desire. Press through the fear and pain, the doubt and unbelief. Stop waiting for somebody to come along and do it for you. No, take charge and do it yourself. Rise up from the pit of despair and put on the armor of God. With the shield of faith in one hand, and the sword of the spirit in the other, face your enemy and fight the good fight of faith. Run to the roar. Heb. 13:15,16 says, "Therefore by Him let us continually offer the sacrifice of praise to God, that is, the fruit of our lips, giving thanks to His name. But do not forget to do good and to share, for with such sacrifices God is well pleased." One way to get the devil to leave you alone is to praise God continually and to be good to other people. Doing this will help take your mind off your problems. What you focus on, you magnify. It is better to think about Jesus and to focus on how good He is. His name is higher than any problem you have.

Aggressively expect something good to happen to you. Rom. 8:24, 25 says, "For we were saved in this hope, but hope that is seen is not hope; for why does one still hope for what He sees? But if we hope for what we do not see, then we eagerly wait for it with perseverance." Paul is saying that you are to wait for the manifestation with patience and composure. This means that your emotions are under control. The Message Bible says, "We are enlarged in the waiting. We, of course, don't see what is enlarging us. But the longer we wait, the larger we become, and the more joyful our expectancy." Don't let your feelings control you for it is impossible to stay calm with a negative attitude. Look your problem in the eye and say, "Something good is going to happen to me today. Greater is He who is in me than he who is in the world." Read out loud Eph. 1:3, "Blessed be the God and Father of our Lord Jesus Christ, who has blessed us with every spiritual blessing in the heavenly places in Christ." Rejoice for you are blessed with everything you'll ever need.

In Matt. 7:13,14 your walk with the Lord is compared to being on a straight and narrow road. Another similar example would be to say that you are traveling down the journey of life on a set of railroad tracks. The train you are on travels on two railings, one being love and the other faith. Hope is the wooden ties that hold love and faith together. The fruit of patience and long-suffering are the spikes that secure the two railings onto the wooden ties. This railroad line is owned and operated by the Heavenly Father. The powerful engine pulling the train is the Holy Spirit and Jesus is the conductor. All the members of the body of Christ are passengers on this train. As a born-again believer you are to be led by the Lord Jesus Christ and are pulled through life by the power of the Holy Spirit. You travel on love and faith which are held together by hope. Many Christians do not understand what true Biblical hope is and its importance to faith and love. In Heb. 6:19 hope is called "an anchor of the soul." If a person doesn't have an anchor they'll just float off in the direction of the current.

Hope is steadfast and sure. It holds you in place and builds in your mind a confident expectancy that comes when you get an inner image of something that hasn't happened yet. With hope comes peace and joy. Rom. 15:13 says, "Now may the God of hope fill you with all joy and peace in believing, that you may abound in hope by the power of the Holy Spirit." The Message Bible says, "Oh! May the God of green hope fill you up with joy, fill you up with peace, so that your believing lives, filled with the life-giving energy of the Holy Spirit, will brim over with hope!" Hope builds a picture in your mind based on the promises of God found in His Word. As you continue to concentrate on the mental picture that is formed, it will begin to grow stronger and become more clear. Hope takes that image from your mind and puts it in your spirit. Through prayer and meditation, what hasn't manifested yet begins to become more real to you. Eventually you'll begin to act and talk like it has already happened. This is called "faith" and, before you know it, that image will become a reality in your life.

1 Thess. 5:8 says, "But let us who are of the day be sober, putting on the breastplate of faith and love, and as a helmet the hope of salvation." These three spiritual forces work hand-in-hand in the fulfillment of your destiny. Faith works through love (Gal. 5:6) and is the substance of things hoped for (Heb. 11:1). Faith begins in the spiritual realm of love, passes through the mental realm of hope, and concludes in the physical realm of works (James 2:26). Faith is a substance from heaven that comes and empowers you when you put actions to what you believe. There is power in faith that gets charged up and energized by hope. God intended for His people to be dreamers. He has built into each person the capacity to dream. Hopes and dreams are what motivate you to keep moving forward in your walk with the Lord. You should always be content where you're at but never satisfied because satisfaction brings complacency. Striving for something better will place a motivating spirit in your heart and will give you reason to get up each and every morning.

Rom. 5;5 says, "Now hope does not disappoint, because the love of God has been poured out in our hearts by the Holy Spirit who was given to us." Expectancy will keep you watchful and on the alert for whatever God will do next. The more hope in God you have, the more happy you will be. Hope will give you a good, positive outlook on life. Things just don't seem so bad when you're always expecting something good to happen. David wrote in Ps. 16:8,9, "I have set the Lord always before me; Because He is at my right hand I shall not be moved. Therefore, my heart is glad, and my glory rejoices; My flesh also will rest in hope." The Message Bible says, "Day and night I'll stick with God; I've got a good thing going and I'm not letting go. I'm happy from the inside out, and from the outside in, I'm firmly formed." You can rejoice in hope because every negative problem in your life is subject to change. God will give you beauty for ashes (Is. 61:3) and He'll turn your mourning into dancing (Ps. 30:11). Look your problem in the eye and say, "This, too, shall pass."

Jesus is the Rock on which you stand. He's called that because He never changes and He's not going anywhere. He will never leave you or forsake you. 1 Peter 5:7 says "casting all your care upon Him, for He cares for you." His love for you will bring you into wholeness and this is what you can base your hope on. If your life is founded on the Rock then you can stay filled with expectancy when the storms of life blow your way. You look to Jesus in the midst of things you can't control, believing that somehow, some way, everything will work out in your favor. He never changes (Heb. 13:8) but your negative circumstances sure can. Job 14:14 says, "All the days of my hard service I will wait, till my change comes." When you truly believe that God is at work in your life then the level of your expectancy will rise to a higher level. Why? Because down in your heart you believe that something good is about to happen to you. The God who never changes will turn around those negative things in your life which are subject to change.

Rom. 8:31 says, "If God is for us, who can be against us?" You need to renew your mind and have the attitude that you can never be defeated in the game of life. In the natural the odds may be against you and your situation may seem hopeless. If that be the case then be like David who believed his God was bigger than the giant who stood before him. He later wrote in Ps. 41:11,12, "By this I know that You are well pleased with me, because my enemy does not triumph over me. As for me, You uphold me in my integrity, and set me before Your face forever." David had the right attitude. He knew God was on his side and that he could never be defeated. He was not intimidated by the size of Goliath but with bold confidence and expectation he ran toward his adversary knowing that victory was only moments away. When tempted to be discouraged always remember that one touch of God's favor can turn any situation around. The bigger God is in your eyes, the smaller your giants will become.

When you fight the good fight of faith you can never give up because if you do, there is nothing God can do to help you. You need the heart of a warrior who will stand and fight until the very end. Whether you win or lose depends on your attitude which is yours to command and is something nobody can control but you. You need to be determined that you will finish your course, enjoy your life as you're doing it, and that you will fulfill your destiny. You need to make up your mind what you want, and then remain steadfast in what you say and do. You can't be in faith one day and doubt and unbelief the next. If you're double-minded James 1:7 says, "For let not that man suppose that he will receive anything from the Lord." In order to receive from God, you need a peaceful, wholesome attitude that will not waver but stay committed to the truth of God's Word. You overcome the wiles of the enemy by having a joyful, confident expectation that something good is going to happen in your life today. That's what hope-energized faith will do for you.

Doubt and unbelief is a problem and you need to do something about it. There is no such thing as a person who can't believe. A person in unbelief is a person who is unwilling to believe. Because of a bad attitude this person has chosen purposefully not to believe. To walk in faith, one must be willing to change their lifestyle and most people don't want to do that. Every unbeliever in the world today would get saved if God would allow them to keep doing what they're doing. The bottom line is that most people don't want to change the way they live. It's far easier to sin than it is to resist sin and walk the straight and narrow path. People choose the path of least resistance and this is why Jesus said "wide is the gate and broad is the way that leads to destruction, and there are many who go in by it" (Matt. 7:13). It takes strength to do what's right and to follow in the footsteps of Jesus. Christianity is not a wimpy man's religion. No, it's a way of life where only the strong in Christ survive, a life where only true warriors become more than conquerors in Christ Jesus.

To overcome doubt and unbelief you need to do what Abraham did "who, contrary to hope, in hope believed" (Heb. 4:18). The Message Bible says, "When everything was hopeless, Abraham believed anyway, deciding to live not on the basis of what he saw he couldn't do but on what God said He would do." He got his hopes up and looked not at what was seen but looked at the unseen. He considered not his own body, already old and nearly dead, nor the deadness of Sarah's womb, for he was fully convinced that what God had promised He was able to bring to pass (vs. 20,21). Faith believes God anyway, no matter what the circumstances may be. In the natural you don't have to see the answer, you just have to believe that God has one. Don't let the devil steal your peace and joy but be like Abraham who "was strengthened in faith, giving glory to God" (vs. 20). Laugh in the face of the devil and boldly proclaim that you are never going to give up. Keep standing and keep pressing forward. Know in your heart that as you put one foot in front of the other, God is leading you to victory.

The devil does not know what to do with a happy person. Hope raises your expectancy level and this makes you excited. This joy you feel is proof that your faith is working and the devil has to weapon to combat that. He knows he's defeated when he throws a trial at you and all he sees is a smile on your face. Hope gives you the assurance that God is going to do something great in your life and this puts joy in your heart and a radiant glow on your face. Hope overflows when you get God's perspective on everything that happens to you. It makes you see the potential in everything, knowing that what the enemy means for evil, God means it for good (Gen. 50:20). Hope makes you happy and this joy gives you the energy to face every trial and to keep moving forward in life. As a believer in Christ, you don't have to be sad and depressed over what's happening to you because what's inside of you is greater than anything that's on the outside. Greater is He who is in you than he who is in the world.

When a trial comes your way, you need to get happy and you need to do it on purpose. You have control over how you feel and being negative all the time only assists the devil in his endeavor to destroy your life. You need to remember that you get what you believe for. Don't sit around waiting for things to change on their own because more times than not it won't happen. No, you've got to get aggressive in the things you hope for. You've got to believe that good things will happen to you and be expecting that you'll soon be walking in the promises of God. Your destiny is determined by what you decide to believe. Yes, God has a glorious plan for your life but that doesn't change the fact that your future is in your hands. Every morning when you wake up you need to say out loud that something good is going to happen to you today. How you begin the day often sets the pace for the direction the rest of your day will go. Always begin your day with a smile on your face and your expectancy level raised high.

Set a goal for yourself to have a positive attitude every hour of every day. That's what Bible hope is. It's a commitment to see good in everything. Problems will come but in the midst of what's happening you can have the joyful anticipation that God will lead you to victory. Remain hopeful in thought, attitude, and in the words you speak. Take control of your life and do the right thing. Why be miserable when you can be happy every day of your life? When you walk in faith, God will fill you completely with His joy and His peace because you trust in Him. Ps. 25:5 (NIV) says, "Guide me in Your truth and teach me, for You are God my Savior, and my hope is in You all day long." Get radical in what you hope for. God is good and something good is going to happen to you. Never settle for second best but always strive to reach the top of your mountain. God is great and there is nothing second best about Him.

If you want to enjoy your life then you've got to maintain a good, positive attitude. This is what hope and expectation does for you. Prov. 13:12 says, "Hope deferred makes the heart sick, but when the desire comes, it is a tree of life." Good things won't happen to you until you get positive in the way you act, think, and talk. This has got to become a daily lifestyle for you. You need to convince yourself that your hardships are only temporary and, in the hands of the great God of the universe, are subject to change. Stay in hope which is "a happy anticipation of something good." If you're full of expectation then you're going to be happy and you'll enjoy your life. Paul endured great hardship but he had the right attitude. He wrote in 2 Cor. 4:17,18, "For our light affliction, which is but for a moment, is working for us a far more exceeding and eternal weight of glory, while we do not look at the things which are seen, but at the things which are not seen. For the things which are seen are temporary, but the things which are not seen are eternal."

If you want good things to happen to you, your attitude has to change during the hard times. Jesus said in John 10:10, "The thief does not come except to steal, kill, and destroy. I have come that they may have life, and that they may have it more abundantly." Jesus died so you wouldn't be miserable, so make up your mind not to be that way no matter what's going on around you. Jesus did His part and you must now renew your mind and get in agreement with what He said is rightfully yours. Amos 3:3 says, "Can two walk together, unless they are agreed?" Change your attitude until it lines up with the will of God. Jesus came to give you peace so refuse to be down and depressed. If He says you're healed, you're healed. If He says all your needs are met, they're met. Why be concerned when the need has already been provided for? Rom. 14:17 (NLT) says, "For the Kingdom of God is not a matter of what we eat or drink, but of living a life of goodness and peace and joy in the Holy Spirit?" Get in agreement with God who wants you to enjoy every single day of your life.

With God on your side, you can be positive in the midst of negative circumstances. Just because things aren't going good for you at the moment does not mean you can't be happy. The joy of the Lord is your strength and the more happy you are, the less grip the enemy will have on your life. Expecting good things to happen to you will naturally make you happy, and the more happy you are, the more you'll expect good things to happen. You are a soldier in the army of the Lord and you've got to fight against those things that will take your joy away. Be like Paul who said "none of these things move me" (Acts 20:24). Be on your guard. Watch and pray. Expect good things to happen to you. Believe that when the enemy comes in, the Spirit of the Lord will lift up a standard against him (Is. 59:19). God will arrive like a river in flood stage and will bless you above what you can ask or think. Nothing is too big or too hard for God and it is your blood bought right to enjoy your life.

Get aggressive and constantly be looking for good things to happen in your life. Not only do you stop being negative but, at the same time, you need to raise the level of your expectancy. When you walk in faith, the thing you aggressively expect to happen is the very thing God will do. You determine what happens in your life, not God, and it's all based on what you believe and what you're expecting to happen. Jesus said, "Be it done to you according to your faith." Stop leaving everything up to God for He has already done everything He's ever going to do. Take charge of your life and, with faith and a confident expectation, receive everything Jesus died to give you. You may know God is good but without expectancy all you're doing is spinning your wheels in the mud. You're going nowhere and nothing good is happening in your life. You need to do something; the responsibility is yours. You've got to know who you are in Christ and the things He died to give you. Once you know those things you can use your faith and expect good things to happen. You'll never be the same if you do.

| 11 |

"THE PERSISTENCE OF FAITH"

Veteran newscaster Paul Harvey once said, "You can tell when you're on the road to success because it's usually uphill all the way." And so it is with the believer who has been anointed by God to be co-laborers with Him. Know with certainty that your trial is no accident. Satan has issued an assault against the beloved children of God and it's going to get worse the closer we get to the end of the age. The good news is that in the midst of a mega-storm Jesus can give you a mega-calm. We read in 1 Peter 1:6-10, "In this you greatly rejoice, though now for a little while, if need be, you have been grieved by various trials, that the genuineness of your faith, being much more precious than gold that perishes, though it is tested by fire, may be found to praise, honor, and glory at the revelation of Jesus Christ, whom having not seen you love. Though now you do not see Him, yet believing, you rejoice with joy inexpressible and full of glory, receiving the end of your faith - the salvation of your souls."

The Message Bible records Peter's words this way, "What a God we have! And how fortunate we are to have Him, this Father of our Master Jesus! Because Jesus was raised from the dead, we've been given a brand-new life and have everything to live for, including a future in heaven - and the future starts now! God is keeping careful watch over us and the future. The Day is coming when you'll have it all - life healed and whole. I know how great this makes you feel, even though you have to put up with every kind of aggravation in the meantime. Pure gold put in the fire comes out proved pure; genuine faith put through their suffering comes out proved genuine. When Jesus wraps this all up it's your faith, not your gold, that God will have on display as evidence of His victory. You never saw Him, yet you love Him. You still don't see Him, yet you trust Him - with laughter and singing. Because you kept on believing, you'll get what you're looking forward to: total salvation" (1 Peter 1:3-9).

To the early church Peter was a breath of fresh air and his influence was enormous and acknowledged by all. His letters reveal the qualities of Jesus that the Holy Spirit wants to shape in all believers. God wants all believers to have a readiness to embrace suffering rather than prestige, wisdom developed from experience rather than a book, and a humility that lacks nothing in vigor and imagination. Peter had all these qualities and was so humble that when he was put to death by crucifixion, he asked to be hung upside down instead of upright like the Lord had been. And it was this same apostle who says that our faith will be "tested by fire." This epistle presents Christ as the believer's example and hope in times of suffering in a spiritually hostile world. Jesus is the basis for the Christian's "living hope" and "inheritance" (1:3,4), and the love relationship available with Him by faith is a source of inexpressible joy (1:8). His suffering and death provide redemption for all who trust in Him. He is the Chief Shepherd and Overseer of all believers, and when He appears those who know Him will be glorified.

Peter addresses this epistle to those believers who are pilgrims in a world that is growing increasingly hostile to those anointed by God. Knowing that his readers will be facing more persecution than ever before, Peter writes this letter to give them a divine perspective on these trials so that they will be able to endure them without wavering in their faith. They should not be surprised at their ordeal because Jesus also suffered and died and they should count it a privilege to share in the sufferings of Christ. He goes on to exhort them to be sure their hardships are not being caused by their own wrongdoings but rather for their Christian testimony. Peter wants you to not be overcome with attitudes of bitterness and anxiety but instead replace those negative feelings with confidence in God. By standing firm in the grace of God through faith you'll be able to endure the fiery trials that all believers are sure to face.

Yes, you've got to fight for your faith and Paul told Timothy that if you don't, you'll suffer shipwreck in your ability to believe God. 1 Tim. 1:18,19 (MSG) says, "All those prayers are coming together now so you will do this well, fearless in your struggle, keeping a firm grip on your faith and on yourself. After all, this is a fight we're in. There are some, you know, who by relaxing their grip and thinking anything goes have made a thorough mess of their faith." A stern warning is given in Heb. 3:12, "Beware, brethren, lest there be in any of you an evil heart of unbelief in departing from the living God." In this verse faith that has been shipwrecked is called "an evil heart of unbelief." The Message Bible says, "So watch your step, friends. Make sure there's no evil unbelief lying around that will trip you up and throw you off course, diverting you from the living God." This verse was written in response to the story of those who refused to enter into the Promised Land after being rescued from the bonds of slavery in Egypt. They could not enter into the rest of God because of unbelief.

When their faith got tested their hearts got hardened. They suffered shipwreck with their faith. They did not understand that having faith is not the absence of distress, trials, or heaviness of heart. Faith is about whether or not you'll go forward with Jesus and cross over into your own personal promised land. God wants to bring you into a place of total dependence on Jesus where all your confidence is in Him and not your own ability. Num. 13:30,31 tells what was said when the twelve spies returned from the land of promise and shows a stark contrast between faith and unbelief. "Then Caleb quieted the people before Moses, and said, 'Let us go up at once and take possession, for we are well able to overcome it.' But the men who had gone up with him said, 'We are not able to go up against the people, for they are stronger than we.'" Unbelief says "we are not able" whereas faith says "we are well able." If you are weak in your own eyes, so will you be weak in the devil's eyes.

The Christian life is full of giants and there are strongholds and walled cities everywhere you look. This is what the battle of faith is all about. Don't let the giants in your life scare you and cause you to run away. People who want to take the easy route don't enter in. Understand that your problems are not there to keep you down but instead are there to keep you out of that place where you have absolute confidence in Jesus. Faith is a daring, reckless abandon to the absolute, ultimate power of Jesus Christ to keep you and sustain you in this present age. It brings you to a place where you're resting in His faithfulness and you'll have no doubt that God's eternal purpose for your life will be fulfilled. We all have dreams, desires, and visions to take us beyond where we're at now but those dreams don't come to pass immediately. The desire to quit will be one of the major temptations the enemy will bring against you, but God says to enter into your promised land. Press on and never give up! Trust Jesus and be determined to press through to the end.

You were not anointed with the power of God so you could quit. The journey is not easy but it's worth the challenges that go along with it. And remember, it's those who finish the race that get the prize. When you have a passion for what you're doing it will override the negative circumstances that rise up against you. Is. 41:10 says, "Fear not, for I am with you; Be not dismayed, for I am your God. I will strengthen you, Yes, I will help you, I will uphold you with My righteous right hand." Probably the first thing a person learns when they make a quality decision to live by faith is that the answer to their prayers is almost never manifested immediately. The Bible says that it is through faith and patience that we inherit the promises of

God (Heb. 6:12). Timing is of the utmost importance when it comes to receiving from God. All believers need the confident assurance that God is never late when it comes to answering our prayers. On the other hand, neither is He early.

Patience is what God uses to keep you in His timing and faith is your positive response to His ability to perform what He has promised (Rom. 4:21). Jesus, when informed of the sickness of His friend Lazarus, stayed two more days in the place where He was at. His explanation for His delay in going to the scene of His friend's eventual death is found in John 11:14,15, "Then Jesus said to them plainly, 'Lazarus is dead. And I am glad for your sake that I was not there, that you may believe.'" Going through a phase of waiting from the time you first believe to the time of manifestation will build your faith and help you to believe to a greater degree. It is during this time of waiting that persistence and tenacity needs to be built up in the life of all believers who sincerely wish to walk by faith. Faith that is persistent is faith that gets the job done. It is a quality of faith that forces its way into the kingdom, takes it by storm, and remains there and does not rest satisfied until it receives what it is believing for.

Persistence is the power of continuing in some effort of course of action in spite of difficulty or opposition. It means 'to be steadfast in purpose, to pursue to an end, to go on stubbornly, to remain unchanged in the repetition of a test or trial, to stay fixed on a character, to hang on tenaciously.' The word "tenacious" means 'to be tough.' Persistent faith is tough faith and doesn't look at the failures of the past but at the promises of the Word of God. It is a faith that refuses to be denied. The story of Caleb going in to the promised land is a tale of a man who did not let go of a promise made to him many years before. With possessive boldness the old man Caleb stood before his longtime friend Joshua who was now leader of the Israeli people and made the proclamation, "Give me this mountain!" Like Joshua, Caleb had been one of the twelve spies Moses sent into the Promised Land to spy out the land of Canaan. Caleb reminds Joshua of this in Josh. 14:7, "I was forty years old when Moses the servant of the Lord sent me from Kadesh Barnea to spy out the land, and I brought back word to him as it was in my heart."

Ten of the twelve spies brought back an evil report saying, "We are not able to go up against the people, for they are stronger than we" (Num. 13:31). They later said in vs. 33, "We were like grasshoppers in our own sight, and so we were in their sight." Caleb and Joshua, however, came back with a good report. They believed they could take possession of the land and, because of this good report, Caleb now reminds Joshua of a promise made to him by Moses. "So Moses swore on that day saying, 'Surely the land where your foot has trodden shall be your inheritance and your children's forever because you have wholly followed the Lord my God" (Josh. 14:9). The old generation of murmuring and disbelieving Israelites had died off in the wilderness and now the new generation, along with Joshua and Caleb, were ready to take possession of the Promised Land. Caleb was now eighty-five years old and he felt he was still just as strong as he had been when he went into Canaan as a spy.

The land now had rest from war and Caleb was ready to go on with his life. Before Joshua divided the promised land among the other tribes, he would give his faithful friend first choice of what land he wanted. As his inheritance Caleb had chosen Mount Hebron where a race of giants called the Anakims still had control of the land. Moses had promised him a place of his own and now he wanted to take over that land. Josh. 14 tells us, "Then the children of Judah came to Joshua in Gilgal and Caleb the son of Jephunneh the Kenizzite said to him, 'You know the word which the Lord said to Moses the man of God concerning you and me in Kadesh Barnea. As yet, I am as strong this day as I was on the day Moses sent me; just as my strength was then, so now is my strength for war, both for going out and for coming in. Now therefore, give me this mountain of which the Lord spoke in that day; for you heard in that day how the Anakam were there, and that the cities were great and fortified. It may be that the Lord will be with me, and I shall be able to drive them out as the Lord said.' And Joshua blessed him and gave Hebron to Caleb the son of Jephunneh as an inheritance" (vs. 6, 11-13).

In order for Caleb to take possession of his inheritance he would have to once again go to war and risk his life and those of his men. To gain what was rightfully his Caleb would have to force his way onto the mountain and take it by storm. Josh. 15 goes on to tell us that this is precisely what he did. For those living today under the new covenant Mount Hebron symbolizes any one of the many blessings God promises you in His Word. The promises available to you today are greater than those in the day of Joshua and Caleb. 2 Peter 1:4 says "by which have been given to us exceedingly great and precious promises." You may not be living in the promised land but you are living in the land of promises. The good news is found in 2 Cor. 1:20 which says, "For all the promises of God in Him are Yes, and in Him Amen, to the glory of God through us." Notice that God gets glory when you partake of His promised blessings. Because of this verse and your relationship with Jesus Christ you can boldly go before the throne of God and say, "Give me this mountain! It's mine! Your Word promised it to me and I take possession of it now! In the Name of Jesus Christ, I believe I receive! So be it!" Hallelujah!

All faith needs is "Thus saith the Lord." Caleb held on to the promise of God and waited forty-five years to receive his inheritance. Sad to say, most people give up if they have to wait forty-five days or for that matter forty-five hours. Like Caleb, you must learn Paul's message in Gal. 6:9. "And let us not grow weary while doing good, for in due season we shall reap if we do not lose heart." The Message Bible states, "So let's not allow ourselves to get fatigued doing good. At the right time we will harvest a good crop if we don't give up, or quit." The mountain is yours! Do not lose possession of it because of a simple thing called "time." Be like David who said in Ps. 31:14,15, "But as for me, I trust in You, O Lord; I say, You are my God. My times are in your hand." If you have made Jesus the Lord of your life, then also make Him the Lord of your time. You can trust Him. He will not let you down. And if you do not lose heart you can count on Him to give you your mountain. Receive it today!

Paul wrote in 1 Cor. 16:9, "For a great and effective door has opened to me, and there are many adversaries." The Message Bible says, "There is also mushrooming opposition." He went on to say in 1 Thess. 3:3,4 "that no one should be shaken by these afflictions; for you yourselves know that we are appointed to this. For, in fact, we told you before when we were with you that we would suffer tribulation, just as it happened, and you know." When you rise up and set your heart like flint to fulfill the call of God on your life, then you can be certain opposition will come. The Lord said this about the apostle Paul, "He is a chosen vessel of Mine to bear My Name before Gentiles, kings, and the children of Israel. For I will show him how many things he must suffer for My Name's sake" (Acts 9:15,16). All this opposition should not cause you to give up and walk away, but instead to rise up with a holy determination to do that which the Lord wants you to do.

Paul said in Phil. 3:7-9, "But what things were gain to me, these I have counted loss for the excellence of the knowledge of Christ Jesus my Lord, for whom I have suffered the loss of all things, and count them as rubbish, that I may gain Christ and be found in Him." How did Paul respond to all the trials and opposition in his life? Vs. 13-15 says, "But one thing I do, forgetting those things which are behind and reaching forward to those things which are ahead, I press toward the goal for the prize of the upward call of God in Christ Jesus. Therefore, let us, as many as are mature, have this mind." What did Paul do? He pressed on! He never gave up and he kept going forward. He then told those who are mature to do the same thing. In Phil. 4:1 he said to "stand fast in the Lord." This means you never give up in the face of opposition. Remember, being a servant of God is not for the faint hearted and it is only those who finish the race that receive the prize. Ps. 34:19 says, "Many are the afflictions of the righteous, but the Lord delivers him out of them all."

God will tell you what He is going to do in your life but rarely will He tell you when He's going to do it. This is so because He wants you to keep pressing on. If He told you the answer was soon forthcoming, you'd be tempted to slack off in your good fight of faith, and if He revealed you'd be in this season of affliction for a long time to come you may get discouraged and quit. Not knowing when the breakthrough will come keeps hope alive and Heb. 11:1 says, "Now faith is the substance of things hoped for, the evidence of things not seen." Faith is your handle on what you can't see and vs. 6 says that without faith it is impossible to please God. David wrote in Ps. 31:14,15, "But as for me, I trust in You, O Lord; I say, 'You are my God.' My times are in Your hand; Deliver me from the hand of my enemies, and from those who persecute me." He told God what he wanted but he left the decision of when this would happen in the hands of God. He said, "My times are in Your hand."

You must accept God's timing to have peace. Without peace, there is no joy. Without joy, there is no strength. Without strength, there is no breakthrough. Let's face it, everybody waits. Waiting is a fact of life and everybody does it. Moses waited 40 years on the backside of the desert, Caleb waited 45 years to get his mountain, Abraham waited 25 years for the birth of Isaac, Joseph waited 14 years for the fulfillment of his dream, and David ran and hid from the evil King Saul for 13 years as he waited to be made king over all of Israel. Job, Ruth, and Esther all waited on God to move in their lives. Even today Jesus is waiting for His enemies to be made His footstool. As you can see, everybody waits. If the truth be told, you will spend more time waiting than you will receiving. For the rest of your life, you will have to deal with things for which you'll be required to wait. Like it or not, this is the lifestyle all believers are required to live. You are always going to have to wait for something so you better get used to it.

So, you can do it the right way or you can do it the wrong way. Either way, you're still going to have to wait. If you do it the wrong way you're going to be miserable and if you do it the right way you'll live a happy, victorious life. Yes, good things come to those who wait properly. The Bible says that it is through faith and patience that you inherit the promises of God (Heb. 6:12) which, of course, includes your much needed breakthrough. Patience is so important that God is called "the God of patience and comfort" (Rom. 15:5). Notice that when you wait properly your life will be filled with comfort. Understand that patience is not the ability to wait. It's how you act while you wait. It's an attitude of hope and expectancy and it grows only under trial. God determines the timing of things in your life and you chose the attitude you'll have. You need to wait on God with a good attitude. As you endure the trials of life with a good attitude, patience is given and developed. The more you wait the better your patience will be.

James 1:4 says, "But let patience have its perfect work, that you may be perfect and complete, lacking nothing." That's a powerful promise! The Message Bible says, "So don' try to get out of anything prematurely. Let it do its work so you become mature and well-developed, not deficient in any way." Vs. 12 says, "Anyone who meets a testing challenge head-on and manages to stick it out is mighty fortunate. For such persons loyally in love with God, the reward is life and more life." Wait with a good attitude and don't murmur and complain. You don't have patience if you have a bad attitude. You should not shun patience but instead should embrace it as if it were your best friend. Jesus said, "In your patience possess your souls" (Luke 21:19). One way to possess your soul is to understand that God is different from us. He sees things and does things in a way that is different from your choosing and understanding.

Is. 55:8,9 says "'For My thoughts are not your thoughts, nor are your ways My ways', says the Lord. 'For as the heavens are higher than the earth, so are My ways higher than your ways and My thoughts than your thoughts.'" God made man in His image but since the fall in the Garden of Eden man has set out to do things his own way. As evidenced in scripture and your own private life, things almost never turn out the way you want then to when you get stubborn and insist on doing things according to how you want them done. Thankfully God, in His infinite mercy, sent Jesus to earth for the purpose of getting man back on track and in line with God's perfect will. In the Garden of Gethsemane Jesus set the example for all believers to follow when He prayed "Nevertheless, not My will but Yours be done" (Luke 22:42). In the Lord's prayer Jesus taught you to pray to the Father and say, "Your kingdom come. Your will be done on earth as it is in heaven" (Matt. 6:10).

Later in the same chapter He tells you what to do in order to transfer the priority of doing things your way to the submissive action of allowing God to have His way in your life. Matt. 6:33 says, "But seek first the kingdom of God and His righteousness." What does it mean to "seek first the kingdom of God"? It means to seek God's way of doing things. Remember, His ways are above your ways. There are certain things involved with Christian growth and development that if not understood can cause a believer to get discouraged and walk away from their faith. One of these areas is the subject of time. 2 Peter 3:8 says, "But beloved, do not forget this one thing, that with the Lord one day is as a thousand years and a thousand years as one day." Notice the importance Peter puts on you learning this concept. He says "do not forget this one thing." What he is saying must therefore be important. A similar passage of scripture is found in Ps. 90:4, "For a thousand years in Your sight are like yesterday when it is past and like a watch in the night."

These scriptures verify that God does not see time in the same light as people do. For example, in Rev. 22:7 Jesus said, "Behold, I am coming quickly!" This was spoken two thousand years ago and Jesus calls this time frame "quickly." Here is another example. After the rapture of the church all believers will attend a reward ceremony called "the Marriage Supper of the Lamb" which will take place during the seven-year tribulation period on earth. The deeds of all believers will be reviewed at this time and rewards will be given out for service done unto the Lord during one's lifetime. It has been estimated that if each believer stood before the Lord for only one minute this ceremony would still take thousands of years to complete. But in time as we know it the event will take place in seven short years. These scriptures make it clear that what time means to God and what it means to people are as opposite as night and day. It would benefit all believers to search the scriptures and seek out God's way of measuring time and apply the same principle to their everyday lives.

Man measures his existence on planet earth in quantities of time commonly known as seconds, minutes, hours, days, weeks, months, years, decades, centuries and millenniums whereas God measures time in seasons. Eccl. 3:1 says, "To everything there is a season, a time for every purpose under heaven." Webster's dictionary defines "season" as 'a time characterized by a particular circumstance or feature.' A season also has a beginning and an end. In nature there are four seasons that we go through in a calendar year. There is winter, spring, summer and fall. Each one has particular features and different characteristics from the others but it is important that we go through each and every season. Likewise, in the realm of the Spirit it is also important that you experience all of God's seasons and go through the different things you go through so that you will develop and grow and mature properly in the things of God. Some things just don't happen instantly in the Christian life.

Christian maturity is developed and not received and this takes
time. Yes, you do receive the fruit of the Spirit when you get
born-again but none of these qualities begin to operate fully
and automatically when you get saved. These are developed
and this takes time. It takes growth and this is a process. Any
farmer will testify that in order to receive a crop from his efforts the seeds he sows must go through a planting season, a
watering season, a growth and development season, and finally
there is the harvest season. All these seasons have different
characteristics and features that surround the different stages
of growth that the plant is in. A full-grown plant doesn't mature instantly; therefore, it is vitally important for that plant to
go through each and every season in its growth and development. It is the same way with those in the body of Christ. 2
Cor. 6:2 says, "For He says, 'In an acceptable time I have helped
you.' Behold, now is the accepted time; behold, now is the day
of salvation."

There was a time when people could not get born-again because Jesus had not come to earth yet. There was a time for Jesus to come, a season for Him to walk the earth. Thankfully,
now is the time. Today is the day of salvation. You can get
saved now, healed now, and delivered now. At the same time,
we are told in Phil. 2:12 to "work out your own salvation with
fear and trembling." The Word must be planted and given time
to grow. Since God is a "now" God, people think that if the answer to their prayer is not manifested immediately then something is wrong. This is not necessarily so. There is a process of
time involved in walking in the things of God. The Bible says
it is through faith and patience that we inherit the promises

of God (Heb. 6:12). Patience is a vital ingredient in the walk of faith and is only developed by remaining strong and steadfast in the season of tests and trials (James 1:2-4). If things are not going right for you at this time, then you can rejoice knowing that your time of trial is but for a season.

Don't forget, every season has a beginning and an end. With confidence you can look at your problem and say, "This, too, shall pass." With every Godly principle that you try to inhabit into your life comes with it a season of testing and growth. God will take you through different seasons that will have particular features designed to change your life into His image. Learn to recognize the seasons in your spiritual life. Many times, you'll grow rapidly but other times you'll go through a longer period of stabilizing and growth. With God a delay is not a denial. When He wants to make a mushroom, He does it overnight but when He wants to make a giant oak tree, He takes a hundred years. The best things in life take time. You gave your life to God, now give Him your time also. Pray as the psalmist did in Ps. 31:15, "My times are in your hand." Then stand back and watch the blessings come.

| 12 |

"THE CRUCIBLE OF FAITH"

Did you know that there is a way to tell how strong you are in the Lord? There is. If you want to know how much you weigh, you go step on a scale. If you want to know how tall you are, you go get a tape measure. If you want to know how strong you are physically, you go to the weight room and see how many pounds you can lift over your head. But what about spiritually? How can you tell how strong you are spiritually? The answer is found in the trials you face. God promises that there will be no trial in your life that you can't overcome. In other words, you are stronger in the Lord than anything the devil throws your way. A baby Christian will have "baby" trials. As one grows in the Lord, the trials also will grow and increase. New level, new devil. So, if you're having big, hard trials, that means you are big and strong spiritually. A baby Christian can defeat and overcome baby trials and a strong Christian can have a breakthrough over strong trials. God says that in Him you are all stronger that any trial that comes your way. And it's the size and intensity of the trial that indicates how strong you are spiritually.

During those times when it seems like your world is falling apart, rise up and rejoice because in Jesus you are stronger and mightier than that trial. A trial is your "strength indicator." Don't fret or worry during hard times but rejoice because the enemy just showed you how strong you are in the Lord. If it's a big trial then say, "Thank you, devil, for recognizing how strong I am in the Lord." Yes, there is a limit on how much he can attack you. He cannot attack you beyond your level of spiritual strength. You cannot be overcome by the enemy unless, of course, you let him. Daily confess out loud, "Greater is He that is in me than he that is in the world." Paul says in Eph. 6:16 what to do when trials come knocking on your door, "Above all, taking the shield of faith with which you will be able to quench all the fiery darts of the wicked one." Faith is taught throughout the Bible and is the thread of the fabric of God's Word. It is a spiritual force that is established in the heart and is based on the Word of God.

Faith is a substance from heaven that like the wind cannot be seen but the results thereof can be. It is everlasting in its nature and eternal in its operation. Faith is the ability to believe what you have heard, yet have not seen, based solely on your confidence in the speaker. It means to have confidence in the testimony of another. The obvious question to be asked then is, "Who's doing the speaking?" Is the person speaking reliable and dependable? God is. Malachi 3:6 says, "For I am the Lord, I do not change." Faith, therefore, means to have a confidence in the absolute truthfulness of every word that comes from the mouth of God. The level of your faith is determined by how well you trust the Creator of the universe. The basis of that trust begins with a thorough knowledge of God Who is revealed in and throughout His holy Word. The more you read and study the Bible, the greater you will come to know Him, thus increasing your potential for faith.

Daniel had more knowledge of God than he did of lions. Three times a day he diligently knelt before the Heavenly Father and communed with the King of kings and Lord of lords. As a result of this, Daniel had a God Who was larger than all the lions in the world. The more you know somebody and see what their character is like, the more you'll be willing to put your trust in them and what they say. Trusting in the Lord, therefore, is a sure thing because He is an absolute. He never changes. People everywhere, no matter who they are, have the capability of letting you down. This is not so with God. God is love (1 John 4:8) and love never fails (1 Cor. 13:8). When you put your trust in the Lord you will discover that He is more than worthy of your confidence. People crave for the opportunity to put their trust in someone other than themselves. People want to believe, they need to believe. They want to be able to put their confidence in someone that will not let them down or bring disappointment to their lives.

The problem most people have is they believe in people who are always changing and going through various mood swings and are thus not always dependable. Still, people continue to believe in them because they are tangible and can be related to with the five physical senses. They can see their doctor and the mechanic down the street who promises to have their car repaired by the end of the day but rarely does. True Biblical faith, however, is to believe in the unseen. Natural faith says "I'll believe it when I see it" whereas Biblical faith says "You'll see it when you believe it." You cannot please God by believing what you can see. Even the heathen do that. In reality, natural faith is nothing more than wishful thinking. The God kind of faith, however, is not based on feelings or the five physical senses but on the written and revealed Word of God. A familiar passage of scripture concerning faith is Rom.10:17, "So then faith comes by hearing, and hearing by the Word of God."

To better understand faith and how it comes and how it works, one must go back to their first encounter with faith, the day they got born-again. Paul said in Rom. 10:8-10, "But what does it say? 'The Word is near you, even in your mouth and in your heart' (that is, the word of faith which we preach): that if you confess with your mouth the Lord Jesus and believe in your heart that God has raised Him from the dead, you will be saved. For with the heart, one believes to righteousness and with the mouth confession is made to salvation." This is how faith comes and works. You hear the Word by confessing it out loud with your mouth. Eventually, if you will do this long enough, you will come to believe in your heart those same words you've been hearing yourself speak. The moment you do, the exact moment you believe in your heart what you've been confessing with your mouth, God will bless you by giving you the faith you need to receive from Him that which you've been believing for. It's that simple.

Eph. 2:8 says, "For by grace you have been saved through faith, and that not of yourselves; it is the gift of God." What is the gift of God? Faith. Rom. 12:3 says that "God has dealt to each one a measure of faith." It goes without saying that whoever gives a gift must first own and possess the gift before they can give it away. The faith God giftsyou as a gift is the same faith He possesses. It's His faith. 1 John 5:4 says, "For whatever is born of God overcomes the world. And this is the victory that has overcome the world - our faith." The faith you have as a born-again believer is "born of God" and is the same faith God used to create the universe. This is what is meant by saying faith is a heavenly substance (Heb. 11:1). It comes from heaven. It comes from God. It's His faith and He gives it to you as a gift when you believe. If giving you His faith were not enough, God has also taken on the responsibility of performing His Word when you apply your faith to any given situation.

God is faithful and the integrity of the Lord is unquestionable to those who know Him. Num. 23:19 says, "God is not a man that He should lie, nor a son of man that He should repent. Has He said, and will He not make it good?" Faith is when you trust God enough to believe that He will perform that which He promised in His Word. Jer. 1:12 says, "Then the Lord said to me, 'You have seen well, for I am ready to perform My Word.'" Abraham had a strong conviction in his heart concerning the faithfulness of God to perform His Word. Rom. 4:20,21 says, "He did not waver at the promise of God through unbelief, but was strengthened in faith giving glory to God, and being fully convinced that what He had promised He was also able to perform." In other words, God has given you His personal guarantee that He will cause to happen whatever it is you are believing Him for based solely on the Word of God. Your faith moves the hand of God "who is able to do exceedingly above all that we ask or think" (Eph. 3:20).

The Amplified Bible says God will "do super-abundantly, far over and above all that we dare ask or think - infinitely beyond our highest prayers, desires, thoughts, hopes or dreams." This is what is meant when Jesus is called "the finisher of our faith" (Heb. 12:2). You do the believing and He does the performing. Plus, it's His faith! What more could anyone ask? You must forever be armed with the shield of faith because without exception tests and trials come into the lives of every born-again believer. Oftentimes they come when you least expect it, when everything seems to be going good for you. They come and will continue to come until we all go home to be with the Lord. Jesus said, "In the world you will have tribulation but be of good cheer for I have overcome the world" (John 16:33). Since tests and trials will always come your way, the attitude you have when they do come and what you decide to do about them will be the deciding factor as to whether or not you live a victorious Christian life.

Tests and trials are not easy and were never meant to be. They do, however, serve a purpose. Jer. 9:7 (AMP) says, "Therefore, thus says the Lord of hosts, 'Behold, I will melt them by the process of affliction to remove the dross and test them; for how else should I deal with the daughters of My people?" Ps. 66:10-12 states, "For You, O God, have proved us, You have refined us as silver is refined. You brought us into the net, You laid affliction on our backs. You have caused men to ride over our heads; we went through fire and through water but You brought us out to rich fulfillment." The Bible talks of God's children being refined as silver and gold. This metaphor is borrowed from the technology of refining precious metals which included heating them in a crucible to see if all impurities had been removed. These metals pass repeatedly through the furnace until all the dross breaks away and floats to the top. The refiner then removes all the impurities and disposes of them. It is said that the refiner knows the process is completed when he is able to see his image reflected in the precious metal purified.

God is compared to a refiner of silver and gold which means He allows His people to be cast into the furnace of affliction (Is. 48:10) until they are purified and clearly reflect His image in their lives. Dan. 12:10 says, "Many shall be purified, made spotless and white, and be tried, smelted and refined." Job, a man who definitely passed through the fire when Satan brought several tests and trials into his life said, "But he knows the way that I take. When He has tested me, I shall come forth as gold, pure and luminous" (Job 23:10). Indeed, fire is a blessing if you know how to use it. From one point of view, times of distress constitute a testing of God's people as to their trust in and loyalty to God. Sometimes the best place to be is in a position where there is nothing else you can do but sit back and trust God. Passing through the fire is a sign of your commitment to Him. If you run away from every test and trial that comes your way, "if you faint in the day of adversity, then your strength is small" (Prov. 24:10).

Many people run away from making a commitment to God or anybody else because with it comes responsibility. In the day and age in which we now live people do not want to be responsible for anything. They "don't want to get involved" or they're "too busy." Tests and trials that come as a result of being anointed to serve God will bring change into your life and many people don't like or want to change. They run away from responsibility and change as if it were some incurable plague. They run away from the effort, work, and pain that the changes to serve God and to become Christlike require. Daily they avoid the challenges of improving themselves with spiritual growth and are content to lay back and live the easy life. Tests and trials will require work on their part and most people don't like to work. They want to take the path of least resistance. They enjoy living in their comfort zone and they crave the quiet life with as little distractions as possible.

People like this need their microwaves and remote-control switches. They wouldn't think of getting out of their easy-chair and walking across the room to turn on the television set themselves. These people are not workers, they're floaters. They float through life and take whatever this world throws at them. Whatever will be, will be. It is these lazy people who will never gain prominence in the kingdom of God. They are satisfied at being where they're at, wherever that might be, and will never rise above the level of being mediocre believers. These are the people who back away from the heat of walking through the fire of spiritual growth. They pull back and become only "half-baked." The Bible calls these people "lukewarm" and says that God will spew them out of His mouth

(Rev. 3:16). This statement is hard but true and the sooner the decision is made to face your trials head on and not run away from them the better off you'll be.

When a test or trial comes your way the first thing you should do is determine the cause of the fire. God does not ordain all fire and it's not always the devil's fault either. Many times, you bring fire into your own life. You cannot blame God or the devil if you are facing a financial crisis because you violated the proper use of credit cards at Christmas time. You need to accept responsibility for your circumstances because where you're at today is a result of the decisions you've made through-out your life. You need to be teachable and learn from your mistakes because Satan will fight and attack you through your lack of knowledge. If you will refuse to panic when the tests and trials come, if you will stay connected to Jesus through the fire, then ultimately spiritual growth will come. Pain always precedes promotion. Many Christians fail to grow because they never see the connection between their problems and their future dreams and victories. A crisis is a signal for you to learn and grow, not lose.

Your problem is your promotion. A problem will introduce you to yourself and cause you to find out what you're made of. Every obstacle will bring change into your life. You'll either be stronger because of it or you'll be weaker. Great leaders are those who do not quit but with grit and determination rise above their problems. You should view the tests and trials that come your way as an opportunity for your life to be built up and molded until you become mature in the Lord. This is how holiness comes and God Himself said, "Be holy, for I am holy" (1 Peter 1:16). Do not let your head hang low and confess that you're walking through the valley. In Christ there are no valley experiences, some mountains are just higher than others. Your primary desire should not be to live a trouble free life but rather to develop inside yourself those qualities that will mold and shape you into the very image of Christ. Surprisingly, this is the purpose hardships serve. No pain, no gain.

Maturity and strength of character will come when you respond to the tests and trials of life in the proper way. It is faith that causes you to rise up in triumph over your troubles and to rejoice in the midst of your sufferings. Pressure, hardship, and affliction produces patience inside of you and, as you put your faith and hope in Jesus, unwavering endurance will create in you the character needed to stand tall as you walk through the pitfalls of life. This in turn produces joy and the strength you receive from this spiritual fruit will give you the confidence and hope to put your faith in God "Who always leads us to triumph in Christ" (2 Cor. 2:14). God never promised you an easy life but He did say in Jesus you could have a victorious life. Life is what you make it, whether good or bad. On the evil day when calamity strikes go to Ps. 91 and meditate therein day and night. As you do you will come to realize that like the three Hebrew children you can be in the midst of the refiner's fire and not be burned. And when you exit the furnace of affliction you will come out smelling like a rose.

Every day you should be living on the high clouds of victory, success, and spiritual fulfillment because all this has been made available to you. 2 Peter 1:2-4 boldly proclaims, "Grace and peace be multiplied to you in the knowledge of God and of Jesus our Lord, as His divine power has given us all things that pertain to life and godliness through the knowledge of Him Who called us to glory and virtue, by which have been given to us exceedingly great and precious promises, that through these you may be partakers of the divine nature, having escaped the corruption that is in the world through lust." Since God has already given you all things that pertain to life and godliness, you must ask yourself how determined you are to receive what God has already provided for you. How determined are you? Are you willing "to contend earnestly for the faith which was once and for all delivered to the saints" (Jude 3)? Are you willing to stand up and "fight the good fight of faith" (1 Tim. 6:12)?

A good fight is a fight you win. 1 Cor. 15:57 says that God always causes you to triumph through the Lord Jesus Christ. There is no failure or defeat in the good fight of faith. Most people do not fail, they simply give up trying. They lay back and expect God to do all the fighting for them. Too often people are waiting for God to do something while He's waiting for them to do something. People need to understand that they have as much to do with the answer to their prayers as they expect God to be. There is a sign on the Colorado River which instructs whitewater rafters, "If you fall overboard, you must be an active participant in your own rescue!" For those who have the misfortune of falling into the swirling waters of the raging Colorado River, they must take charge of the situation even though thousands of gallons of water are flooding over them. They must participate in their own rescue and cannot lay back and let the rescuers do all the work. There is a part they have to play and so it is in the believer's fight of faith.

The day will come when the rain will descend, the floods will come, and the wind will blow and beat upon your spiritual house (Matt. 7:25). It is times like these when you must take charge of your situation and rise up and fight the good fight of faith. It is time for action and resolve. God gave the people of Israel the promised land but wars had to be fought before they could possess it. Likewise, to fight the good fight of faith you must press in to the things of God with a persistence and determination that will not rest satisfied until it receives what is desired. Heb. 10:35,36 (AMP) says, "Do not, therefore, fling away your fearless confidence for it carries a great and glorious compensation of reward. For you have need of steadfast patience and endurance, so that you may perform and fully accomplish the will of God, and thus receive and carry away [and enjoy to the full] what is promised."

Is. 53:12 says, "Therefore I will divide Him a portion with the great, and He shall divide the spoil with the strong." The Amplified Bible says that "He shall divide the spoil with the mighty." This verse clearly states that you must become strong and mighty in order to partake of the abundant riches of the spoil that is available to you. There is strength to be had in being a Christian and it is your faith in God that makes you strong. And what is that strength and power to be used for? Phil. 4:13 (AMP) gives the answer, "I have strength for all things in Christ Who empowers me - I am ready for anything and equal to anything through Him Who infuses inner strength into me, [that is, I am self-sufficient in Christ's sufficiency]." Are you "ready for anything"? Are you prepared to stand and fight for those things that rightfully belong to you? Know for certain that there is no place on the victory platform for laid back and easy-going Christians. The only place where "success" comes before "work" is in the dictionary.

Matt. 11:12 (AMP) says, "And from the days of John the Baptist until the present time the kingdom of heaven had endured violent assault, and violent men seize it by force [as a precious prize] - a share in the heavenly kingdom is sought for with most ardent zeal and intense exertion." This verse could also be rendered, "The kingdom of heaven is being taken by storm and the strong and forceful ones claim it for themselves eagerly." It is the responsibility of every Christian who seeks to live a victorious life to storm into the kingdom and take it by force. Phil. 2:12 clearly tells believers to "work out your own salvation with fear and trembling." In order to live up to the potential that your faith would allow you must go to work, pick up our sword, and "fight the good fight of faith, lay hold on eternal life" (1 Tim. 6:12). There is no other way. God is looking for a faith that is genuine and true. If you don't go through the tests and trials that come your way then all you'll be in the kingdom of God is a pretender.

Members in the body of Christ must wake up and realize that the days of passive Christianity are over. This Christian life you've been called to is no Sunday picnic and neither is it all peaches and cream. It is a war and you have been called to battle. You cannot ignore the devil because the devil will not ignore you. 1 Peter 5:8 (AMP) says, "Be well-balanced, temperate, sober-minded; be vigilant and cautious at all times, for that enemy of yours, the devil, roams around like a lion roaring [in fierce hunger], seeking someone to seize upon and devour." So what are you to do when attacked by the enemy? Peter says in vs. 9, "Withstand him; be firm in faith [against his onset], - rooted, established, strong, immovable and determined." This is what it means to fight the good fight of faith. The availability of the blessings of God are abundant on the earth here in the last days but instead of growing stronger the Church has instead become complacent, indifferent, and unassertive.

A lot of people know the Word but only quote it in peace time. Churches are to train people to be an army and fight but, sad to say, most only go through the motions and don't produce anything. Satan has mounted an all-out assault against the faith of the brethren which means you've got to fight for your faith. God never intended for you to run from the devil and his cohorts. Why run from an enemy who was defeated two thousand years ago on Calvary's tree? Although his future is forever sealed in scripture, the devil still continues his onslaught against the body of Christ, against which you must fight the good fight of faith. By using the armor of God, you must stand up and defend what belongs to you. This is what it means to have a warrior spirit. The armor of God (Eph. 6:13-17) gives you equipment for your head, your chest, your loins, and your feet. There is a sword in one hand and a shield in the other. There is no protection for the back because you are to face the enemy head-on and put him under your feet where he belongs.

Zech. 10:5 (AMP) says, "And they shall be as mighty men, treading down their enemies in the mire of the streets in the battle and they shall fight because the Lord is with them, and the [oppressors'] riders on horses shall be confounded and-put to shame." David says in Ps. 18:39, "For You have armed me with strength for the battle; You have subdued under me those who rose up against me." Our soon-coming King is coming back not for a defeated church but for a victorious body of believers who are "more than conquerors through Him Who loved us" (Rom. 8:37). Jesus came to earth as the Lamb of God but will return with His followers as the Lion of Judah. Is. 43:12 says, "The Lord shall go forth like a mighty man; He shall stir up His zeal like a man of war. He shall cry out, yes, shout aloud; He shall prevail against His enemies." Jesus was, is, and always will be a winner! The problem with those believers who refuse to go forward is that many of them still see Jesus hanging on the cross and have developed a mentality of Him as a dead man Who was a loser.

It is time these people start building within themselves a picture of a resurrected Christ Who now sits at the right hand of the Heavenly Father clothed with power and majesty! The good news is that God wants this same power demonstrated in and through your life. The avenue through which He desires to do this is your faith. It is essential, therefore, that you develop a deep hunger and thirst for the Word of God and keep your eyes focused on Him. Jesus said, "I am the way, the truth, and the life." (John 14:6a). Satan will bring persecutions, trials, and afflictions into your life and try to take away from you your hunger for the Word. It is the enemy's purpose to take your attention away from God and His eternal Word and have you focus on natural things. Do not allow him to prosper in this evil endeavor. Jesus said in John 16:33, "These things I have spoken to you, that in Me you may have peace. In the world you will have tribulation; but be of good cheer, I have overcome the world."

If you are in a struggle then take courage and rejoice because that means you haven't been defeated yet. Nahum 1:7 says, "The Lord is good, a stronghold in the day of trouble; and He knows those who trust in Him!" The Message Bible says, "God is good, a hiding place in tough times." With Jesus as the center of your life you can't get lost, you can't be deceived, and the devil can't defeat you. Those who God calls, He will defend. He is called El Shaddai, the all-mighty One! With Jesus as your King, you can rule in the midst of your enemies. All this being said, and true, you must not forget that there is still a battle to be fought. It is called the good fight of faith. Until the day you go home to be with Jesus, you must continually force your way into the kingdom and take it by storm. You need to boldly face your enemy and claim for yourself the benefits of eternal life in greater fullness. Eternal life is the crown prepared for you and is to be your encouragement for war.

| 13 |

"THE SHIELD OF FAITH"

A student in a Bible college was talking with one of his professors and was excited to tell his mentor how well his life was going. "When I first came here I was so tempted and tested I could barely keep my head above water. But now, praise God, my life at seminary has smoothed out. I'm not being tempted at all." The professor looked deeply alarmed and this was not the reaction the student was expecting. "That's about the worst thing I could have heard," he told the surprised student. "That shows me that you're no longer in the battle. Satan isn't worried about you anymore." Since the enemy only opposes those who are the greatest threat to him, all those anointed by God should forever be prepared to confront spiritual attack. The devil walks about like a roaring lion seeking whom he can devour (1 Peter 5:8) and, because of that, Paul writes in Eph. 6:11, "Put on the whole armor of God that you may be able to stand against the wiles of the devil."

Putting on the whole armor of God should be a one-time event. You need to put it on and never take it off. Sleep with the armor on and get up with it on. Work in it and play in it. Never take it off. The Message Bible says, "God is strong, and He wants you strong. So, take everything the Master has set out for you, well-made weapons of the best materials. And put them to use so you will be able to stand up to everything the devil throws your way. This is no afternoon athletic contest that we'll walk away from and forget in a couple hours. This is for keeps, a life-or-death fight to the finish against the devil and all his angels." You are not strong in yourself but you are strong in the Lord and in the power of His might (Eph. 6:10). He gives you armor and weaponry to use in the good fight of faith but to most people this is not real to them. Their knowledge is vague and their understanding is too general, causing them to need a divine revelation of all that's been made available to them.

This equipment is called the "armor of God" because He both prepares and bestows it. You have no armor of your own that will be armor of proof on the day of battle. Nothing will hold up under the onslaught of the enemy but the armor of God. It's there so you can stand against the deceptive tactics that the enemy is bringing against you. As a child of God, you should have no fear of the devil at all. You know the truth and this sets you free from all fear. Yes, the devil is real and his influence is everywhere but be cannot do anything to you unless you yield to him. That's the gospel truth that many people have not seen. If he had the power most people give him credit for then you would have been dead a long time ago. You are alive today because you have been kept by the mercy of God. The devil can't touch you as long as you don't give in to his trickery and deceptive ways. This is why you need to be alert and on the watch so you won't be devoured through the avenue of deception.

Eph. 6:12 says, "For we do not wrestle against flesh and blood, but against the rulers of the darkness of this age, against spiritual hosts of wickedness in the heavenly places." Paul is saying that you have to deal with those principalities and powers that are trying to get at you through your flesh and things that come through natural desires. There are spiritual forces that are trying to get involved with your carnal mind and get you away from faith and into fleshly thinking. If you think you're immune from the lying schemes of the devil then you're just the person he's looking for. He'll even agree with you that you're too smart to be taken captive by his evil ways, all the while he's taking your hand and leading you down the paths of destruction. "Pride goes before destruction, and a haughty spirit before a fall" (Prov. 16:18) but protection comes when you put on the whole armor of God.

You no longer have to fight the devil because the battle has already been won. Jesus defeated him at the empty tomb. Col. 2:15 says He "disarmed principalities and powers, He made a public spectacle of them, triumphing over them in it." The word "disarmed" means 'to strip off; unclothe.' Jesus stripped the enemy of his authority and his ability to harm you. He said in Luke 10:19, "Behold, I give you the authority to trample on serpents and scorpions, and over all the power of the enemy, and nothing shall by any means hurt you." The "power of the enemy" is not referring to authority because the devil doesn't have any. You have to have a physical flesh and bone body in order to have authority on this planet. The devil doesn't have one. In the Garden of Eden, he had to use the body of a serpent in order to manifest himself. The only power and authority he has is what he can take illegally from somebody. He has to have a body from which to take authority from.

The devil is a defeated foe but you have to enforce his defeat. There is no need to fight the devil because you are an over-comer. You overcome him by the blood of the Lamb and the word of your testimony (Rev. 12:11). The problem is some people don't have any Word in their testimony. They can always tell you what the devil is doing and it's with these words that they give him the authority to come in and steal, kill, and destroy their lives. Those who say they're going to fight the devil are going to lose because they're trying to do it in their own power. They're trying to fight a battle that's already been won. This proves they don't believe Jesus has already won the battle and the Word of God does not mean anything to them. They didn't submit to God and when they resisted the devil, he didn't flee from them. The power of the devil comes through deception and each piece of armor is designed to keep the lies of the enemy from getting into your life and doing great damage.

Eph. 6: 13 says, "Therefore take up the whole armor of God, that you may be able to withstand in the evil day, and having done all, to stand." The Message Bible says "that when it's all over but the shouting you'll still be on your feet." Putting on the armor is something you do. God has given it to you but you have to receive it and by faith put it on. Most people don't know how to do this. It's not complicated but people are destroyed by a lack of knowledge (Hos. 4:6). Calling the day the devil attacks you an "evil day," Paul goes on to list the various items of armor that the believer must put on in order to fight the good fight of faith. He says in vs. 14, "Stand therefore, having girded your waist with truth, having put on the breastplate of righteousness." Flaming arrows of lies and evil thoughts and imaginations are being shot at you every day, and this is why the first piece of armor you are to put on is the belt of truth. If you know the truth then you won't be pierced with the arrows of darkness, deception, and destruction.

The belt of truth encircles you and the World English Bible calls it the "utility belt of truth." Every piece of armor that the Roman soldier wore was fastened to his belt and this signifies that the foundation of all you do is to be based on truth. In Greek the word "truth" is defined as 'the reality lying at the basis of an appearance; the manifested, veritable essence of a matter.' In other words, truth is a growing knowledge and understanding of the scriptures and how they apply to life. Jesus was the perfect expression of truth, not only in what He said but also in sincerity and the integrity of His character. Jesus said, "I am the way, the truth, and the life" (John 14:6). The foundation of truth is that which agrees with final reality and the storms of life bring out into the open and prove what your foundation is. In order to survive the storms of life you must first put on the belt of truth which means to wholeheartedly accept God's Word and His faithfulness in the fulfillment of His promise as exhibited in Christ.

1 Tim. 4:1 says, "Now the Spirit expressly says that in latter times some will depart from the faith, giving heed to deceiving spirits and doctrines of demons." You can't depart from the faith unless you've first been in the faith. The Message Bible says "some are going to give up on the faith and chase after demonic illusions put forth by professional liars." Demons have doctrines and they're not always preached at some satanist church. Satan comes as an angel of light and many of his doctrines are taught by misinformed ministers at the local church down the street from where you live. He does this so that believers will be deceived and turn loose of their faith. There are few things more sad and pitiful than a believer who has lost their faith. There are many who at one time used to believe the truth and were happy and excited about it. Then one day a minister wrongly told them that God was lonely and took their baby in a tragic car accident and now they want nothing to do with Him or the Christian faith. Deception came in and their life was destroyed.

The belt of truth protects you from everything that is not true. Every piece of armor is a piece of truth and light. Righteousness is truth and the breastplate protects the heart and all the vital organs of the upper body. The devil will try to tell you that you're a no good sinner but the truth is you've been made the righteousness of God in Christ Jesus. The breastplate of righteousness keeps you from feeling condemned and believing you're not good for anything. If you don't put on this piece of armor, you will be pierced by the lies of the enemy and will be prevented from fulfilling your destiny. To win a war, a soldier must be well armed for battle but if inwardly he has not a good heart his armor will be of little use to him. 2 Cor. 6:7 (NLT) says, "We faithfully preach the truth. God's power is working in us. We use the weapons of righteousness in the right hand for attack and the left hand for defense" If you are born again, you are righteous in the eyes of God and a bright future awaits you.

Jesus died to make you righteous but still, this is a piece of armor you must put on. If you don't, then quilt and condemnation will pierce your heart and prevent you from living a life of freedom and liberty. In the Bible the word "heart" represents the center of your innermost being which is your spirit. You are a spirit, you have a soul, and you live in a body. Faith proceeds from your heart and allows you to believe the Word of God. Paul said in 1 Thess. 5:8 to put on the breastplate of faith and love. This makes up the righteousness of God for by faith you are united to Him and by love you are united to your brethren. Righteousness is the character or quality of being right or just. It is that which conforms itself to the revealed will of God. For the most part, righteousness can be defined as that gracious gift of God to man whereby all who believe on the Lord Jesus Christ are brought into a right relationship with Him. In Christ you become all that God requires you to be, all that you could never be in yourself because of the bondage of sin.

God smiles when He looks at you because when He sees you, He sees Jesus. You are in Him and He is in you. Your sins are washed away and your past failures He remembers no more. Jesus took your sins and gave you His righteousness. 2 Cor.

5:21 says, "For He made Him who knew no sin to be sin for us, that we might become the righteousness of God in Him." He became what you were so that you might become what He is. He has made you worthy and He has made you righteous. If and when you do miss the mark there is always 1 John 1:9 to fall back on, "If we confess our sins, He is faithful and just to forgive us our sins and to cleanse us from all unrighteousness." When you sin don't run from God, run to Him and He'll forgive your sins and purge you of all wrongdoing. He can be faithful and just because the price has already been paid. You are righteous in Christ so don't let the devil or anybody else tell you otherwise. The breastplate is on and there is no condemnation and guilt in your life.

The good fight of faith is a fight between light and darkness, truth and deception. Billions of people are walking in darkness and most of them don't even know it. They falsely believe that all is well because the god of this age has blinded their eyes through unbelief (2 Cor. 4:4). These people are thinking wrong for Jesus said in John 12:25, "He who loves his life will lose it, and he who hates his life in this world will keep it for eternal life." Jesus is saying that you should hate the deceptive falseness that is causing people to be devoured in this life. Millions of people are living like there's no God and no heaven or hell. They're living as if this life is all there is and with all their might they're trying to get all their satisfaction and fulfillment in what this world has to offer. Millionaires commit suicide because after obtaining fortune and fame they realize there is still a void in their life. They've been living in a world of fantasy and have reasoned that there is no reason to go on with their life. So they end it and die an early death.

Unlike animals who seem quite content to simply be themselves, most people are always looking for ways to be somebody they're not. They look for the meaning of life in all the wrong places. They travel the world seeking adventure and read the writings of ancient philosophers hoping to find out who they are and why they're here. They think wealth and riches is the answer but the more they have it, the less satisfied they are. This is why Solomon said in Eccl. 1:2, "Vanity of vanities, all is vanity." People dream of the day they can retire so they can fish all day and play golf. This may be enjoyable for a season but after a while this too will grow old and stale. There is more to life than putting a worm on a hook or dropping a little white ball into a hole in the ground. None of this satisfies but when you find the plan of God for your life and do what he tells you to do, you will be satisfied from the inside out because you will be doing what you were created to do. There is a light on your path and you're not walking in darkness.

The next piece of armor you are to put on is found in Eph. 6:15, "And having shod your feet with the preparation of the gospel of peace." The NLT says, "For shoes, put on the peace that comes from the Good News so that you will be fully prepared." You don't need shoes if you're not going anywhere but if you're on the road that leads to the fulfillment of your destiny then your feet need to be protected. Shoes, or greaves of brass, were part of the military armor of a fighting warrior (1 Sam. 17:6) and its purpose was to protect the feet from gall traps and sharp sticks which were laid in the way in order to obstruct the marching of the enemy. Since the average ancient soldier marched on hot and rough roads, climbed over jagged rocks, trampled over thorns, and waded through stream beds of sharp stones, his feet needed much protection. The military successes of Alexander the Great and Julius Caesar were due in large measure by their armies being able to undertake long marches at incredible speed and over rough terrain.

The Amplified Bible says, "And having shod your feet in preparation (to face the enemy with the firm-footed stability, the promptness and the readiness produced by the good news) of the Gospel of peace." The shoes of a Roman soldier were usually impregnated with bits of metal or nails to give him better traction as he climbed a slippery hill and greater stability as he fought. A good pair of shoes allowed the soldier to march, climb, fight, or do whatever else was necessary at a moment's notice. God demands the same readiness of His people. The word "preparation" denotes readiness and is a reminder that you are to be eager to preach the gospel of peace to others. Jesus said in mark 16:15, "Go into all the world and preach the gospel to every creature." Take this personally. Some way, somehow, you need to be involved in telling the world about Jesus. Be like Isaiah who said, "Here I am! Send me" (Is. 6:8).

Paul speaks of the preparation of the feet for spiritual conflict. Having the gospel of peace as your footwear suggests that you need to advance into the enemy's territory, aware that there will be traps, with the message of grace so essential to winning souls to Christ. Satan has many obstacles placed in the path of the righteous to halt the gospel message from being preached but the shoes of peace provide you with the ability to face the storms of life knowing you won't slip from your current position. The gospel of peace enables you to walk with a steady pace in the way of the Lord without being hindered or overcome by the difficulties and dangers that may be on the path you are traveling. Going forward is when you become the enemy's worst nightmare for this is when you go on the offensive. You march into the enemy's camp and take back what's he's stolen from you and the body of Christ. You attack the forces of darkness with the truth of the gospel which is the glorious light that liberates and sets free.

Is. 52:7 says, "How beautiful upon the mountains are the feet of him who brings good news, who proclaims peace, who brings glad tidings of good things, who proclaims salvation, who says to Zion, 'Your God reigns!'" Peace is not the absence of tough times nor is there a guarantee that your journey will take you on well-traveled paths. Peace isn't found in your circumstances but rather is found in Christ. In Him you have the refreshment and protection of His presence. Traveling through difficult terrain may be an inevitable part of your journey but still you can experience peace. David wrote in Ps. 23:4, "Yea, though I walk through the valley of the shadow of death, I will fear no evil; For You are with me." When you allow yourself to take comfort in this good news then nothing will be able to trouble your heart or make you afraid. The preparation of the gospel of peace allows you to face the otherwise painful trials and tribulations of life knowing that greater is He who is in you than he who is in the world.

There is one piece of armor which Paul seems to give special attention to. In Eph. 6:16 he writes, "Above all, taking the shield of faith with which you will be able to quench all the fiery darts of the enemy." You are in the crosshairs of the devil. He is shooting flaming arrows at you with the sole purpose of destroying your life. You will be deceived if you're not aware of what's going on and who's behind all this mass confusion and wickedness. The good news is that you have the mind of Christ and God is revealing things to you. You are not ignorant of the devil's devices and his planned out schemes and tactics (2 Cor. 2:11). He is a liar and the father of lies and you can't allow yourself to consider anything that is contrary to God's Word. There is a broad road on which everybody embraces the beliefs of false religions and this leads to destruction and eternal judgment. This is why Paul said in Gal. 1:22, "But even if we, or an angel from heaven, preach any other gospel to you than what we have preached to you, let him be accursed."

The devil is forever seeking to turn you away from the truth. He is full of deceit and all fraud and is the enemy of righteousness. He is a wily adversary and is the master of every form of wickedness, trickery, and restlessness. He is the enemy of everything that is upright and good and continually seeks to pervert the ways of the Lord. 1 John 4:1 says, "Beloved, do not believe every spirit, but test the spirits, whether they are of God; because many false prophets have gone out into the world." The Message Bible says, "My dear friends, don't believe everything you hear. Carefully weigh and examine what people tell you. Not everyone who talks about God comes from God. There are a lot of lying preachers loose in the world." These are the things you need to be on the watch for. These lies are the fiery darts of the enemy and you need to stand behind your shield of faith and be like Abraham who staggered not at the promises of God (Rom. 4:20). He had his shield up and became the father of many nations.

In the good fight of faith, you must walk headfirst into the battle with the shield of faith ever before you. It is important to realize that this shield of faith is not a small, round shield that is held on the arm by two narrow straps thus leaving many parts of the body exposed. A Roman shield covered the whole body which the soldier could hide behind when the enemy shot their arrows at him. The best warriors would have another person called an armor-bearer go before them with the shield and when the onslaught began both would hide behind the shield's wall of protection. Likewise, your whole life is to be protected and shielded by faith. It will guard you when your spiritual values and beliefs come under attack and will allow you to stand resolute and unwavering during times of trial. Satan is always hurling the fiery darts of fear, doubt, and unbelief in your direction but they will be deflected out of the way when your shield is up. When your faith in God is strong it will be impossible for the devil to break through your shield and land an attack.

The Roman shield was a very large, slightly curved rectangular shield featuring at its center a large, metal knob. These shields were often made of wood and then covered with canvas and leather. The edges were bound with rawhide stitched through the wood and sometimes bronze binding was used. When wet these shields could extinguish fiery darts and flaming arrows. Because of its sheer size, soldiers were afforded a great deal of protection from the enemy. Its slight curve was able to deflect attacks without transferring the full force of the assault to the man holding the shield. Because of the knob it was able to deflect even more vicious blows and function in a limited offensive capacity as a means of knocking an opponent backwards. It allowed the Roman soldier to give their enemies a stun-inducing shove that would allow them to follow through with an attack of their own. Your faith in God can also give Satan a shove backwards and give you a chance to fight back by doing the will of God for your life.

The Roman military had an inventive and very effective tactic that made use of their large shields. When the enemy would begin firing arrows and other projectiles at the army, the soldiers would close ranks into a rectangular formation. Those on the outside would use their shields to create a wall around the perimeter and those in the middle would raise their shields over their heads to protect everyone from airborne missiles. When the Roman army joined their shields together it became an unstoppable force. They became like a human tank and their shields were able to quench all the fiery darts of the enemy. When the body of Christ join their shields together, when they strengthen each other with their faith, building up and serving as they are called to do, they also become an unstoppable force able to take on any challenge. You must remember that this is not simply your battle. This is the battle of all your brethren, both near and far. To win the battle all believers must put their faith in God and stand side by side.

The Word of God builds a shield around you and goes wherever you go. Jesus said in John 15:7, "If you abide in Me, and My words abide in you, you will ask what you desire, and it shall be done for you." There are no limits if what you believe is based on the authority of the Word of God. The shield of faith is built with the Word of God and you can make it as strong as you'd like. There is life in the Word of God and death in the words of the devil. You don't want to get caught saying what the devil said. Stop listening to him and concentrate on what God said. When the devil comes to tempt you, you need to know what the Word says about the situation he's trying to tempt you in. Three times on the mount of temptation Jesus told the devil, "It is written." Jesus had a scripture for everything the devil threw at Him. Never again was Jesus tempted in those areas. The devil left and never did return. Don't fight with the devil, just do what Jesus did. Say what the Word says and he will flee from you.

Don't get into a shouting match with the devil. This puts you into the carnal realm whereas the good fight of faith is spiritual. The Word is filled with faith and Rom. 10:17 says, "So then faith comes by hearing, and hearing by the Word of God." Maintaining a constant confession of what the Word says will keep the shield of faith before you at all times. Do not lay down your shield and wait until a problem arises before you confess the Word in that specific area. No, confess and believe for the provision before you need it. Confess by Jesus' stripes you are healed when you are well and whole. Confess that God will supply all your needs when your bank account is overflowing with financial resources. Be offensive minded. Faith is not to be used only when you get hit by an arrow. On the contrary, faith is to be used before the arrow leaves the enemy's hands. Faith is to be a way of life and not just something you use when you get into trouble. The shield of faith must be kept in front of you at all times. Do not lay it down or sit it aside. Be consistent and take it with you wherever you go. Don't leave home without it.

The shield of faith is different from the other pieces of armor. The belt, breastplate, and shoes are items you wear and they essentially hold themselves up. The shield is different. Paul says the shield is something you must take up, something you are required to raise. Just strapping it on your arm won't do any good if you don't make the effort to hold it up and use it. You take up the shield of faith by taking the Word of God because that is what the shield is built out of. The Word of God that abides in you radiates around you and protects you from the fiery darts of the wicked one. Don't be like some who take the shield of doubt and quench all the blessings of God. The shield of doubt comes from negative thinking and negative speaking. Don't get stressed out concerning the necessities of life and don't take thought by questioning God's willingness and ability to provide for you. The children of Israel did this in the wilderness and when they began to murmur and complain fiery serpents came into the camp and killed a great multitude.

As a born-again believer you are not of this world and the shield of faith is needed because the world is engrossed in unbelief and is under the control of the evil one. The evening news will reveal the negativity of this planet and all too often

Christians pick up on this negative spirit. This is why you are to never lay down the shield of faith. Job 22:28 says, "You will also declare a thing, and it will be established for you; So, light will shine on your way." Prov. 20:27 says, "The spirit of man is the lamp of the Lord, searching all the inner depths of the heart." The spirit of man is the light bulb God uses to enlighten you. Prov. 4:23 says, "Keep your heart with all diligence, for out of it spring the issues of life." What gets in your heart will change your life either for the better or for the worse. Let God's Word be the final authority in your life. With it you enforce the devil's defeat. All the pieces of armor are important to the believer but, for sure, the shield of faith needs to be the first thing the enemy sees when he looks your way.

| 14 |

"THE LIGHT OF FAITH"

What most people believe about the devil is a tangled distortion of falseness. They watch horror movies which are designed to put fear and confusion in people and this is what they base their opinions on. What they think simply is not true. The devil is not some spiritual equal opposite to God. He's a created being who has fallen and soon will be cast into the lake of fire. He's been stripped of his power and the only weapon he has to use against people is deception. He is the master con artist and he knows if he can deceive you, he can destroy you. The influence of evil is everywhere and 1 John 5:19 (NLT) says "that the world around us is under the control of the evil one." The world is in the condition it's in today because people have a free choice to believe what they want to believe. Many are yielding to this evil influence and, the more a person yields to a wrong spirit, the more irrational their behavior will become. This is why today's headlines tell of the diabolical things that people are doing all over the world. None of it makes any sense at all.

The mind is the devil's playground and this is why you need to "take the helmet of salvation, and the sword of the Spirit which is the word of God" (Eph. 6:17). The head is the seat of the mind and, when it has laid hold of the truth of God's Word, will not receive false doctrine or give way to the devil's temptations and his deceptive ways. Never fear the devil but know that he'll barge into your life with notions as to why God can't use you, why you'll never be healed, and why your sins are too big to be forgiven. When you wear the helmet of salvation you can take those thoughts captive by replacing them with the truth of God's Word. Speaking scripture gives the devil a potent reminder of everything he lost because of the cross, and it forces him to flee. Paul said in 1 Thess. 5:8 to put on "as a helmet the hope of salvation." A well founded and well-built hope will both purify the soul and keep it from being defiled by the enemy. It will comfort the soul and keep your mind from being troubled and tormented by the storms that come your way.

The soldier's helmet was a single piece of iron molded to fit his head and it was adorned with a peacock-like crest to identify his rank. In ancient times head wounds were the most common and fatal wounds of war and the soldier wouldn't dare enter a battle without his helmet. There are several stories in the Bible that stress the importance of protecting the head while in battle. King Abimeleck died because he charged a city wall without first putting on his helmet. "And a certain woman cast a piece of millstone upon Abimeleck's head, and all to break his skull" (Judges 9:53). In another instance, simply wearing a helmet improperly proved to be a fatal mistake. The giant Goliath became outraged that young David would dare come against him with nothing more than a shepherd's staff and a sling in his hand. Goliath's haughtiness apparently prompted him to carelessly push back his helmet because moments later a smooth stone from David's sling sunk deep into the giant's forehead (1 Sam. 17:40-49).

There is a difference between being religious and being spiritual. There are many religious people in hell today because the devil deceived them into thinking the falseness of what they believed was true. 2 Tim. 2:15 talks about "rightly dividing the word of truth" and this they did not do. The enemy will have an advantage over you if you don't know what's true and what isn't true. The devil will come to you so innocently with thoughts that are more deadly than poison hoping you won't know where they came from. This is how he works. He is very subtle and crafty and if the light of God's Word is not shining in your heart, then you won't know it's him. The devil is counting on you being ignorant of the Word so you won't know the difference. It's only in the light of the truth that you will recognize and be free from the control of the god of this world.

People who don't believe and strive to do their own thing are in truth being dominated and controlled by the darkness that is in the world. The influence of the devil is real and these people are locked into a wrong way of thinking. They are believing lies and because there is a stronghold on their mind, they won't listen to the truth that others want to share with them. If they knew it was a lie they wouldn't be deceived. It matters what you think. To be carnally minded is death (Rom. 8:6) and this is why you need to bring every thought captive to the obedience of Christ. Because of Hollywood and the like there is a grave misconception as to what spiritual warfare is and how it is the devil attacks people. The primary way the enemy will come against you is with thoughts that are contrary to the Word of God. If you don't read and study the Bible then you will be ignorant of the truth and this is what gives your adversary the advantage. This is why Peter says to be sober and vigilant (1 Peter 5:8). You need to be watchful and on the alert because the devil is launching ungodly thoughts at you every day.

There is a fight to be fought and if you don't fight you will be defeated. With the shield of faith in one hand and the sword of the Spirit in the other, you can resist the devil and he will flee from you. Like Jesus, you can say, "Get behind Me, Satan! You are an offense to Me, for you are not mindful of the things of God, but the things of men" (Matt. 16:23). The biggest trick of the devil is he tries to get people to think he doesn't exist. Like the prodigal son, millions of people are trying to live a life of fantasy. They're not living in reality but rather in an altered state of mind. They're living in darkness and are not aware of what the devil is doing to them. This is a fatal mistake because people live in their awareness, in what they perceive to be reality, in what they believe to be true. God gave people a free will with which they can choose to believe whatever they want to believe, whether it be true or not. Millions are praying to statues and worship Mother Earth all the while thinking they're doing the right thing. These people are deceived for the devil has blinded their eyes.

Take captive those thoughts that are contrary to the Word of God. Refuse to consider it and refuse to think about it. Cast it away and instead think about what God said. In the wilderness Jesus was tempted for forty days with thoughts and suggestions and feelings. He had not eaten during this time and He was hungry. The devil knew this and applied more pressure to get Jesus to do the wrong thing. This was a true spiritual battle. It happened to Jesus and it will happen to you. Even the most holy Christians will at times have thoughts come to their mind that are unclean and perverted and wrong. These thoughts are from the devil yet he'll do everything he can to keep you from seeing they're from him. He'll bring guilt and condemnation your way in hopes of getting you to blame yourself for the thoughts he sent to you. If your eyes are on yourself then you won't see the craftiness of how he operates. The Message Bible says in 1 Peter 5:8, "Keep a cool head. Stay alert. The devil is poised to pounce, and would like nothing better than to catch you napping. Keep your guard up."

Two of the devil's favorite words are "do it." He'll bring a thought and a suggestion to your mind and then he'll tell you to "do it." The serpent told Adam and Eve that if they ate of the forbidden fruit they'd be like God, knowing good and evil. He then said "do it" and they did. From a rooftop David saw Bathsheba bathing and he longed to have her. The devil said "do it" and he did. In the wilderness Jesus was hungry and the devil told Him to command the stone to be turned into bread. "Do it," he said. "Do it." Pressure was being applied and the devil was relentless in his attack. "Do it! Do it! Do it!" This was the real deal. This is what spiritual warfare is all about. Three times the devil tempted Jesus and told Him to do what he suggested. It was a real temptation for Jesus was hungry and He wanted to eat. What would He do? How would He respond? His destiny and the purpose for which He came to earth hung in the balance right here. This was the moment of truth. As hungry and as tempted as He was, Jesus dug deep inside Himself and responded with three of God's most favorite words, "It is written."

1 John 3:8 says, "For this purpose the Son of God was manifested, that He might destroy the works of the devil." Jesus came to dissolve and undo the works that the devil has done. 2 Tim. 1:10 says Jesus "abolished death and brought life and immortality to light through the gospel." You are a soldier in the army of the Lord and this is to be your mission as well. In a war you must know who your enemy is and what he's capable of. You must know him frontwards and backwards. In the good fight of faith, you need to know that the devil has been stripped of all his power. However, one thing he does do is lie, and this he does very well. For the most part, he has been quite successful and darkness has covered the face of this planet. You overcome darkness with light and this is why Paul tells you to take the helmet of salvation and the sword of the Spirit which is the Word of God. John 1:1 says, "In the beginning was the Word, and the Word was with God, and the Word was God." Vs. 4,5 says, "In Him was life, and the life was the light of men. And the light shines in the darkness, and the darkness did not comprehend it."

Light dissolves darkness but darkness can never overtake light. Never has happened, never will. 1 John 2:8 (NLT) says, "For the darkness is disappearing and the true light is already shining." Darkness can only exist in the absence of light and the purpose of the devil is to blind the minds of those who do not believe "lest the light of the gospel of the glory of Christ, who is the image of God, should shine on them" (2 Cor. 4:4). The devil and his cohorts are called "the rulers of the darkness of this age" (Eph. 6:12) because they can only operate when there is no light. There is nothing the devil can do to you when you walk in the light of God's Word. It's a simple concept but the problem in the world is that most people don't want to see the light. Matt. 13;15 says "their eyes they have closed." Jesus is ready to save these people, and heal them, but they want nothing to do with it. These are the ones who will listen to and believe the lies of the devil until the day they die. They've been deceived and will be devoured by the enemy of light.

Jesus said in John 3:19-21, "And this is the condemnation, that the light has come into the world, and men loved darkness rather than light, because their deeds were evil. For everyone practicing evil hates the light and does not come to the light, lest his deeds should be exposed. But he who does the truth come to the light, that his deeds may be clearly seen, that they have been done in God." Those who walk in darkness know what they're doing is wrong but do it anyway. Their lives are bound with the chains of sin and oppression and have become slaves of darkness. They are in the control of the evil one and, if they don't change, their lives will be destroyed. Those who walk in the light, on the other hand, want to hear the truth even if it means there are some areas in their life that needs to be changed. They love the truth more than getting their own way and doing what they think is best. They're willing to change those things that need to be changed and won't feel guilty while they're doing it. Light has shone on their path and they know which direction they should take.

You are a soldier in the army of the Lord which means you are a soldier of light. Jesus said in John 8:12, "I am the light of the world. He who follows Me shall not walk in darkness, but have the light of life." When you follow Jesus, you will have a life filled with light and will never walk in darkness. You live in the light and you walk in the light. Your faith is grounded in the light of God's Word. You know the truth and the truth makes you free. Jesus continued in John 12:35,36, "Walk while you have the light, lest darkness overtake you; he who walks in darkness does not know where he is going. While you have the light, believe in the light, that you may become sons of light." The sword of the Spirit pierces the darkness with glorious light and the devil has no defense against it. Vs. 46 (NIV) says, "I have come into the world as a light, so that no one who believes in Me should stay in darkness." When you see Jesus, you see light. When He was born light was manifested in perfection on the earth. Everything He said and everything He did were demonstrations of light.

The first recorded words of God in the Bible are found in Gen. 1:3, "Then God said, 'Let there be light'; and there was light." Light has been the will of God since the very beginning. Sin prevailed in the Garden of Eden and darkness fell on the face of the earth. But when Jesus was born God said the same thing, "Let there be light!" Jesus is light and He became flesh and dwelt among us and the darkness did not overtake Him. His victory becomes your victory and this allows you to take the sword of the Spirit and fight the good fight of faith. Heb. 4:12 says, "For the word of God is living and powerful, and sharper than any two-edged sword, piercing even to the division of soul and spirit, and of joints and marrow, and is a discerner of the thoughts and intents of the heart." The sword is an offensive weapon and with it you can pierce and penetrate the kingdom of darkness. The only thing that can pierce darkened hearts and minds is the light of the Word of God. It is living and it is powerful. It can do what reasonings and vain philosophies cannot.

Your citizenship is in heaven and as an ambassador for Christ you've been sent to be a beacon of light in this dark world. Jesus said to go into all the world and make disciples of all men. You're in enemy territory and this is why you need to put on the whole armor of God. This world is covered in darkness but Is. 60:1-3 says, "Arise, shine; For your light has come! And the glory of the Lord is risen upon you. For behold, the darkness shall cover the earth, and deep darkness the people; But the Lord will arise over you, and His glory will be seen upon you. The Gentiles shall come to your light, and kings to the brightness of your rising." The enemy will launch an assault against everything God is doing and this is why you can't be passive where the devil is concerned. You are part of a mighty generation chosen by God and you must never run from the enemy. Instead, you must rise up and prepare for war. Much is at stake here and you must step forward and fight the good fight of faith.

You are not here to survive the assaults of the enemy, you are here to start them. The first step in having breakthrough and defeating the enemy is to once and for all get fed up with his efforts to bring you down. In Gen. 27 Esau found out that his brother Jacob had deceived his father into giving him the blessing of the firstborn. Esau lifted up his voice and wept when he found out the blessing could not be reversed so he pleaded with his father to give him a blessing as well. Here is what Isaac told him, "Behold, your dwelling shall be of the fatness of the earth, and the dew of heaven from above. By your sword you shall live, and you shall serve your brother. And it shall come to pass, when you become restless, that you shall break his yoke from your neck" (vs. 39,40). To be restless means to be fed up. You don't get anywhere and you will not accomplish anything until you get fed up with your present condition. You can wish, hope, and cry all day but nothing will happen until you get fed up.

The Message Bible says, "But when you can't take it any more you'll break loose and run free." Things happen when a holy fervor rises up on the inside of you. Your countenance will change, you'll speak with authority and you'll walk in dominion. Jesus said in Matt. 11:12, "The kingdom of heaven suffers violence, and the violent take it by force." Get fed up! Get violent! Draw a line in the sand and tell the enemy, "No more! Enough is enough!" Get aggressive and stirred up once again for what rightfully belongs to you. Get fed up for going without and then rise up and exercise your God-given authority over the devil. Live by the sword and never back off. The victory is yours if you'll get fed up and never back away. War has been declared and to possess your mountain you can't have a lukewarm attitude when it comes to fighting the enemy. Don't be a weak-kneed nobody but rise up and go to war for the glory of God. Don't be afraid of the enemy, make him be afraid of you.

The Complete Jewish Bible says in Eph. 6:10,11, "Finally, grow powerful in union with the Lord, in union with His mighty strength! Use all the armor and weaponry that God provides, so that you will be able to stand against the deceptive tactics of the adversary." You are to never fear the devil but you must take deception very seriously. The problem is that people who are deceived don't know it. They think what they're believing is true when in reality it's a lie from the devil. A lot of these people don't even believe the devil exists yet every day he is leading them down paths of destruction. They are walking in darkness and are being devoured by the evil one. Vs. 12,13 says, "For we are not struggling against human beings, but against the rulers, authorities, and cosmic powers governing this darkness, against the spiritual forces of evil in the heavenly realm. So, take up every piece of war equipment God provides; so that when the evil day comes, you will be able to resist; and when the battle is won, you will still be standing."

You don't fight the devil, you resist him with the light of God's Word. Hollywood would have you believe that you resist the devil by holding a crucifix in front of you as you stomp around your house screaming at the top of your lungs. This is utter nonsense and is precisely what the devil would have you believe. To enhance his deception over you he may even back away for a season causing you to think your silly gestures actually worked. Be forewarned! He will be back! Jesus said in Matt. 12:43-45, "When an unclean spirit goes out of a man, he goes through dry places, seeking rest, and finds none. Then he says, 'I will return to my house from which I came.' And when he comes, he finds it empty, swept, and put in order. Then he goes and takes with him seven other spirits more wicked than himself, and they enter and dwell there; and the last state of that man is worse than the first. So shall it also be with this wicked generation."

You resist the devil with the Word of God. There is an anointing on the Word that will open your eyes and cause you to see the truth. If you don't read and study the Bible then the devil will try to deceive you into resisting the things of God. There are believers all over the world who are resisting prosperity, healing, and speaking in tongues. They'll argue with you night and day over these matters and some may try to engage you in a physical altercation because you don't believe the same way they do. These people are saved and born again yet their eyes have been blinded by the evil one. They have been deceived and in time they'll be even more deceived until one day they'll resist the entire Word of God. A little leaven leavens the whole lump (1 Cor. 5:6). The mind of man has been darkened by sin and must be brought to the place where it thinks as God thinks. To do this you must continually use the sword of the Spirit and say what God says. This comes about when you read, study, meditate, feed on, practice, and confess the Word of God.

The Amplified Bible says the Word is "alive and full of power - making it active, operative, energizing and effective" (Heb. 4:12). When you confess the Word over your storm the enemy will flee and the rough waters and blowing wind will become peaceful and still. Storms such as financial setbacks, health issues, and relationship problems are but a few of the woes that can be quenched with the light of faith which is the Word of God. The Christian life is full of giants and there are strongholds and walled cities wherever you look. This is what the battle of faith is all about. Understand that your problems are not there to keep you down but rather to keep you from having absolute confidence in God. Faith brings you to a place where you're resting in His faithfulness and you'll have no doubt that God's purpose for your life will be fulfilled. You were not anointed with the power of God so you could quit. The journey is not easy but it's worth the challenges that go with it. And remember, it's those who finish the race that get the prize.

To win a battle you must first come to realize that you are in a battle. Most people live life with reckless abandon not even knowing there is an enemy arrayed against them. Job. 1:6,7 tells how Satan presented himself before the Lord and was asked where he came from. "So Satan answered the Lord and said, 'From going to and from on the earth, and from walking back and forth on it.'" People need to awaken to the fact that like a roaring lion the devil is roaming the earth seeking whom he can devour. He is successful when he can get people to not even know he is there. If that doesn't work, he'll make their lives so miserable that all people will do is focus on their problems and not see what's happening in the spiritual realm. Trials can blind your eyes to what the schemes of the devil really are and this is why Paul said in 2 Tim. 2:3,4, "You therefore must endure hardship as a good soldier of Jesus Christ. No one engaged in warfare entangles himself with the affairs of this life, that he may please him who enlisted him as a soldier."

To win the battle you must be entirely devoted to the cause of Christ. You can't walk in light one day and darkness the next. You're not fooling God and you're definitely not fooling the devil. Paul said in 1 Tim. 4:15, "Meditate on these things; give yourself entirely to them, that your progress may be evident to all." You need to diligently apply yourself to the dream God gives you and be willing to exert yourself beyond the norm. Become the kind of person who goes the extra mile, one who believes that whatever you set out to do will succeed and prosper. The Message Bible says in Phil. 4:13, "Whatever I have, wherever I am, I can make it through anything in the One who makes me who I am." Don't let the devil steal your focus and purpose. You are a warrior in the army of the Lord by choice and by command. Your armor is not polished and nice but is tattered and worn. You don't go over the mountain the enemy placed in your path, you go through it. You break through that obstacle and take back what the enemy has stolen. You rise up and take the kingdom by storm.

| 15 |

"THE FIGHT OF FAITH"

The good fight of faith is fought with faith-filled words. Paul mentioned how Timothy had "confessed the good confession in the presence of many witnesses" (1 Tim. 6:12) and how Jesus "witnessed the good confession before Pontius Pilate" (vs. 13). You were made in the image of God, who is a speaking Spirit, and the words you speak are designed to bring forth the same results as when God speaks. Words are powerful, yet most people don't see that the condition their life is in is connected to the words they speak. They talk a lot but in truth don't say anything of value and to them the power of the spoken word has been reduced to nothing. Their words are empty and void of power which means they have no control over the direction their life is going. Words are containers and what you put in them determines what you can or cannot do. Many fill their words with gossip, fear, and unbelief and then wonder why nothing good ever happens to them. Then there are those who fill their words with faith, hope, and love and these are the ones who live a victorious life.

Paul said that you lay hold of eternal life by making a good con- fession and this is what the good fight of faith is all about. You don't fight to get God to bless you because He's already done it. And you don't fight to defeat the devil because he's already defeated. No, you fight against those things which would stop you from making a good confession. The devil is a liar and a deceiver and he'll drop little hints of doubt and unbelief into your mind in hopes of getting you to speak negative words out your mouth. He'll try to get you to say things like "Whatever will be, will be." Those words sound innocent enough but in truth they will destroy your life. It's like eating sugar-coated rat poison. It's sweet on the outside but deadly on the inside. If the devil can't get you to say things like this then he'll be unable to stop the miracle-working power of God from operating in your life. He can't stop the faith-filled words you speak from producing and multiplying grace into your circumstances. This is why when you resist the devil his only option is to flee from you.

Every day Jesus walked the earth He fought the good fight of faith. He continually pleased the Father and had victory wher- ever He went. Today, He is seated at the right hand of the Fa- ther watching to see if you will do the same things He did. Rev. 1:16 says "out of His mouth went a sharp two-edged sword, and His countenance was like the sun shining in its strength." Rev. 2:16 says, "Repent, or else I will come to you quickly, and will fight against them with the sword of My mouth." The words Jesus speaks are fighting words and this is how He fights the good fight of faith. This is how you also tear down those barri- ers that stand against the truth of God, "bringing every thought into captivity to the obedience of Christ" (2 Cor. 10:5). You fight the good fight by speaking words that are filled with faith. This is how Jesus does it and this is how you do it. Rom. 10:8 says, "The word is near you, even in your mouth and in your heart." You getting your bills paid is near you and so is the healing of your body. Where is it at? In the words you speak.

The answer to all your problems is right under your nose. Rom. 10:9 says "that if you confess with your mouth the Lord Jesus and believe in your heart that God raised Him from the dead, you will be saved." Many believers have become silent believers who would prefer to say nothing at all. This is precisely what the devil wants them to do. People who say nothing don't get born again and never get their prayers answered. Jesus works with the faith-filled words you speak and if all you say is nothing then He has nothing to work with. Words are how you make known what's in your heart (Matt. 12:34) and it's what you used to get born again. Salvation is the greatest miracle of all and if you have faith to get saved, then you also have the faith to receive anything and everything you'll ever need in life. If you can get a salvation miracle, you can get a healing miracle. It all works the same way. You believe it in your heart and speak it out your mouth. This is how you fight the good fight of faith.

Paul said Jesus witnessed the good confession before Pontius Pilate. The Message Bible says He "took His stand before Pontius Pilate and didn't give an inch." You, also, must take a stand against the enemy and not give an inch. Pilate was an evil, cruel man but Jesus was full of faith and had no fear when He stood before him. Many people had died at the hands of Pontius Pilate but still Jesus spoke the truth to him and not just what he wanted to hear. Pilate asked Jesus, "Do You not know that I have power to crucify You, and power to release You?" (John 19:10). Most people would have bowed down at this point and begged for mercy. Not Jesus. He had faith, He was bold, and He didn't give an inch. Jesus answered, "You could have no power at all against Me unless it had been given you from above" (vs. 11). This is not what you say to an egotistical ruler such as this but Jesus took a stand and said it anyway. He did not waver and right here He is fighting the good fight of faith. He was looking the enemy in the face and didn't back down.

This is how you fight cancer and depression and poverty. You look them in the eye and say, "You have no power over me!" You don't lay down and whimper and cry all day. No, you take a stand. There is a two-edged sword in your mouth and you use it. You say out loud, "Greater is He who is in me than he who is in the world." When you say that in faith, the power of God will come on the scene and change things around in your favor. Lay hold of the fact that Jesus bled and died for your healing and that on the cross He was made poor so that you may be rich. Wrap your arms around the truth that you are the righteousness of God in Christ Jesus. You are who God says you are and you can have what He says you can have. You are not moved by what the devil or people like Pontius Pilate say to you or about you. Jesus is watching you and He is pleased when He sees you speaking the Word over every storm that blows your way. You are imitating Jesus "because as He is, so are we in the world" (1 John 4:17).

Jesus is the Apostle of what you say, the High priest of what you speak (Heb. 3:1). He fought the good fight of faith with words, and so do you. God works with what you say out of a heart that's filled with faith. 1 Peter 5:9 says you resist the devil by being "steadfast in the faith." You resist the devil and keep on resisting him by standing firm in the faith. Your mind is daily being assaulted with negative thoughts and feelings and it is time for you to spring into action. Continually, faith-filled words need to be coming out of your mouth. Speak the Word and hold on to it. Heb. 3:6 (NLT) says, "And we are God's house, if we keep our courage and remain confident in our hope in Christ." Vs. 14 says, "For we have become partakers of Christ if we hold the beginning of our confidence steadfast to the end." You need to hold on to the Word and not let go. Heb. 4:14 says, "Seeing then that we have a great High Priest who has passed through the heavens, Jesus the Son of God, let us hold fast our confession."

The Bible tells you to hold fast onto your confession because there are forces that are trying to get you to turn loose of what you believe and say. This is where the fight comes in. Heb. 10:23 (NLT) says, "Let us hold tightly without wavering to the hope we affirm, for God can be trusted to keep His promise." The Message Bible says, "Let's keep a firm grip on the promises that keep us going. He always keeps His word." You confess the things that God has promised and, since He does not change, neither should your confession of faith change. If you want to win, you can't waver. You must remain confident and stead-fast in what you say until the end. Be aware of how deceptive and subtle the enemy is. He'll shoot the fiery darts of thought, feelings, and imaginations at you in such a way that you won't even know it's him. If you don't know you're being attacked, you may put your guard down and not pick up your shield of faith. This is what happened to Adam and Eve in the garden. The devil didn't come knocking on the front door, he slid in unawares through the back door.

You lose the faith fight by losing your faith. You got your faith by hearing the anointed Word of God, you lose your faith by hearing the wrong things, the lies and deceptions of the enemy. Adam and Eve walked with God in the cool of the evening and heard from Him all the time. Their faith was strong and they had the power to rule the entire planet. They lost their faith when they listened to the deceptive reasonings of the serpent. They turned loose of their trust in God and lost the fight of faith that day. Nothing has ever been the same since. The devil was so cunning that they never knew they were being attacked. Don't let this happen to you. If need be, be like Joseph who ran away from the lustful advances of Potipher's wife. Humility does not overrate your ability to deal with the temptation. Many people think they can watch and listen to the wrong things and it won't hurt them. This is pride and these people have just been sucked into the deadly snare of the enemy. Like Adam and Eve, they didn't run away and now their lives are in the hands of the one who comes to steal, kill, and destroy.

When you are in a fight there are many things you can't listen to. If the devil can't get you to listen to him directly, he'll then use your friends and loved ones to speak wrong things into your life. They may be innocent pawns and not even know what's going on behind the scenes but this does not change the fact that you are in a fight. You need to treat it as such and excuse yourself and walk away. You can't just sit there and listen to what's being said. Yes, their feelings may get hurt but this is truly a matter of life and death. Their words are fiery darts and they're being aimed at the core of your being. Who cares what they think? Walk away as quickly as you can and, if need be, run! Adam and Eve didn't run and look what happened to them. Joseph did run and became one of the greatest heroes in all the Bible. You are in a fight and you can't sit there and do nothing. You lose your faith by listening to the wrong things so be like a gazelle and run away as fast as you can.

2 Tim. 2:16-18 says, "But shun profane and vain babblings, for they will increase to more ungodliness. And their message will spread like cancer. Hymenaeus and Philetus are of this sort, who have strayed concerning the truth, saying that the resurrection has already past; and they overthrow the faith of some." Some of the words you hear are like cancer and can be as fatal as poison. These two men were instruments of the enemy and were preaching a false message. Many people listened to them when they should have run away and, as a result of all this, they lost their faith. This is precisely what the enemy wanted to happen. These men were disguised as preachers and the people put their guard down assuming everything they said was the truth. Just because a person stands behind a pulpit doesn't mean they're always correct in what they say. If you believe a non-truth, it will affect the way you live your life. In time you'll lose your faith and this opens the door and allows the enemy to come in and destroy your life.

Stop listening to the wrong things and start saying things that will help you. Give the High Priest of your confession something to work with. Stop talking about how bad the economy is and start confessing that God will supply all your needs. Don't moan and groan over the bad report the doctor gave you but rejoice as you confess that by Jesus' stripes you are healed. Your mouth can be your worst enemy or your best friend. You choose which one it's going to be by the words you speak. Use your words to help your finances and to affect the health of your body. Use your words to restore a broken relationship and to bring home a wayward child. Use your words the same way a fighter uses his fists to defeat his opponent. Paul said in 1 Cor. 9:26 (NIV), "Therefore I do not run like someone running aimlessly; I do not fight like a boxer beating the air." Paul wasn't running in circles and when he throws a punch it connects and does some damage. He "knows the weapons of our warfare are not carnal but mighty in God for pulling down strongholds" (2 Cor. 10:4).

You can't win the good fight of faith if all you're doing is shadow boxing and beating the air. You've got to know who the enemy is and what it is you're fighting. 2 Cor. 10:5 says "casting down arguments and every high thing that exalts itself against the knowledge of God, bringing every thought into captivity to the obedience of Christ." The good fight is over what you believe and the thoughts that come to your mind. The Message Bible says, "We use our powerful God-tools for smashing warped philosophies, tearing down barriers erected against the truth of God, fitting every loose thought and emotion and impulse into the structure of life shaped by Christ."

What you believe makes up the majority of who you are for it covers every aspect of your life. Because of this, the purpose of every attack from the enemy is to blind your spiritual eyes and prevent you from seeing and walking in the light of God's Word. The thoughts the enemy throws at you are more deadly than a poisonous snake and if you're not resisting these thoughts and imaginations, you are only beating the air and will eventually lose the fight.

People don't realize how deadly some thoughts are. The devil is out to kill you and you need to know that there are some thoughts you must not allow yourself to think. The thoughts the enemy sends to you is a personal attack on your well-being with the purpose of destroying your life. When they do come, it's time to rise up and fight the good fight of faith. Say out loud, "No! I do not receive that thought! I will not lose my job and my marriage will be restored! No, I will not die of cancer and my children will not pull away from the faith." No! No! No! Tell the devil that you can do all things through Christ who strengthens you. Tell him that you are more than a conqueror and no weapon formed against you will prosper. With long life God will satisfy you and you will fulfill your destiny. This is how you fight and win the good fight of faith. This is how you throw a punch that lands and does some damage. You are strong in the Lord and in the power of His might. Greater is He who is in you than he who is in the world.

Your beliefs are everything and this is why the war is over what you believe. The enemy will try to get you to believe the wrong things by bringing thoughts and reasonings to you. The devil is a liar and everything he says is contrary to the Word of God. Don't listen to him. Cast down those thoughts and imaginations that he tries to get you to meditate on. If you don't, then eventually you'll speak these wrong thoughts out of your mouth and in time what you say will come to pass. This is how you lose the good fight. Don't ever underestimate the influence of the enemy. If you give him an inch, he'll take a mile. Adam and Eve should never have given the serpent a chance to speak in the first place. They gave the enemy the opportunity to deceive them and moments later they chose to believe him rather than God. To win the good fight you never get in a conversation with the devil. You cut him off and do what Jesus did when the devil tempted Him. You say, "Devil, it is written!"

Jesus said in John 8:31,32, "If you abide in My word, you are My disciples indeed. And you shall know the truth, and the truth shall make you free." You cast down the lies of the enemy with the truth of God's Word. In truth is life and liberty and it has the power to break the chains of darkness that the enemy tries to bind you with. Jesus is the light of the world and when there is light, darkness must flee. On purpose speak the truth wherever you go. Don't give the devil a chance to get a word in edgewise. Be proactive instead of reactive. 2 Cor. 4:6 says, "For it is the God who commanded light to shine out of darkness who has shone in our hearts to give the light of the knowledge of the glory of God in the face of Jesus Christ." The Message Bible says "our lives filled up with light as we saw and understand God in the face of Christ, all bright and beautiful." When the light comes in, your faith will grow and the enemy will flee.

Truth wins the battle every time. You are a well-armed soldier in the army of the living God.

1 Peter 5:8 says, "Be sober, be vigilant; because your adversary the devil walks about like a roaring lion, seeking whom he can devour." You have an enemy, he is real, and he is opposed to everything about you, especially your walk with God and the call that is on your life. You need to stay alert and be on the watch because the attacks of the enemy are sure to come. If he's seeking whom he can devour, then that means there are some he can't devour. If you will always stay alert and remain ready to fight, then the enemy won't be able to destroy your life. The word "devour" means to 'gulp up and swallow' and you prevent this from happening by fighting the good fight of faith. The devil tries to swallow you up with ungodly thoughts and imaginations that can lead to unbelief. These are the things you need to be made aware of. This is the arena where the good fight of faith is fought. You must be on guard because wrong beliefs will turn into wrong words and wrong actions. When that happens, watch out for you will soon be swallowed up in darkness and devoured.

Be aware of the things you think about. Take charge of your thought life. Jesus said in Matt. 5:28, "But I say to you that whoever looks at a woman to lust for her has already committed adultery with her in his heart." If you are not resisting these thoughts that can destroy your life then you are only beating the air. Most people don't know who or what their real enemy is. They are looking for a guy in a red suit with horns and a pitchfork when the real enemy is right between their two ears.

2 Cor. 10:3 says, "For though we walk in the flesh, we do not war according to the flesh." This is not a flesh and bone fight. It's a war that determines what you think about. 2 Cor. 10:5 (NLT) says, "We capture their rebellious thoughts and teach them to obey Christ." There are thoughts that contradict what God has said and these are the things you need to be on the watch for. This is why you need to read your Bible every day. This is where you find out what God has said and know which thoughts to resist and cast away.

David wrote in Ps. 141:3, "Set a guard, O Lord, over my mouth; Keep watch over the door of my life." Words give voice to what you're thinking and you set a guard over your mouth by first putting a guard over your mind and what you think about. Eph. 6:11 says, "Put on the whole armor of God, that you may stand against the wiles of the devil." You don't stand against the power of the devil because he has no power. All he has is deceit and this is what he uses to gulp up and swallow people who don't guard what goes into their mind. Every hour of every day you need to be on the alert watching for all the lies and deceptions of the enemy. When you agree with a person who says the economy is bad or that the flu season is here, you have opened your mind to the schemes and wiles of the enemy. You have opened the door to your life and have given him access to come in and swallow you up. This is not a small matter. What you think about determines the direction your life will go. It truly is a matter of life and death.

The word "deceive" means 'to cause to go astray' and this has been the devil's weapon from the very beginning. He didn't force Adam and Eve into submission, he lied to them and deceived them into questioning what God had originally said to them. He attacked their mind with carefully crafted thoughts and questions with the intention of getting them off the path of truth. He came to sift them as wheat (Luke 22:31) and it worked. Jesus said in Matt. 24:4, "Take heed that no one deceives you." If you don't take heed and stay on the alert the enemy will drop little thoughts and suggestions into your mind and you won't even know it's him. He doesn't bang a drum and announce with a loud voice that he's here. No, he's quiet and he's subtle. He talks in a whisper so you won't know it's him. He's trying to draw you into his deadly snare. People who are proud and don't think they can be deceived already have one foot in the trap. You must keep watch and stay on the alert because if you don't the enemy will sneak in unawares and before long tragic things will begin happening in your life.

The devil does not fight fair. If you are in Christ you don't have to fear getting deceived but you must always be aware of how the devil works. He is continually trying to sneak up on you trying to get you to think and say the wrong things. If he can do that then he can defeat you and swallow you up. You must also walk away from the fantasy of what spiritual warfare is all about. It's not what you see in some Hollywood production up on the movie screen. Stop worrying that some devil is going to jump out of your bedroom closet and tear you to pieces. No, the battlefield is in your mind and you must resist those thoughts that rise up against the knowledge of Christ. These thoughts are deadly and they come to you in a subtle way. Do not listen to the devil when he asks, "Did God really say that?" Shut down those thoughts immediately! Cast them away! Adam and Eve got deceived because when the serpent first talked, they continued to listen to him. They didn't walk in the authority God had given them and were soon cast out of the garden.

The good fight of faith is fought with the truth of God's Word. You must get in the truth and stay in the truth. The Bible is the anointed Word of truth and if you know what it says then you won't be deceived by the lies of the devil. You don't have to fear the devil but never take him for granted. He's out there and he's seeking whom he can devour. The world is in spiritual darkness because the devil, who is the god of this world system, has blinded the minds of those who don't believe (2 Cor. 4:4). Their lives have been swallowed up by the evil one and they are being devoured. They're living in vanity and darkness and most of them don't even know it. They've been deceived by the subtlety of the devil and are on their way to eternal judgment. It doesn't have to be that way for the born-again believer. Paul says in 2 Cor. 4:1,2, "Therefore, since we have this ministry, as we have received mercy, we do not lose heart. But we have renounced the hidden things of shame, not walking in craftiness nor handling the word of God deceitfully, but by manifestation of the truth."

Eph. 5:8 says, "For you were once darkness, but now you are light in the world. Walk as children of light." There is always hope in Jesus. Vs. 14 says, "Awake, you who sleep, arise from the dead, and Christ will give you light." When those who are in darkness hear and believe the truth of God's Word, they will "come to their senses and escape the snare of the devil, having been taken captive by him to do his will" (2 Tim. 2:26). People who don't even believe in the devil are being used by him like a puppet on a string. They've been deceived and are walking in darkness. The good news is that when light comes, darkness leaves. The key to victory is to never turn the light off. Get in the Word and stay in the Word. This is what spiritual warfare is all about. The truth will liberate you and set you free from the chains of darkness that bind your life. Jesus said in John 8:12, "I am the light of the world. He who follows Me shall not walk in darkness, but have the light of life." The Message Bible says, "I am the world's Light. No one who follows Me stumbles around in the darkness. I provide plenty of light to live in."

In Paul's final letter before his death, he wrote in 2 Tim. 4:7, "I have fought the good fight, I have finished the race, I have kept the faith." You also have a race to run. There is a calling on your life, an assignment you've been commissioned to complete, and to run your race and finish your course you've got to learn to fight the good fight of faith. There is an enemy out there whose sole purpose is to stop you from doing what God told you to do. Because of this, there is a fight to be fought and, if you don't fight, you won't finish your course. This world is a cruel place and the devil's influence is everywhere. He comes to steal, kill, and destroy and, if you do nothing, you will be caught in his web of death and destruction. You must rise up with the spirit of a warrior and take a stand against the onslaught of the enemy. Fight you must do for if you do nothing, you lose. If a nobody like Gideon can be called "a mighty man of valor" (Judges 6:12), just imagine what God is calling you since Jesus is living in your heart.

| 16 |

"THE STAND OF FAITH"

Paul wrote in 2 Cor. 4:8,9, "We are hard pressed on every side, yet not crushed; we are perplexed, but not in despair; persecuted, but not forsaken; struck down, but not destroyed." It discourages the enemy when he gives you his best shot and you act like you're not bothered by it at all. No matter how much trouble is in your life, you don't have to be distressed about it, you don't have to be in despair. This is faith. If God be for you, who can be against you? Paul earlier wrote in 2 Cor. 2:14, "Now thanks be to God who always leads us in triumph in Christ." How often? Always! The devil can be defeated by you confessing that one word. He will come and say you won't be victorious this time and you'll look him in the eye and say God "always" leads me in triumph! Always! You will be victorious this time, you will be victorious next time, you will be victorious all the days of your life when you build your faith in the word "always." You are an overcomer because you walk in faith always.

In order to overcome and walk in victory there must first be a war to fight. The problem is a lot of believers don't know what they're fighting against. They think and say they're fighting the devil but how can you fight an enemy that's already been defeated at the empty tomb? Paul tells us in Eph. 6:11 what the real enemy is, "Put on the whole armor of God, that you may be able to stand against the wiles of the devil." You don't fight the devil; you stand against the wiles of the devil. Be aware of the subtlety and craftiness of your enemy. The devil never comes in the front door, he comes in through the back door. He is a deceiver and at times he comes as an angel of light (2 Cor. 11:14). He'll tell you things and you won't even know it's him. He'll make you think it's God talking to you. He'll tell you something is good for you when in reality it will destroy your life. Satan is a despicable foe and he doesn't fight fair. If given the chance he'll stab you in the back and kick you when you're down. He hates faith and he'll do anything and everything he can to make it ineffective in your life.

Rev. 12:1-4 teaches us the ways of this fallen angel, "Now a great sign appeared in heaven: a woman clothed with the sun, with the moon under her feet, and on her head a garland of twelve stars. Then being with child, she cried out in labor and in pain to give birth. And another sign appeared in heaven: behold, a great fiery red dragon having seven heads and ten horns, and seven diadems on his heads. His tail drew a third of the stars of heaven and threw them to the earth. And the dragon stood before the woman who was ready to give birth, to devour her Child as soon as it was born." The Message Bible translation says, "The dragon crouched before the woman in childbirth, poised to eat up the Child when it came." Likewise, the devil wants to eat you up! Anytime a person tries to give birth to a God-given vision by using their faith Satan will be right there trying to devour the "Child."

In the parable of the sower Jesus said, "The sower sows the Word. And these are the ones by the wayside where the Word is sown. And when they hear, Satan comes immediately and takes away the Word that was sown in their hearts" (Mark 4:14,15). When does the enemy come to steal your vision and your faith? Immediately! An example of this happening is seen in the Old Testament book of Ezra. This book continues where Second Chronicles ends and shows how God fulfilled His promise to return His people to the land of promise after seventy years of exile. Ezra was a godly man marked by a strong trust in the Lord, moral integrity, and a deep grief over sin. He knew God was with His people and although their days of glory seem to be over their spiritual heritage still remained.

The basic theme of Ezra is the restoration of the temple and the spiritual, moral, and social restoration of the returned remnant in Jerusalem. We read in Ezra 4:1,2, "Now when the adversaries of Judah and Benjamin heard that the descendants of the captivity were building the temple of the Lord God of Israel, they came to Zerubbabel and the heads of the fathers' houses, and said to them, 'Let us build with you, for we seek your God as you do; and we have sacrificed to Him since the days of Esarhaddon king of Assyria, who brought us here.'" Deception is one of Satan's most often used tactics as he tries to eat you up and if he can't hinder you directly, he'll try to sneak in through the back door. Jesus exposed this evil scheme of the enemy in the parable of the wheat and tares. He said in Matt. 13:24,25, "The kingdom of heaven is like a man who sowed good seed in his field; but while men slept, his enemy came and sowed tares among the wheat and went his way."

This is what happened here in the story of Ezra. Immediately Satan sent the adversaries of God's people to get involved with what they wanted to do. Satan always opposes you when you're birthing or building. If you're doing nothing for God, he'll leave you alone because you are not a threat to him. We read in Gal. 5:9, "A little leaven leavens the whole lump." The Message Bible says, "It only takes a minute amount of yeast, you know, to permeate an entire loaf of bread." In the Bible leaven is never used to symbolize anything good (see Mark 8:15). What Paul is telling us is that one bad apple will indeed spoil an entire basket of good apples. The leaders in Ezra's time knew this and responded in vs. 3, "But Zerubbabel and Jeshua and the rest of the heads of the fathers' houses of Israel said to them, 'You may do nothing with us to build a house for our God; but we alone will build to the Lord God of Israel, as King Cyrus the king of Persia has commanded us.'" These leaders knew that yeast may be a small thing but it works its way through a whole batch of bread pretty fast. It's the small foxes that spoil the vine.

1 Cor. 15:33 says, "Do not be deceived: Evil company corrupts good habits." If they would have accepted the offer of their adversaries it is a sure reality that the temple of God would not have been rebuilt. The devil won't appear to be opposing you

if you let him get involved but do not be deceived. He is a thief who comes to kill, steal, and destroy and he did not stop his efforts to hinder the work of God's people. "Then the people of the land tried to discourage the people of Judah. They troubled them in building, and hired counselors against them to frustrate their purpose all the days of Cyrus king of Persia, even until the reign of Darius king of Persia" (Ezra 4:4,5). Jesus said in Rev. 3:20, "Behold, I stand at the door and knock. If anyone hears My voice and opens the door, I will come in to him and dine with him, and he with Me." People everywhere love this verse and the sentimental value it brings but they also need to realize that Satan is saying the exact same thing. The devil is also knocking on the door of your life. The devil don't bother folks who don't bother him. However, if you and your faith are a threat to him then for sure he'll come knocking at your door.

2 Cor. 2:11 says "we are not ignorant of his devices." Underestimating your enemy is not how you win. The way he destroys people is through his wiles and schemes and one of the biggest ways he's been able to do that is by getting people to back away from faith. You overcome by faith and he knows that. This is why he tries to get you out of the realm of the unseen and into the realm of the seen. 2 Cor. 4:18 says "we do not look at the things which are seen, but at the things which are not seen. For the things which are seen are temporary, but the things which are not seen are eternal." The devil tries to get you out of faith and into the realm of reason where you will begin to question the Word of God. If you are depressed because you haven't seen the manifestation of what you're believing for then you have left the realm of faith. You are walking by sight, looking at the

seen and not the unseen. When you fight the good fight of faith you're fighting against the wiles of the devil, those thoughts and imaginations that are designed to get you to see, feel, and reason.

Heb. 11:1 says that faith is the evidence of things not seen. Real faith overcomes every obstacle and can move you from one realm into another. Vs. 5 says, "By faith Enoch was translated so that he did not see death, 'and was not found because God had translated him'; for before his translation he had this testimony, that he pleased God." Enoch believed for this to happen. He enjoyed his time with God so much that he used his faith to have God translate him so he wouldn't see death. He moved from one realm into another but before this happened, he pleased God with his faith. When Jesus was baptized a voice came from heaven and said, "This is My beloved Son, in whom I am well pleased" (Matt. 3:17). The Father was well pleased with Jesus before His first miracle was ever performed or His first sermon ever taught. In like manner you must also please God with your faith before you see the manifestation. You please God when symptoms of sickness cling to your body. You please God when you're got no money in the bank to pay your bills. You walk by faith and are not moved by what you see and feel.

If you will cast away those bad thoughts and imaginations and trust God anyway then He will be well pleased with you right now. And like what He did with Enoch, He will translate your situation from bad to good. He'll make you the head and not the tail. He'll see to it that you come behind in no good thing

(1 Cor. 1:7). The more you step out in faith, the more the presence of God is manifest. You don't wait on God to decide to do something, you take the first step by pleasing God with your faith. Enoch initiated his translation the same way the woman with the issue of blood initiated her healing. They both pleased God with their faith. When they did, they both received what they were believing for. Nothing gets done in the kingdom of God without faith. People don't get saved or filled with the Holy Spirit without faith. They don't get healed or delivered without faith and neither do they fulfill their destiny without the great and mighty working power of faith. Miracles happen by the grace of God and by the faith of God that is in you. It's discernable and when faith shows up good things start to happen.

1 John 5:4 (NIV) says, "For everyone born of God overcomes the world. This is the victory that has overcome the world, even our faith." The spirit of faith overcomes the spirit of the world because the Holy Spirit moves in an environment of respect, appreciation, and faith. You don't believe based on what you see or feel but your faith is fixed on the Word of God which does not change. To be spiritually minded is life and peace (Rom. 8:6) because you believe every word that proceeds out of the mouth of God. When trials come you don't talk about how you feel, you talk about what you believe. You don't operate in the realm of the seen but in the realm of the unseen. This is where the fight is fought and won. The weapons of your warfare are not carnal but mighty in God for pulling down strongholds (2 Cor. 10:4). You cast down arguments and imaginations and confess those things that be not as though

they were. If you can see the answer with eyes of faith, you will receive and become what you see.

You are in Christ and when you see Him you see yourself. Always look to Jesus who is the author and finisher of your faith because what you behold is what you will become. You are changed into His image from glory to glory and faith to faith. Take a stand and believe every word God says. If He says you're righteous, stand on that word and confess "I am righteous." If He says you are healed, say you are healed. If He says you're prosperous, say you're prosperous. You stand on whatever He says about you and when you do the enemy will flee from you. Faith always takes a stand and doesn't quit or give up. The spirit of faith is the spirit of victory and it wins every time. Your situation may seem hopeless but faith believes that God will supply all your need according to His riches in glory by Christ Jesus (Phil. 4:19). The devil tries to keep you in the realm of reason but you overcome because you walk by faith, not by sight. When you stand on faith you are standing on something that cannot fail. You don't quit when others do because you believe something they don't believe.

God said in Josh. 1:9, "Have I not commanded you? Be strong and of good courage; do not be afraid, nor dismayed, for the Lord your God is with you wherever you go." In other words, take a stand. This is not a suggestion. God is commanding you to take a stand of faith for this is what causes you to be strong and of good courage. This world is under a blanket of darkness and the spirit of fear is everywhere but when you're in faith you have hope, confidence, and expectation. Nothing moves you for you are more than a conqueror in Christ Jesus (Rom. 8:37). If you don't yield to fear and doubt you will never be defeated. No weapon formed against you will prosper because for every attack there is a spiritual weapon to retaliate with. For every lie there is a truth to confess and an action to take. Be strong and resist every thought that says you can't fulfill your destiny. Take a stand and cast down those arguments and every high thing that exalts itself against the knowledge of God. Be the overcomer you are called to be and don't let the enemy push you around.

Jesus said of the devil, "He was a murderer from the beginning, and does not stand in the truth, because there is no truth in him. When he speaks a lie, he speaks from his own resources, for he is a liar and the father of it" (John 8:44). Satan is the master of deception and you are to never let him get involved in your personal life and that which you desire to do for the Lord. James 4:7 says, "Therefore submit to God. Resist the devil and he will flee from you." The Message Bible says, so let God work His will in you. Yell a loud 'no' to the devil and watch him scamper." You need to steadfastly resist the enemy but you're not going to be able to exercise any power and authority over Satan until you first submit yourself to God. You need to be radically and outrageously obedient to God and His Word. Phil. 2:8 says Jesus humbled Himself and became extremely obedient to the point of death, even the death of the cross. Don't let the devil steal your vision and the faith you have. Overcome him by the power of the Word and the word of your testimony.

Paul says to "Watch, stand fast in the faith, be brave, be strong" (1 Cor. 16:13). The Message Bible says, "Keep your eyes open, hold tight to your convictions, give it all you've got, be resolute, and love without stopping." Yes, sometimes it is lonely at the top but you and Jesus will always be a majority. If God be for you, who can be against you? So stand your ground! Protect what is yours! Eph. 6:13,14 says, "And having done all, to stand. Stand therefore." David had three mighty warriors who did just that. Soldiers in the time of David were professional warriors whose job it was to protect and defend the honor of the king. His wish was their command. Once, when David was driven out of the city of Bethlehem and forced to live in the stronghold of the cave of Adullam, he said in longing, "Oh, that someone would give me a drink of water from the well of Bethlehem, which is by the gate!" (2 Sam. 23:15).

At the time, Bethlehem was the garrison of the evil Philistine army. Nevertheless, when three of David's men heard the desire of their king they went down and broke through the enemy's camp, drew water from the well, and brought it back to David. Because these three brave men risked their lives to satisfy the thirst of their king, David refused to drink the water and instead poured it out as an offering to the Lord (2 Sam. 23:16). Just who were these three men who served under David? What was the special quality in their character that earned them eternal recognition as David's mighty men? Each of these three men performed heroic feats in battle with tenacious determination that allowed each of them to come out victorious and receive the honor of being called "mighty." They refused to run when the going got tough as the children of Israel did when challenged by the giant Goliath. They stood their ground and fought a good fight because the honor of their king would be determined by the outcome of their battle.

One of these men was called Adino the Eznite and he was chief among the captains of David's army of mighty men. One day he went to war and killed eight hundred men at one time (2 Sam. 23:8). With unrelenting tenacity and aggressiveness, he vigorously fought on until the last enemy was overtaken and destroyed. The magnitude and vastness of this great victory is beyond human comprehension. Adino was a true warrior and for him defeat was not an option. Like Gideon, this man can also be called "a mighty man of valor." The word "might" means to 'have the ability to do anything,' and any man who can stand his ground and kill eight hundred men at one time has earned the right to be called "mighty."

In a similar story, King Jehoshaphat once went to war and was outnumbered by great proportions and this is what the Lord said to him, "Do not be afraid nor dismayed because of this great multitude, for the battle is not yours, but God's" (2 Chron. 20:15). Another time a wicked king once sent horses and chariots and a great army to surround a city occupied by the prophet Elisha. When informed by his servant of this evil deed the man of God said, "Do not fear, for those who are with us are more than those who are with them" (2 Kings 6:16). The great prophet then asked the Lord to open the eyes of his young servant who then saw that the mountains was full of horses and chariots of fire all around Elisha. The battle indeed is the Lord's. Is 59:19 (AMP) says, "When the enemy shall come in, like a flood the Spirit of the Lord will lift up a standard against him and put him to flight - for He will come like a rushing stream which the breath of the Lord drives."

2 Sam. 23:9,10 gives the description of another of David's mighty men, "And after him was Eleazar the son of Dodo, the Ahohite, one of the three mighty men with David when they defied the Philistines who were gathered there for battle, and the men of Israel had retreated. He arose and attacked the Philistines until his hand was weary, and his hand stuck to the sword. The Lord brought about a great victory that day; and the people returned after him only to plunder." When the time for battle came the men of Israel retreated. They ran away and refused to fight for their king and for what rightfully belonged to them. Ps. 78:9-11 says, "The children of Ephraim, being armed and carrying bows, turned back in the day of battle. They did not keep the covenant of God; they refused to walk in His law, and forgot His works and His wonders that He had shown them." These people, just like the men with Eleazar, were well able to be victorious, but instead of fighting they turned back. Likewise, those who only try to live a lifestyle of faith will oftentimes in the face of contradictory circumstances waver in their faith and give up, thus forfeiting the victory and promise of God that rightfully belongs to them.

The thing that causes people to retreat and not go forward when tests and trials come for the Word's sake is panic. Panic is nothing more than distrust, which is the exact opposite of faith. It is a sudden, unreasonable, overpowering fear. When overtaken by panic a person will begin to react and respond in the natural rather than in the spiritual. Peter panicked when he was walking on the water toward Jesus and began to sink. He took his eyes off Jesus who is the Living Word and focused instead on the stormy circumstances around him. People who panic will retreat in the day of battle and will not go forward. What, then, should a person do? The same thing Eleazar did! He grabbed onto his sword and wouldn't let go. He was tired from all the fighting and his hand was weary. Still, he wouldn't let go of the one thing that for him represented the difference between life and death, victory and defeat. Eph. 6:17 tells us that the sword of the Spirit is the Word of God. The worst thing you can do when the pressure is on is throw down your sword and retreat.

Ps. 68:1 says, "Let God arise, let His enemies be scattered." The Message Bible says, "Up with God! Down with His enemies! Adversaries, run for the hills!" Since God is represented by His Word, this verse can also be rendered, "Let the Word of God arise, let the enemies of His Word be scattered." Eleazar refused to drop his sword. He was so determined that he was going to be victorious that his hand clung to his sword until God had given him a great victory. When it was all over, his comrades had to pry his hand off his sword. If you are to live a victorious life as a successful believer, where you force your way into the kingdom of God and take it by storm, you must have the same attitude and determination as Eleazar. You need to grab hold of the Word of God and refuse to let go of your faith. This persistence will give you the ability and strength to go forward and not panic in the day of battle. And if you will stand your ground and fight the good fight of faith God, like He did with Eleazar, will bring about a great victory in your day of battle.

The last of David's three mighty men is described in 2 Sam. 11,12, "And after him was Shammah the son of Agee the Hararite. The Philistines had gathered together into a troop where there was a piece of ground full of lentils. Then the people fled from the Philistines. But he stationed himself in the middle of the field, defended it, and killed the Philistines. And the Lord brought about a great victory." Once again, we see the Philistine army arrayed in battle against the people of Israel. This time the enemy had gathered near a field of beans and the people of Israel, as they had done with Eleazar, had fled at the time of battle. One man, however, decided to stand his ground and fight for what was his. Shammah stationed himself in the middle of the field, and boldly proclaimed, "This bean patch is mine! This harvest belongs to me!" Shammah made up his mind that this bean patch belonged to him and no man or army was going to take it away from him. Shammah stood his ground and single handedly fought the enemy until the Lord gave him a great victory.

God made a special promise to the children of Israel in Deut. 20:1, "When you go to battle against your enemies, and see horses and chariots and people more numerous than you, do not be afraid of them; for the Lord your God is with you, who brought you up from the land of Egypt." Vs. 4 says, "For the Lord your God is He Who goes with you, to fight for you against your enemies, to save you." Shammah understood this and he won his war because he decided that he was going to keep what was his and that he would not panic. Knowing that the battle was the Lord's, Shammah fought a good fight and won. His bean field, like the mountain that belonged to Caleb, represented all the blessings and promises of God that are available to all who will believe. When you make the commitment to live and walk by faith it will not take long for you to realize that sometimes you have to fight for the things that already belong to you. For certain, the day will come when you will have to stand your ground and fight the good fight of faith.

It would be interesting to find out what happened to those people who ran away the day Eleazar and Shammah went to war. Jesus said in Luke 9:62, "No one, having put his hand to the plow, and looking back, is fit for the kingdom of God." Like those who were in the company of David's three mighty men, all too often many Christians will run away and give up on something the minute their faith is tried. They fall by the wayside and relinquish their faith because they fail to recognize that it is Satan who is trying to keep them from receiving the blessings God has promised in His Word. Prov. 24:10 says, "If you faint in the day of adversity your strength is small." The Message Bible says, "If you fall to pieces in a crisis, there wasn't much to you in the first place." The sad part is that the answer to their prayers is usually waiting on their doorstep ready to be received at the very moment they decide to give up and run away on the day of battle.

So what happened to those Israelites who decided to retreat instead of heeding the call to go forward? The answer can be found when we consider what happened to the people of

Ephraim who also ran away on the day of battle (Ps. 78:9). The book of Hosea says, "Ephraim shall be desolate in the day of rebuke. Ephraim is oppressed and broken in judgment, because he willingly walked by human precept" (Hosea 5:9,11). "O Ephraim, what shall I do to you? For your faithfulness is like a morning cloud and like the early dew it goes away" (Hosea 6:4). "Ephraim also is like a silly dove, without sense" (Hosea 7:11). "Woe to them, for they have fled from Me! Destruction to them, because they have transgressed against Me! Though I redeemed them, they have spoken lies against Me" (Hosea 7:13). So, what happens to those who run away on the day of battle? Need anymore be said?

There are several fighting warriors listed in the Hebrews 11 "Hall of Fame" of faith. Names such as Gideon, Barak, Samson, Jephthab, and David (vs. 32) grace the pages of this chapter to be an example to all who walk by faith. These are men who fought a good fight and did not run away on the day of battle. These are warriors "who through faith subdued kingdoms, worked righteousness, obtained promises, stopped the mouths of lions, quenched the violence of fire, escaped the edge of the sword, out of weakness were made strong, became valiant in battle, turned to flight the armies of the aliens" (Heb. 11:33,34). Make no mistake about it, Christianity is a confrontation and you must realize that there are no victories when there are no wars. You must, therefore, develop within yourself a warrior spirit so that you can force your way into the kingdom and take it by storm. With determined confidence you can boldly proclaim, "I can do all things through Christ who strengthens me. Greater is He who is in me than he who is in the world" (Phil 4:13;1 John 4:4).

The day of battle means greater victories because as 1 Cor. 15:57 says, "But thanks be to God who gives us the victory in Christ Jesus." We are told in Is. 54:17 that "no weapon formed against you shall prosper." The Message Bible says, "Any accuser who takes you to court will be dismissed as a liar. This is what God's servants can expect. I'll see to it that everything works out for the best." Rom. 8:31 says, "If God be for us, who can be against us?" Because of who you are in Christ, the persistent believer with a warrior spirit can just as easily say, "If God be for us, who cares who is against us?" Unlike those mighty men from the Old Testament, you are engaged in a different type of battle. Eph. 6:12 (AMP) says, "For we not wrestling with flesh and blood - contending only with physical opponents - but against the powers, against [the master spirits who are] the world rulers of this present darkness, against the spiritual forces of wickedness in the heavenly (supernatural) sphere."

Neither do we use natural weapons such as a sword, spear, or the jawbone of a dead animal. 2 Cor. 10:3-5 says, "For though we walk in the flesh, we do not war according to the flesh. For the weapons of our warfare are not carnal but mighty in God for pulling down strongholds, casting down arguments and every high thing that exalts itself against the knowledge of God, bringing every thought into captivity to the obedience of Christ." The battle is still the Lord's and our weapons today consist of the mighty Name of Jesus, His shed blood, and the

Word of God. The good news is that the victory has already been won. In His death, burial, and resurrection, Christ "disarmed principalities and powers, He made a public spectacle of them, triumphing over them in it" (Cor. 2:15). Christ did not run away on the day of battle although He was tempted to do so in the Garden of Gethsemane. Heb. 12:3 says, "For consider Him who endured such hostility from sinners against Himself, lest you become weary and discouraged in your souls."

Christ faced the enemy and reduced them to nothing (1 Cor. 2:6) and as a result of His obedience to the point of death, even the death of the cross, God has highly exalted Him and given Him the Name which is above every name (Phil. 2:8,9). Today, He is seated at the right hand of God waiting for you to do the same thing He did. Christ is "waiting till His enemies are made His footstool" (Heb. 10:13) and this happens when you stand your ground and fight the good fight of faith. It is encouraging to know that you are fighting a defeated foe and one day you will gaze at the devil, consider him, and say, "Is this the man who made the earth tremble, who shook kingdoms, who made the world as a wilderness and destroyed it's cities, who did not open the house of his prisoners?" (Is. 14:16,17). Because the battle has already been won, then victory is assured every time you fight the good fight of faith. If you will trust God and go forward there is no way you can lose. Greatness is ahead of you for mighty are those who walk by faith. So, what are you waiting for? Let the battle begin!

| 17 |

"THE COURAGE OF FAITH"

The good fight of faith is a fight about trust. Will you trust God in the midst of hard times even when you don't know what's going on or why it's happening? Many people get mad at God when questions about their problems don't get answered. The reality of life, however, is that there are always going to be things you don't know. On purpose, God is not going to tell you everything. The good news is that you don't have to know all the answers to fight and win the good fight of faith. All you have to know is that God is a good God and He will never leave you or forsake you. He will set your feet on a solid rock and will uphold you with His righteousness. If you will believe that and trust Him, you can have the confidence that He will deliver you from the situation you are currently in. It all comes down to trust. You need to have a close, personal relationship with God and a willingness to trust Him completely no matter what's going on in your life. This is how the battle is won and is what causes you to live a victorious life.

Trust is the key to victory but for sure it does not come easily. You will have to fight to keep and maintain the trust you have in the Lord your God. Problems will come and questions will arise in an attempt to shake the faith you have in the God you serve. You will have to fight to hold on to your trust in Him. You will need to take a stand against what you see and hear, those things that rise up against the knowledge of God (2 Cor. 10:5). With a strong, spiritual conviction in your heart you need to resist and oppose those things that will try to take that trust away from you. Paul said in 2 Tim. 4:5, "But you be watchful in all things." Be aware of what's going on around you "lest Satan should take advantage of us; for we are not ignorant of his devices" (2 Cor. 2:11). The Message Bible says, "After all, we don't want to unwittingly give Satan an opening for yet more mischief - we're not oblivious to his sly ways!" Set a goal for yourself so that one day you can say what Paul said in 2 Tim. 4:7, "I have fought the good fight, I have finished the race, I have kept the faith."

You should never want to die and go home to be with the Lord too early. As wonderful as that may be, you have a job to do and you shouldn't leave until you've run your race and finished your course. Who wants to stand before the Lord having not finished the work He gave them to do? Spiritual weaklings and spiritual babies want to go home early but the true warriors are willing to stay and fight. They know that laid up for them in heaven is a crown of righteousness. If they finish their course, they know one day the Lord will say to them, "Well done, good and faithful servant; you were faithful over a few things, I will make you rulers over many things. Enter into the joy of your

Lord" (Matt. 25:21). The Message Bible says, "Good work! You did your job well, From now on be My partner." Who doesn't want to hear the Lord say that? Jesus will not say this to everybody, only those who remain and finish the work He gave them to do. If you willingly leave too soon then you're not a good and faithful servant.

It takes courage to trust God in the midst of overwhelming circumstances, a willingness to not fear in spite of what you may see and feel. You need to be determined that you are going to do what God is telling you to do, confront what you need to confront, and to receive everything Jesus died to give you. God told Joshua to take the people into the promised land and said in Josh. 1:3, "Every place that the sole of your foot will tread upon I have given you, as I said to Moses." God had already given them everything they needed to live an amazing life and now they had to go face the giants in the land and take what was rightfully theirs. If you are not determined and courageous you will never have what God wants you to have. Life is what you make it and your destiny is in your hands. Nobody can be determined for you but, if you are determined, nobody can stop you. Vs. 5 says, "No man shall be able to stand before you all the days of your life; as I was with Moses, so I will be with you. I will not leave you nor forsake you."

Only do what God tells you to do. If He put a dream in your heart then go after it with everything you've got. Josh. 1:9 says, "Have I not commanded you? Be strong and of good courage; do not be afraid, nor be dismayed, for the Lord your God is with you wherever you go." God is on your side and the same power that raised Jesus from the dead dwells in you. Jesus is the strength of your life and this is what allows you to do what you need to do. Never again say that life is too hard. You are "strong in the Lord and in the power of His might" (Eph. 6:10). God is strong and in Him you are strong also. There is no mountain too high to climb and no giant too big to slay. You can do all things through Christ who strengthens you (Phil. 4:13) but, if you don't act on that truth, it's never going to happen. You've got to get out of the boat and take what belongs to you. His power is working in you and this gives you the courage to face your enemy and fight the good fight of faith.

Courage is faith in action. It's when you put your trust in God and cross over to the other side knowing there are giants in the land. Courage is when you know the battle won't be easy but you decide to fight anyway. It confronts feelings of fear but goes forward knowing that the battle is the Lord's. You need to have the courage to find the will of God for your life and the boldness to do what He tells you to do. You cannot fail as long as you don't look back but keep going forward in the pursuit of the fulfillment of your destiny. The blessings of God were in the promised land but the people had to cross over the Jordan River to get them. Don't let anything hold you back. If God says to cross over to the other side, then cross over. If He says to take the land, take the land. Courage gives you the ability to believe that if God says you can do it, then you can do it. It's what causes you to put one foot in front of the other and march boldly into the camp of the enemy knowing the blessings of God are there.

There is nothing more important than to know and fulfill the call of God that's on your life. It takes courage and strength to lay your life at the feet of the Master and say, "Not my will, but Your will be done." With that comes a willingness to get out of the boat and do what He tells you to do. 1 Chron. 28:9,10 says, "As for you, my son Solomon, know the God of your father, and serve Him with a loyal heart and with a willing mind; for the Lord searches all hearts and understands all the intent of the thoughts. If you seek Him, He will be found by you; but if you forsake Him, He will cast off forever. Consider now, for the Lord has chosen you to build a house for the sanctuary; be strong, and do it." You need to be brave and determined to do the will of God and to trust Him when the going gets tough. It takes courageous faith to hold on and not give up when the storms of life blow your way. The best things in life are worth fighting for and, for sure, there is nothing better and more important than to fulfill your God-given destiny.

Courage gives you the confidence to get out of the boat. Know this, if you're lacking in courage, you're lacking in faith. God will give you everything you need to fulfill your dream and your trust in Him is the foundation courageous faith is built on. Faith activates your confidence and gives you the courage to step out and do what you're supposed to do. You are trusting God and nothing else matters. You've got a positive attitude because you know that you can do all the things God has called you to do through Christ who strengthens you. Getting out of the boat will be no problem because God told you to do it. Where God guides, God provides. You know deep inside that once your foot touches the top of the water, the power of God will be there to hold you up and keep you from sinking. You've got the confidence that you can do what God has called you to do. Your eyes are on Him and you never look back to the comfort and protection of the boat. Faith always looks forward believing that God is directing your life with each step you take.

With a backbone of courage, you never have to fear again. 2 Tim. 1:7 says, "For God has not given us a spirit of fear, but of power and of love and of a sound mind." Courage is the spirit of power that causes you to be bold, loving, and sensible. It propels you forward with a confidence that you will never be defeated. Yes, trials will come, they'll always come. If they didn't come you wouldn't need courage. The good news is found in Ps. 34:19, "Many are the afflictions of the righteous, but the Lord delivers him out of them all." Look the devil in the eye and say, "Do not rejoice over me, my enemy; When I fall, I will arise; When I sit in darkness, the Lord will be a light to me" (Micah 7:8). Courage gives you the confidence that you will be the person God called you to be and will do what God has called you to do. Follow what's in your heart and step out of the comfort of your boat. That boat has no anchor and is floating aimlessly on the water going wherever the winds and waves take it. This is not the kind of life God has planned for you.

Paul got out of his boat because he had the attitude of a winner. When he said "I can do all things through Christ who strengthens me" he was saying he had a commitment to win. He had a strength and a power to get into the arena of action not because of self-confidence but because of an awareness that God was with him every step of the way. Daily he would travel to the "land of confidence" and this is what caused him to run his race and finish his course. He knew what he was called to do and, as he set out with passion to fulfill his destiny, his confidence in God grew to a high level. Passion builds confidence and this is why your call-in life is centered around that which you're passionate about. When you care about something enough you won't be intimidated by the enemy nor will you be defeated. Never will you stay in the boat when the things you're passionate about are out there in front of you. With the confidence of a lion, you'll get out of the boat and go after it with everything that's in you.

It was because of passion that Paul wrote in Phil. 3:13,14, "But one thing I do, forgetting those things which are behind and reaching forward to those things which are ahead. I press toward the goal for the prize of the upward call of God in Christ Jesus." Passion energizes your confidence so that you'll run your race in such a way that you'll obtain the prize (1 Cor. 9:24). There is a fire burning inside of you that can't be quenched when the trials of life come knocking on your door. When they do come, you'll soar like an eagle and rise above the clouds of hardship and pain. Nothing can stop you from fulfilling your destiny because you have passion for what you're doing. It's the compelling motivator that drives you forward no matter what roadblocks stand in your way. You have passion and you have energy and you cannot be defeated. Paul endured great hardship in his life but his passion caused him to think of his trials as "a light affliction, which is but for a moment" (2

Cor. 4:17). Paul thought this way because he had the confidence of a winner.

Passion gives you the confidence and the energy to do what you've been called to do. It will cause you to say things you didn't know you could say and do things you didn't know you could do. Passion reveals what you're good at and where your strengths are. Stop trying to develop skills you don't have but rather stay focused on the strengths you do have. Your calling is based on the things you're good at so don't get off track trying to do something else. Many people have wasted years of their lives trying to do something they're not good at. The passion wasn't there and neither was the energy to do it. They were doing the wrong thing when they could have been doing that which they were passionate about. Confidence comes when you do the things you do well. It puts you in your strength zone and gives you the motivation to keep moving forward where otherwise you might quit and give up if you were doing something you really didn't want to do. Only do the things you're passionate about for this is what God wired you to do.

There are two great days in a person's life, the day they're born and the day they understand why. When you know what God's will is for your life you will begin to cultivate an unshakable confidence that can withstand even the greatest of fears and doubts. You will develop a trust in the unchanging, all-powerful source of everlasting strength, Jesus Christ. Jer. 17:7 (NIV) says, "But blessed is the man who trusts in the Lord, whose confidence is in Him." Paul told King Agrippa what Jesus said to him on the road to Damascus, "I am Jesus, the One you're hunting down like an animal. But now, up on your feet - I have a job for you. I've handpicked you to be a servant and witness to what's happened today, and to what I am going to show you" (Acts 26:15,16 MSG). Paul found out what his calling was and said in vs. 19, "What could I do, King Agrippa? I couldn't just walk away from a vision like that! I became an obedient believer on the spot." Paul was bold and confident because he knew what God's will was for his life.

When you obey what God tells you to do the confidence will be there. It's in the act of obedience that faith and courage rises up inside of you. It's the power that causes you to walk on water. Many believers know the Bible inside out but they're far more educated than their level of obedience. They'd rather go to another Bible study than go out into the world and act on what they already know. Never try to explain God to people until you first learn to obey Him. Don't practice what you preach, preach what you practice. Obedience is a choice you make. You don't choose your calling, you discover it, but you do choose whether or not you're going to get out of your boat and fulfill your destiny. It's all up to you. Josh. 24:15 says, "Choose for yourselves this day whom you will serve. As for me and my house, we will serve the Lord." There is a choice you have to make in everything you do. When you choose the same things God has chosen, the passion you have will ignite your courageous faith and nothing will be impossible for you.

If you want to walk on water, you've got to get out of the boat. When Peter saw Jesus walking on the water, he decided in his heart that he wanted to do the same thing. You need a vision for your life that is greater than anything you've ever done before. You don't want to be like the eleven disciples who stayed in the boat when Jesus passed by or like the ten spies who went into the promised land and brought back an evil report. You've got the ability to do what God has called you to do but it won't do you any good if you don't get out of the boat. It takes courage to do that which means you must be bold and confident. You need an unshakable trust in the Lord because without a doubt the winds will blow and the waves will roar. But so what if they do? Your eyes are locked on Jesus and your trust is in Him. You've just stepped out of your comfort zone and have embarked on the greatest adventure of your life. Pick up your sword and say, "Giants, here I come."

The truth be told, the place of comfort is a place of misery and, if you stay there long enough, you can get addicted to doing nothing. In your comfort zone there is always an excuse as to why you can't get out of the boat. People say they'll serve God tomorrow or next week but, of course, that day never arrives. Instead of getting out of the boat, they choose to lay back and do nothing and watch the world pass them by. They don't do anything but they're the very ones who always murmur and complain about everything that's wrong in the world. These people are all talk and no action. They need to get out of the boat and do what's right in spite of what others may think. John 12:42, 43 says, "Nevertheless even among the rulers many believed in Him, but because of the Pharisees they did not confess Him, lest they should be put out of the synagogue; for they loved the praise of men more than the praise of God." These rulers never got out of the boat and it stopped them from having a personal relationship with Jesus who was standing there in their midst.

You need to decide right now if you're going to stay in your stinking boat where everybody likes you or if you're going to walk on water and fulfill your destiny. It really shouldn't be a hard decision to make. Jesus is passing by and He is inviting you to come follow Him. Since He is on the water, to follow Him you must get out of the boat, take a risk, and walk on water also. It's time for you to make a change from your dreary, dull, miserable life. It's time for an adventure that will take you to the high places of God. It's time for your passion to flow and your zeal to rise up and take you away from the mundane routine of life to an exciting place of joy and happiness. The happiest you will ever be is when you're at the place God wants you to be and doing what God wants you to do. Why stay in the boat and be miserable? Why be unhappy just because those around you are unhappy? Jesus said, "For many are called, but few are chosen" (Matt. 20:16). Everybody is called to get out of their boat, those who are chosen are those who do.

Passivity is one of the biggest enemies you will ever face. Adam was passive as he stood by his wife and did nothing as the serpent tempted her to eat the fruit. He didn't get out of his boat. The army of Israel was passive when taunted by Goliath but David got out of his boat and slew the giant. It's easy to pass the responsibility off on someone else when you're passive. The problem with that is God never uses people who are lazy and passive because at the first hint of trouble these are the people who turn and run back to the comfort of their boat. No, God only uses warriors who put on their armor and fight the good fight of faith. There is no such thing as a passive warrior for all warriors get out of the boat and run to the battle. They have the same attitude as Caleb who quieted the people before Moses and said, "Let us go up at once and take possession, for we are well able to overcome it" (Num. 13:30).

Believe with confidence that you can do whatever you need to do. God will never allow more to come on you than what you can bear and overcome. Matt. 11:12 says, "And from the days of John the Baptist until now the kingdom of God suffers violence, and the violent take it by force." There is nothing passive about that. There is more involved here than sitting in church on Sunday wishing you were home watching the ball game on television. To fight the good fight of faith you need to be courageous and you need to get violent as far as the devil is concerned. The kingdom of God is under attack more now than ever before because the devil knows his time is short. Those who are passive lay down and let the devil walk all over them but the true warriors stand up and fight for what's right. These are the ones who are energetic, confident, courageous, bold, and brave. These are the ones who stand their ground and live out what they say they believe. These are the warriors of God.

People who are passive cling too much to the things of this world while warriors fight believing they'll live forever. They are eternally minded and this causes them to stand tall on the day of battle. It gives them courage to get out of their comfort zone and press on to do the work God gave them to do. They look at the giants who stand in their way and say, "This day the Lord will deliver you into my hand, and I will strike you and take your head from you" (1 Sam. 17:46). They've grasped the reality that they are to rule and reign through Christ. Rom. 5:17 (MSG) says, "If death got the upper hand through one man's wrongdoing, can you imagine the breathtaking recovery life makes, sovereign life, in those who grasp with both hands this wildly extravagant life-gift, this grand setting-everything-right, that the one-man Jesus Christ provides?" Warriors maintain their peace and joy when trials come and continually strive to be a blessing to other people no matter what's happening in their personal life. Jesus walked on water in a storm and so do they.

With courageous faith warriors believe the words Jesus spoke in Luke 10:19, "Behold, I give you the authority to trample on serpents and scorpions, and over all the power of the enemy, and nothing shall by any means hurt you." Warriors believe they can do whatever they need to do. They then get out of the boat and act on what they believe. They know that each trial they face only makes them stronger for the next battle. David faced and killed the lion and the bear before he fought Goliath. He knew that if God delivered him then, He would deliver him this day as well. With bold confidence he ran toward the enemy and won a great victory. This young teenager did what an entire army refused to do because fear kept them in the boat. David had no such fear and had the confidence that God would do exceedingly, abundantly above what he could ask or think. He backed up what he believed with action and moments later the head of Goliath was held up in the hand of David for all the world to see.

God is calling you to be a warrior and with the courage of faith you are being commissioned to go take the world by storm. You can be today what David was in his day. He didn't know he was a hero but he knew God was. Because of that, he became the greatest king ever seen in the land of Israel. Is Jesus your hero? If so, He's standing on the water with an outstretched hand calling you to get out of the boat and come out to Him. He knows that you are destined to do something great in this world, to leave your mark in this sin-filled, confused generation. He knows that if you will trust Him and get out of the boat that nothing will be impossible to you. The trials you face today is not because of what you've done in the past but is the devil's attempt to keep you in the boat so you won't fulfill your destiny. The devil knows your potential more than you do and this is why he's trying so hard to keep you from grabbing hold of the hand of Jesus. Don't let him stop you! Jesus is saying "Come" so get out of the boat and go to Him. Your future depends on it.

| 18 |

"THE ASSURANCE OF FAITH"

P rison is the last place from which to expect a letter of encouragement but that is where Paul's second letter to Timothy originates. This is Paul's last epistle before his death and he begins by assuring Timothy of his continuing love and support. He reminds his young protege of his spiritual heritage and responsibilities and that only the one who fights the good fight of faith and perseveres will reap the reward. Fortunately, Timothy had Paul's example to guide him and God's Word to fortify him as he faced the challenges and growing opposition of serving the Lord his God. To win the good fight of faith you must pay close attention to what Paul said in vs. 12 of the first chapter, "For this reason I also suffer these things; nevertheless, I am not ashamed, for I know whom I have believed and am persuaded that He is able to keep what I have committed to Him until that day." How well you know God will determine how well you receive from Him and whether or not you'll stand strong on the evil day when the enemy comes knocking on the door of your life.

When you walk in faith you are bold and confident because you know in whom you have believed. You are fully persuaded and thoroughly convinced that you are who God says you are and that all things will work out for your good in Christ Jesus. There are no restrictions in your life for all things are possible to them that believe. You overcome when you have living faith in a living God. This is how you walk in victory. You're pressed on the outside but free on the inside. Ps. 91:7 says, "A thousand may fall at your side, and ten thousand at your right hand; But it shall not come near you." That is victory! Faith allows you to rest in God even when you see no end to the situation you are in. In the midst of chaos and the unknown you can walk around with your head held high and a smile on your face. You have been born of God and greater is He who is in you than he who is in the world. You have the assurance that faith works and you know in your heart that everything will turn out all right.

The heart of what Paul was saying here is that people put too much emphasis on what they believe and not enough on who they believe. There is a difference between knowing God and knowing about Him. Jesus prayed to the Father in John 17:3, "And this is eternal life, that they may know You, the only true God, and Jesus Christ whom You have sent." You don't have eternal life until you know God. The Lord said in Jer. 9:23,24, "Let not the wise man glory in his wisdom, let not the mighty man glory in his might, nor let the rich man glory in his riches;

But let him who glories glory in this, that he understands and knows Me, that I am the Lord, exercising loving, kindness, judgment, and righteousness in the earth. For in these I delight." Spending time with God and getting to know Him is the most important thing you will ever do. It takes time to get to know somebody so make time with Him the top priority of your day. God will not force His way into your life but only goes where He is invited.

In John 4 Jesus witnessed to the woman at the well and so astonished was she at what He said she immediately left and told the men of the city what had happened. "And many of the Samaritans of that city believed in Him because of the word of the woman who testified, 'He told me all that I ever did.' So when the Samaritans had come to Him, they urged Him to stay with them; and He stayed there two days. And many more believed because of His own word. Then they said to the woman, 'Now we believe, not because of what you said, for we have heard for ourselves and know that this is indeed the Christ, the Savior of the world'" (vs. 39-42). For faith to come you have to hear from God for yourself. Eph. 1:3 says, "In Him you also trusted, after you heard the word of truth, the gospel of your salvation; in whom also having believed, you were sealed with the Holy Spirit of promise." The Holy Spirit is the revealer of truth and it is He who enables you to hear from God and this is how faith comes.

Your life depends on you hearing from God and so often you will need His assistance in doing this. Just like those Samaritans who believed the testimony of the woman at the well, so also will the Holy Spirit put His anointing on gifted preachers who proclaim the good news all over the world. Paul said in Rom. 10:14, "How then shall they call on Him in whom they have not believed? And how shall they believe in Him of whom they have not heard? And how shall they hear without a preacher?" He then said in vs. 17, "So then faith comes by hearing, and hearing by the word of God." You should always hear yourself confessing the Word of God and when you believe what you hear yourself say, faith will come. However, you can't overlook the context in which this verse was written so never minimize the value of good preaching. Is. 52:7 says, "How beautiful upon the mountains are the feet of him who brings good news, who proclaims peace, who brings glad tidings of good things, who proclaims salvation, who says to Zion, 'Your God reigns!'"

A preacher is a "proclaimer" and with the call comes the anointing that will allow you to hear things you wouldn't normally hear. Faith comes by hearing the anointed preaching of the Word and this is why Jesus said in Matt. 11:15, "He who has ears to hear, let him hear." The NLT says, "Anyone with ears to hear should listen and understand!" The anointing can be described as "God on flesh doing only what God can do" and it isn't given just so preachers can say nice spiritual things. More than that, it is given so the listener can hear and properly discern what's being said. An example of this not happening is found in Mark 16. Jesus had just risen from the dead and vs. 9-11 says, "Now when He rose early on the first day of the week, He appeared first to Mary Magdalene, out of whom He had cast seven demons. She went and told those who had been with Him, as they mourned and wept. And when they heard He was alive and had been seen by her, they did not believe."

Mary Magdalene was no stranger to these mourning disciples and there was no reason for them not to believe her. God, however, in His infinite mercy, was willing to give them another chance to believe. Vs. 12,13 says, "After that, He appeared in another form to two of them as they walked and went into the country. And they went and told it to the rest, but they did not believe them either." These two men were on the road to Emmaus and the scripture says they were of them who had been with Jesus. They also were not strangers to all the others but still the disciples did not believe their report. Let's also not forget doubting Thomas who did not believe the others whom the Lord appeared to and talked with (John 20:24,25). What was the Lord's response to all this? Mark 16:14 says, "Afterward He appeared to the eleven as they sat at the table; and He rebuked their unbelief and hardness of heart, because they did not believe those who had seen Him after He had risen."

The Message Bible says, "He appeared and took them to task most severely for their stubborn unbelief, refusing to believe those who had seen Him raised up." Why does Jesus rebuke unbelief in such a hard way? Because He knows you and He wants you to know Him. God wants you to know that He is mighty and His strength is in you. You access this power with faith that comes from knowing Him. When you walk in faith you don't yield to panic and fear for you believe what Paul said in 2 Cor. 4:17, "For our light affliction, which is but for a moment, is working for us a far more exceeding and eternal weight of glory." The NLT says, "For our present troubles are small and won't last very long. Yet they produce for us a glory that vastly outweighs them and will last forever." Battles are won when you don't look at the things which are seen but at the things which are not seen. Things that are seen with the human eye are temporary but what you see with the eye of faith is eternal (vs. 18).

James 1:2 says that you are to shout and count it all joy when you fall into various tests, trials, and challenges. You can't count it joy if you don't know God and if you're looking at the problem. If all you do is think and talk about how bad life is and how much pain you're in, you will not be able to do this. To count it all joy you have to look at something else. When you walk by faith you don't look at the problems that are temporary anyway, you look at the promises of God and the unseen things that will turn your situation around. You look to Jesus who is the author and finisher of your faith. Peter was able to walk on the water as long as he was looking at Jesus. But when he took his eyes off of Jesus and looked at the wind and the waves, he began to sink. It matters what you look at. The only way to count it all joy and maintain your faith and confidence in an environment that's filled with doubt and unbelief is you've got to look at the right thing. You have to know God and you have to choose to set your eyes on Jesus.

Nothing you're facing is a surprise to God. There were giants in the land of promise but to God it was no big deal. After all, He flung stars into existence. David faced Goliath but to him it was a simple thing because he knew God was on his side.

With faith you can have the assurance that one touch of God's favor can thrust you to a higher level. Your health will be restored and your finances will turn around. God will lead you to a place where you'll be able to leave your mark on this generation. Your destiny will be fulfilled and one day God will say to you, "Well done, good and faithful servant" (Matt. 25:21). What greater blessing is there than that? If you will keep moving forward in faith, honoring God as you go, you will cross over into your promised land. The giants will be defeated and the walls will come tumbling down. The next time a storm rises up in your life, decide quickly and firmly that you are going to trust God. No if's, and's, or but's about it.

2 Tim. 1:7 says, "For God has not given us a spirit of fear, but of power and of love and of a sound mind." The spirit of fear is the spirit of defeat whereas the spirit of faith is the spirit of victory. Your faith in God is bigger than any storm that blows your way. His Name is above sickness and disease, poverty and lack, divorce and loneliness. God has a plan and a purpose for your life and when you truly know Him as Lord and Master you will not hesitate to do what Heb. 4:16 tells you to do, "Let us therefore come boldly to the throne of grace, that we may obtain mercy and find grace to help in time of need." The Message Bible says, "So let's walk right up to Him and get what He is ready to give. Take the mercy, accept the help." Boldness is needed to fight the good fight of faith and it comes when you know God in an intimate way. David was a man after God's own heart (Acts 13:22) and you can hear the boldness in what he told the giant Goliath, "This day the Lord will deliver you

into my hand, and I will strike you and take your head from you" (1 Sam. 17:46).

Paul said in Eph. 3:12 (NLT), "Because of Christ and our faith in Him, we can now come boldly and confidently into God's presence." Having confidence eliminates all doubt from your life and allows you to forever walk in faith. When you're confident, you're bold, and when you're bold, you'll be sure that God will do what He says He will do. It blesses the Father when you know He wants to be good to you. It warms His heart and makes Him want to bless you even more. He'll want to bless you exceedingly, abundantly above what you could ask or think. Walking in faith and getting in agreement with Him is what releases the blessing. You are one of a kind and you've been crowned with favor. Blessings and mercy follow you wherever you go. You are royalty and this means you can eat the good of the land and partake of the best things life has to offer if you will have the courage and the boldness to go get it.

There are blessings with your name on it and, as far as God is concerned, they already belong to you. He had given the children of Israel the promised land but it was up to them to use their faith and go in and possess it. The same is true for you today. With unrestricted boldness you need to rise up and go get what rightfully belongs to you. 2 Cor. 1:9 says, "For all the promises of God in Him are Yes, and in Him Amen, to the glory of God through us." God says yes, you will fulfill your destiny and be a blessing to others. Yes, you are healthy and strong. Yes, you are rich and prosperous. God says "Yes" but you must say "Amen. So be it." God has already blessed you so do not consider what the doctor's report says or what's in your bank account. Faith never looks at what is seen but at the unseen. Faith rises up and openly declares, "I am blessed. I am healthy. I am prosperous. I'm the head and not the tail, above and not beneath. I come behind in no good thing."

You need to talk like you're blessed and act like you're blessed. This is how you possess the land. This is how you take back what the enemy has stolen from you. Throw your shoulders back, stand tall, and put a smile on your face. You are a child of the Most High God and you have the assurance that He is on your side. Ps. 84:11 says, "For the Lord God is a sun and shield; The Lord will give grace and glory; No good thing will He withhold from those who walk uprightly." God says you are blessed so get in agreement with Him. You are victorious. You're more than a conqueror. God is not limited by your past experiences or how much education you have or don't have. Jesus said in Luke 12:32, "Do not fear, little flock, for it is the Father's good pleasure to give you the kingdom." God said in Deut. 1:6, "You have dwelt long enough at this mountain." He then said in vs. 8, "See, I have set the land before you; go in and possess the land which the Lord swore to your fathers."

The land of promise is yours but you've got to go in and possess it. Don't wander aimlessly in the wilderness for forty years like the children of Israel did. Put on your crown, pick up your sword, and go take your mountain. With confident assurance you know God is on your side so you don't have to fear or be discouraged. This is your time. This is your moment. Joel 3:9

says, "Prepare for war! Wake up the mighty men, let all the men of war draw near, let them come up." Just as it is impossible to please God without faith, so also is it impossible to please Him without confidence and boldness. Put your wavering and questioning aside. Don't wonder anymore and don't try to believe. Just do it! If you are not sure that God will move on your behalf then you are in trouble. You win the good fight of faith by being sure. The word "faith" means 'to be form, stable, to build up and support.' Faith will build under you a firm foundation and is something to stand on without fear of falling.

Faith is a spiritual force that you can lean on, depend on, and rest your weight upon without concern that it will collapse under you or let you down. It means 'to be certain, to be true, permanent, established, to believe in or to trust.' A person of faith is a bold person and because your confidence is in God you can speak openly and freely. There will be no uncertainty in your heart thus allowing you to speak plainly without reservation or hesitation. This David did when he faced the giant in the Valley of Elah. When you are bold and have confidence in God you are unstoppable and no enemy can prevent you from going all the way with God. Also, when you fight the good fight of faith, you must finish the same way you began. When Peter walked on the water, he began with boldness but ended in fear and unbelief. Jesus always responded to the disciple's unbelief and when He rescued Peter He said to him, "O you of little faith, why did you doubt?" (Matt. 14:31).

Doubt is the lack of confidence that God will do what He said He would do and will cause boldness to flee from your life. Do not fall into the trap of believing that to walk in faith all you have to do is make faith confessions. You can confess something all day long and not believe in your heart that it will come to pass. Never say something out of desperation because chances are you won't believe it anyway. To walk in faith, you must confess the Word and not doubt in your heart. If you don't truly believe in your heart what you say then it's best not to say anything at all. James 1:5,6 says, "If any of you lacks wisdom, let him ask of God, who gives to all liberally and without reproach, and it will be given to him. But let him ask in faith, with no doubting, for he who doubts is like a wave of the seas driven and tossed by the wind." The word "doubt" comes from the word 'double' and James continues in vs. 7,8, "For let not that man suppose that he will receive anything from the Lord; he is a double-minded man, unstable in all his ways."

Doubt will make your words powerless, null and void. You may be saying the right things but are not fully convinced down in your heart that it will come to pass. People who waver can't make up their minds what they believe. Like a wind-tossed wave they'll be up one minute and down the next. One minute they believe and the next they don't. You can't travel in two different directions at once. Doubt is a serious enemy to your faith and it will prevent you from receiving the will and provision of the Lord. The solution to doubt is to be single-minded. Eph. 4:4-6 says, "There is one body and one Spirit, just as you were called in one hope of your calling; one Lord, one faith, one baptism, one God and Father of all, who is above all, and through all, and in you all." Not two! One! Faith begins where the will of God is known so you must refuse to consider any-

279 BY STORM - 279

thing else. Rom. 15:5 says, "Let each one be fully convinced in his own mind." You've got to be stable. Stop being of two minds and become settled and unmoved in your faith in God.

Continue to study and pray until confidence rises up inside of you. If you are single-minded, the Word of God has to come to pass in your life. When you believe without a doubt, you will receive without delay and without fail. God said you would receive what you say if you doubt not. When you cast doubt out of your life, you will not fret or have anxiety about anything (Phil. 4:6). Jesus said in Matt. 6;25, "Therefore I say to you, do not worry about your life, what you will eat or what you will drink; nor about your body, what you will put on. Is not life more than food and the body more than clothing?" Worry is of the world and it will get you nowhere. In fact, it only makes the situation worse. Peter learned this lesson well when he began to sink in his quest to walk out to Jesus on the water. Worry chokes the Word and will choke Jesus out of your life. The devil is the author of alternate choices. He offered Adam and Eve a different lifestyle than the one God intended. Likewise, he wants you to live a life of worry and doubt instead of a life of faith and confidence.

Never worry about anything. Instead, cast all your care on Jesus and fight the good fight of faith. 1 Peter 5:7 (AMP) says, "Casting the whole of your care, all of your anxieties, all your worries, all your concerns, once and for all on Him, for He cares for you affectionately and He cares about you watchfully." The Living Bible says, "Let Him have all your worries and cares for He's always thinking about you, and watching everything that concerns you." When you cast your care on the Lord, confidence will come and with it the boldness to fight and win the good fight of faith. Heb. 10:22 says, "Let us draw near with a true heart in full assurance of faith." The Message Bible says, "Let's keep a firm grip on the promises that keep us going." Vs. 35 goes on to say, "Therefore do not cast away your confidence, which has great reward." You can boldly have confidence that good things will happen in your life. Faith draws near so never draw back and play it safe. Live confidently and always encourage yourself in the Lord knowing that He cares for you.

Don't be passive, be possessive. Paul told Timothy, "Fight the good fight of faith, lay hold on eternal life" (1 Tim. 6:12). The Message Bible says, "Run hard and fast in the faith. Seize the eternal life, the life you were called to." The Greek word for "lay hold" is 'take' so stand up and take what God says you can have. Consider the woman with the issue of blood. She didn't stand in the back of the crowd and do nothing. No, with boldness she pushed through the crowd, pressed in, and took her healing. She had confidence and the full assurance of faith that if she could but touch the hem of His garment she would be healed. She fought and won the good fight of faith and was completely set free from her ailment. You also can receive from God. With confidence that is sure and bold you must believe that you can take what belongs to you. You have to lay hold! People who possess the promises are not weak and passive, they're bold and aggressive.

The blessings of God are forever available but they won't fall on you from out of nowhere. No, you must go and possess them. When the manna fell in the wilderness the people still had to go pick it up. They learned that if you don't take it, you won't possess it. The word "possess" is used over 300 times in scripture with none as meaningful as Num. 13:30, "Then Caleb quieted the people before Moses, and said, 'Let us go up at once and take possession, for we are well able to overcome it." Caleb had a different spirit about him (Num. 14:24) and he knew what it took to fight the good fight of faith. He had a spirit of faith and a spirit of victory. He had the spirit of an overcomer. He followed God fully and overcame fear and the temptation to doubt and walk in unbelief. He knew that God provides His blessings by grace but you must go in and possess them with the full assurance of faith, a faith that is bold and confident.

Heb. 10:38 says, "Now the just shall live by faith; But if anyone draws back, My soul has no pleasure in him." When you walk by faith you don't quit and you don't back off. Like Caleb, you take possession of what is yours. You possess your possessions based on what God said you could have. Real faith is based on what God said and if He doesn't change, then what you believe in also should not change. People who draw back focus on the giants in the land, but those who go forward focus on the promise. They walk by faith, not by sight. They believe they are well able to live a victorious life and that nothing is too big for their God. If you can understand what God said to you, then you can believe it. It's a choice you make. You either believe it or you don't. The faith that you have, if you'll hold on to it, is a sustaining faith that will be with you for the rest of your life. If you know what belongs to you, you can rise up and use that faith to take possession of what is rightfully yours.

Heb. 3:6 (NLT) says, "But Christ, as the Son, is in charge of God's entire house. And we are God's house, if we keep our courage and remain confident in our hope in Christ." If you truly believe that something good is about to happen to you, then it is impossible for you to be down and depressed. No matter how bad it seems to be at the present moment, you know that soon and very soon God will turn it all around in your favor. A good life is when you've always got something good to look forward to. This is what happens when you walk in faith. To possess what belongs to you takes endurance and so you must maintain your faith even in an environment of doubt and fear just like Joshua and Caleb did. In the midst of people laughing at you and mocking you, always maintain a spirit of faith. When people like Job's wife tell you to "curse God and die" (Job 2:9) you can be like Job who said, "Though He slay me, yet will I trust Him" (Job 13:15).

There were some things happening to Job that he didn't understand but the bottom line is that he trusted God with all his heart and soul. This is the attitude you must have to get the miracles God wants to perform in your life. You can't let the cares of this world choke the seed that's been planted in your heart (Matt. 13:22) and you are to never give fear your stamp of approval. Fear is totally unacceptable for the child of God. Fear is what caused Peter to sink in the water and it's what kept the children of Israel out of the promised land. Fear can affect the environment around you so stay away from it at all costs. Stay away from people who speak doubt and fear all the time. 1 Cor. 15:33 says, "Evil company corrupts good habits." The enemy will try to use negativity in other people to influence you.

You must take charge of the situation and control what you allow to get inside of you. Will it be fear and doubt, or faith and courage? You can't believe God for just a day or two. You must do it every single day of your life.

James 1:3 (Young's Literal) says "knowing that the testing of your faith does work endurance." This means that what you believe today, you will believe tomorrow. If you're expecting this week, you'll be expecting next week. You don't change because what He told you doesn't change. This works only when you believe for the things God told you to believe for. You can't go off and believe for just anything that comes off the top of your head. You won't be able to stand very long on some whim you decided one day to believe for because you'll have nothing on which to base your faith. You base your faith only on what God says to you, either in the Word or by His Spirit. Joshua and Caleb had such a word. God said He had given the children of Israel the promised land and they believed Him. They had a word to stand on, a solid rock on which to base their faith. They stood strong for forty years and went in with the new generation and possessed the land. James 1:4 says, "But let patience have its perfect work, that you may be perfect and complete, lacking nothing."

How can you do what Joshua and Caleb did? They were in a scorching hot desert in an environment of overwhelming fear and unbelief for forty years. How do you hold on to your faith in circumstances such as these? First, you've got to know you've heard from God. You must be thoroughly convinced that you did because the first thing the devil will say to you is

"Has God indeed said...?" (Gen. 3:1). Even if you are sure, the devil will still try to wear you down. This is why you need to endure until the promise is manifested. Heb.11:27 said about Moses, "By faith he forsook Egypt, not fearing the wrath of the king; for he endured as seeing Him who is invisible." Moses looked at the unseen and so did Joshua and Caleb. They did not focus on where they were currently at and the fact that they were getting older every year. You can't keep looking at the calendar and the things that are seen. That's how you get a hard heart and grow bitter. You must look at the unseen and that which God specifically told you to believe for.

Joshua and Caleb's focus was on the land flowing with milk and honey, not the hot and dry desert. God told them they could have the land and this is the word they held on to. They didn't look at where they were at, they looked at where they were going. Heb. 12:2 says that Jesus "who for the joy that was set before Him, endured the cross." Jesus endured the cross because He wasn't looking at the cross. You don't look at your symptoms, you look at by Jesus' stripes you are healed. You don't look at your weakened body, you look at with long life He will satisfy you. You don't look at your debt, you look at your God who will supply all your needs. Talk and act like your destiny is already fulfilled and that your body is already healed and that your bills are already paid. You endure when other people don't because you look at what other people aren't looking at. You endure as seeing Him who is invisible. You look at the unseen.

| 19 |

"THE ENDURANCE OF FAITH"

There is a popular teaching in the body of Christ that is spreading a non-truth to all those who desire to live a good life. Just because something is popular doesn't mean it is accurate and true. Heb. 10:36 (AMP) says, "For you have need of steadfast patience" yet many preachers teach that asking for patience is an open invitation for trials to run rampant in your life. This is total foolishness. Instead of encouraging people to run after patience and seek it with all their heart and soul, they instead use fear of hardship and trial to cause believers to turn and run in the opposite direction. Yes, many translations of James 1:3 does say that "the testing of your faith produces patience." This is an incorrect rendering of this verse and causes preachers to say that if you want patience then get ready for a hard life. The Greek word for "produces" is 'katergazomai' and means "labor, work or engage in an activity involving considerable expenditure of effort." Katergazomai was used by the Romans to describe "working a mine" or "working a field" and in each case there were benefits that followed such diligence. The mine would produce precious metals and the field would yield fruit and crops.

These preachers may be sincere in what they are teaching but they are sincerely wrong. The correct translation of this verse is in the King James Bible that says, "Knowing this, that the trying of your faith worketh patience." Trials work patience, not produce it. This means you use the patience you already have, coupled together with faith, to face head-on the trials that come your way. The Message Bible says, "So don't try to get out of anything prematurely. Let it do its work so you become mature and well-developed, not deficient in any way." Your faith and patience go to work when circumstances contrary to the Word of God rise up and attempt to put a roadblock on the path that leads to the fulfillment of your destiny. Faith comes by hearing, and hearing by the word of God (Rom. 10:17) but how does patience come? James 1:2-4 tells us. "My brethren, count it all joy when ye fall into divers temptations; Knowing this, that the trying of your faith worketh patience. But let patience have her perfect work, that ye may be perfect and entire, wanting nothing."

Faith comes by hearing and patience comes by knowing. In a trial you are to have a future focused mindset. Patience comes by knowing that when all is said and done, all things will work out in your favor. Rom. 8:28 says, "And we know that all things work together for good to those who love God, to those who are called according to His purpose." The word "patience" means 'cheerful endurance' and joy in trials comes from knowing that when the smoke clears the outcome will be good. Knowing that gives you the patience to cheerfully endure whatever it is the enemy may bring your way. On the surface this command to "count it all joy" is one of the most difficult in all the Bible. The Christian life is not all fun and games and there is an enemy out there who comes to steal, kill, and destroy (John 10:10). If what you're facing looked like joy and felt like joy then you wouldn't have to count it as joy. Carnal people act how they feel whereas spiritual people act what they believe.

If a carnal person feels mad, they'll act mad. If they feel upset, they'll act upset. A spiritual person, however, can feel challenged but they'll shout for joy. They can feel worry and fear but let peace flow out of them. They can feel like slapping somebody but speak words of love to them in soft tones. A spiritual person knows something, they've got inside information. They can glory in tribulation because they know in the end, they'll be perfect, complete, entire, wanting nothing. The Phillips Bible says, "When all kinds of trials and temptations crowd into your lives my brother, don't resent them as intruders, but welcome them as friends." With cheerful endurance and a sincere trust in the goodness of God you can look on trials as a welcomed friend, knowing with Joseph that what may have been meant for evil against you, God means for good (Gen. 50:20). The New English Bible says to "count yourselves supremely happy."

James is not saying the trials are joyful in themselves but are a means to an end which is joyful. He is speaking of a unique fullness of joy that the Lord graciously provides His children when they willingly and uncomplainingly endure troubles while trusting in Him, regardless of the cause, type, or severity of the distress. You are not just to act joyful but rather be genuinely joyful. It is a matter of the will, not of feelings, and should be the conscious, determined commitment of every faithful believer. And because God commands it, it is within the ability of every true Christian to do so. When faith in Jesus is genuine, when you have a deep-seated confidence in what the Word promises, Jesus assures us that even the worst of troubles can and should be cause for thanksgiving and rejoicing. The Phillips Bible continues in vs. 3, "Realize that they come to test your faith and to produce in you the quality of endurance." The battle does you good. The conflict educates you, strengthens you, establishes you, and is necessary for you so that you may be grounded and settled and finally approved and rewarded.

When you cheerfully endure trials by faith, your faith is stronger for the next trial. You will know that you can endure whatever happens because you've already been through the previous trial. Patience has not been a greatly desired thing in the body of Christ. People say don't pray for patience because you'll have more problems than you could ever imagine. That is totally absurd, senseless, and moronic. If tribulation produced patience, then everybody would have it and the scriptures wouldn't have to tell you to get it. Heb. 10:36 (AMP) says, "For you have need of steadfast patience and endurance, so that you may perform and fully accomplish the will of God, and then receive and carry away [and enjoy to the full] what is promised." The NLT says, "Patient endurance is what you need now, so you will continue to do God's will. Then you will receive all that He has promised." You need patience and you need a lot of it because cheerful endurance is a necessary prerequisite to receiving the promises of God.

The toughest and most discouraging trials are when you are called to trust and obey God when the fulfillment of His promise seems so far away. This is why you need cheerful endurance. The passage of time will test your trust and faithfulness. What you do when the promise seems unfulfilled will be what measures your spiritual maturity. Endurance means "abiding under" and is courageous gallantry which accepts suffering and hardship and turns them into grace and glory. It is the ability to deal triumphantly with anything that life can do to you. It accepts the blows of life but in accepting them transforms them into stepping stones to new achievement. A person with patience has the attitude of a soldier who in the thick of battle is not dismayed but fights on no matter what the difficulties may be. The Wuest translation of James 1:3,4 states, "Know experientially that the approving of your faith, that faith having been put to the test for the purpose of being approved, and having met the test, has been approved, produces (works) a patience which bears up and does not lose heart or courage under trials."

Patience should be one of the most desirous things to the born-again believer but most people don't know and understand what patience truly is. They think patience is a passive waiting to see what happens next as they struggle to stand when the storms of life blow. No, when you're in faith you already know how it's going to turn out because you've heard from God. Patience is the virtue that can endure not simply with resignation but with a vibrant hope, a triumphant facing of your trials so that even out of evil there can come good, a bearing up in a way that honors and glorifies your Heavenly Father. Prov. 24:10 says, "If you faint in the day of adversity, your strength is small." Many people start out in faith and stay in faith until the passage of time begins to weaken their resolve to stand strong until the manifestation comes to pass. Nothing weakens faith like a few ticks of the clock on the wall. Your flesh don't like to wait. It wants what it wants now! People need to understand that things happen the way they do for a reason.

On purpose God does not tell you when the manifestation will come. He wants you to trust Him because without faith and patience it's impossible to please God (Heb. 11:6). Will you trust God even when circumstances go against what you're believing for? Remember, time tries trust and waiting is the only way for you to grow and become stronger. If everything happened immediately then you wouldn't need any patience and there wouldn't be much opportunity for faith. People would walk by sight and live a life not pleasing to God. The one who truly believes is the one who stands strong over a period of time even when circumstances seem bleak and contrary to what they're believing for. Their faith will shine like gold because it's been tried, tested, and approved. Hab. 2:2,3 says, "Then the Lord answered me and said: 'Write the vision and make it plain on tablets, that he may run who reads it. For the vision is yet for an appointed time; But at the end it will speak, and it will not lie. Though it tarries, wait for it; Because it will surely come, it will not tarry.'"

Know with certainty that when you ask for big things you must be prepared to stand strong for a long time. Not everything happens instantly with God. "With the Lord one day is as a thousand years, and a thousand years as one day" (2 Peter 3:8). God is not in a hurry and neither should you be. Is. 28:16 says, "Therefore thus says the Lord God: 'Behold, I lay in Zion a stone for a foundation, a tried stone, a precious stone, a sure foundation; Whoever believes shall not act hastily.'" The NIV Bible says, "the one who relies on it will never be stricken with panic." Don't panic and be impatient and in a hurry. Strong faith endures and keeps believing no matter how much time has passed by. The flesh says "get it now, anyhow" whereas faith says "if you'll wait, it will be great." Patience patiently endures the passage of time and contradictory circumstances. This long suffering is not added to faith but is an integral part of it because faith's vision will produce patient tenacity. The amount of faith you have is based on the amount of patience you have.

You don't have more faith than you do patience. You don't just believe God, you believe God until the manifestation comes. You believe God and continue to believe Him for as long as it takes even in times of adversity. Fix your eyes on Jesus, looking by faith to see the great unseen realities that await you. Do it with diligence and long-suffering and this will make your hope sure and bring into manifestation that which you have been believing for. Eccl. 7:8 says, "The end of a thing is better than its beginning. And the patient in spirit is better than the proud in spirit." Starting out in faith is good, finishing with patience is better. You'll reap in due season if you faint not (Gal. 6:90). The Message Bible says, "So let's not allow ourselves to get fatigued doing good. At the right time we will harvest a good crop if we don't give up, or quit." Patience is the key to receiving everything you ever believed for, every time. You can't have a "hit and miss" attitude which says, "Sometimes my prayers get answered, sometimes they don't."

While you're being patient you are always expecting God to move. And because you believe what you're expecting will come to pass, you'll have unspeakable joy even in the midst of contrary circumstances. Heb. 6:11,12 says, "And we desire that each one of you show the same diligence to the full assurance of hope until the end, that you do not become sluggish, but imitate those who through faith and patience inherit the promises." The Message Bible says, "And now I want each of you to extend that same intensity toward a full-bodied hope, and keep at it until the finish. Don't drag your feet. Be like those who stay the course with committed faith and then get everything promised to them." Anybody can quit. It's easier to quit and give up but if you do, you're lazy and slothful. In the New Testament "patience" means 'to be long-spirited, long tempered; an abiding under.' It's a long steadfastness no matter what pressures come against you, a long holding of the mind that gives no room to negative actions or passions. It describes a state of emotional calm or quietness in the face of provocation and misfortune.

The Bible says, "Having done all to stand, stand therefore" (Eph. 6:13,14). How long can you stand? With cheerful endurance you can stand and wait a long, long time. Good things come to those who wait and bad things happen to those who don't. God had promised Abraham a son and in Gen. 15:5 told him that his descendants would outnumber the stars in the night sky. "And he believed in the Lord, and He accounted it to him for righteousness" (vs. 6). Abraham is called the father of our faith but many years after the promise had been given his wife Sarah grew tired of waiting. Gen. 16:2 says, "So Sarai said to Abram, 'See now, the Lord has restrained me from bearing children. Please, go in to my maid; perhaps I shall obtain children by her.' And Abram heeded the voice of Sarai." There is no "perhaps" in faith. Faith knows. Faith is aggressive and forever growing. Some people get excited at first but lose heart with the passage of time. Your flesh wants to do anything but wait, but time tries trust.

Sarai's maid Hagar gave Abram a son named Ishmael but because he was conceived through impatience the Bible says in Gen. 16:12, "He shall be a wild man; His hand shall be against every man, and every man's hand against him. And he shall dwell in the presence of all his brethren." If you don't have patience, you won't have victory in your life. You'll forfeit things you could have and should have. You'll always have to settle for second best. Not everything happens instantly with God. What's given by grace must be possessed by faith and patience. Real faith is fully persuaded and does not know how to quit. You need to believe for the promise and cheerfully endure the passage of time until the manifestation comes. The good news is that Abraham eventually did receive the son of promise but only after he patiently endured. Heb. 6:13-15 says, "For when God made a promise to Abraham, because He could swear by no one greater, He swore by Himself, saying 'Surely blessing I will bless you, and multiplying I will multiply you.' And so, after he had patiently endured, he obtained the promise." The Message Bible says "Abraham stuck it out and got everything that had been promised to him."

The book of Exodus tells another story of a people who grew tired of waiting. God had called Moses to the top of Mount Sinai to receive the tablets of stone and Ex. 24:13,14 says, "So Moses arose with his assistant Joshua, and Moses went up to the mountain of God. And he said to the elders, 'Wait here for us until we come back to you.'" A few weeks later the people grew tired of waiting and decided they wanted a new god. A golden calf was made and the people celebrated and proclaimed, "This is your god, O Israel, that brought you out of the land of Egypt!" This angered God and three thousand people were slain with the sword and the Lord plagued the people because of what they did with the calf which Aaron made (Ex. 32:28,35). In another story the prophet Samuel told king Saul, "You shall go down before me to Gilgal; and surely I will come down to you to offer burnt offerings and make sacrifices of peace offerings. Seven days you shall wait, till I come to you and show you what you should do" (1 Sam. 10:8).

Things don't always turn out like you think they should and when Samuel's return was delayed Saul rose up and offered the sacrifices anyway. This never should have happened for Saul was told to wait until Samuel got there. Saul is no priest or prophet and his actions revealed a tremendous amount of pride in his heart. It should come as no surprise that as soon as the offering was made Samuel shows up revealing that, when you feel the most pressure to do something now and not wait, you are the closest to your miracle. When people get tired of waiting they miss God and because Saul did not wait Samuel said to him, "You have done foolishly. You have not kept the commandment of the Lord your God, which He commanded you. For now, the Lord would have established your kingdom over Israel forever. But now your kingdom shall not continue. The Lord has sought for Himself a man after His own heart" (1 Sam. 13:13,14).

Patience should be highly desirable to you for it is that abiding force that keeps you pressing on with steadfast endurance. It causes you to wait with confident expectation. It takes effort to believe God and keep believing Him and not quit when others do. It's a whole lot easier to quit when things go from bad to worse and time goes on and you don't see the manifestation or feel it. This is why it is so important to follow and "imitate those who through faith and patience inherit the promises" (Heb. 6;12). Paul said, "Imitate me, just as I also imitate Christ" (1 Cor. 11:1). Whatever you follow is what you're going to find, and what you fellowship with is what you'll partake of. The people you hang around with are affecting you more than you realize. 1 Cor. 15:33 says, "Do not be deceived: 'Evil company corrupts good habits'" and Prov. 13:20 states, "He who walks with wise men will be wise, but the companion of fools will be destroyed." Good and evil influences are all around you and it's up to you to decide who you will follow and imitate.

When Moses left to get the Ten Commandments the people turned away quickly and built the golden calf. Had Moses been there they never would have done this. We all need spiritual parents, people who will encourage us to hang in there and stand strong during the hard times and never give up. The influence of godly mentors is precious, and you must be thankful for those who lead by precept and example and are not swayed by what other people say and do. Get everything you can from them. Watch them, listen to them, learn all you can get from them now while they're still around. You won't know how much people are influencing you until they are not there. You never miss the water until the well runs dry. Paul said in Phil. 1:27, "Only let your conduct be worthy of the gospel of Christ, so that whether I come and see you or am absent, I may hear of your affair, that you stand fast in one spirit, with one mind striving together for the faith of the gospel." Heb. 10:35 says, "Therefore do not cast away your confidence, which has great reward." It pays to have faith in God.

You can rule and reign with God throughout all eternity because you trusted Him now in an evil, demon-filled world where most people scoff at Him and turn their backs on the one who died for them. You passed tests that others failed. You passed the faith test and the patience test. Heb. 12:1 says, "and let us run with endurance the race that is set before us." The Christian life is not a short sprint but is a long marathon race that requires much endurance. Rom. 5:3-5 (MSG) says,

"There's more to come: We continue to shout our praise even when we're hemmed in with troubles, because we know how troubles can develop passionate patience in us, and how that patience in turn forges the tempered steel of virtue, keeping us alert for whatever God will do next. In alert expectancy such as this, we're never left feeling shortchanged. Quite the contrary - we can't round up enough containers to hold everything God generously pours into our lives through the Holy Spirit."

When you let patience have its perfect work, you'll come out complete, perfect, fully developed, entire, wanting nothing. You'll have everything you need. God said "surely I will bless you and multiply you" but that doesn't mean you'll see it all by the end of the week. Abraham received the promise after he patiently endured and that's how you're going to receive also. Don't quit until you get the manifestation. Don't stop. With cheerful endurance stand in faith for as long as it takes. Glory in your tribulation. The good life is when you've always got something good to look forward to so, if the manifestation has not yet arrived, keep looking. People get frustrated and weary when their situation gets worse instead of better. They give up and concede that it probably wasn't God's will in the first place. They fabricate new doctrines to make up for their lack of faith. They say, "You just never know what God's going to do." They make up a reason to stop expecting and those who doubt shouldn't expect to receive anything from God. Through the power of patience see time from God's perspective and be prepared to stand for as long as it takes.

The longer you wait, the more you show God you trust Him. With cheerful endurance you can be sure that in due season you will reap if you faint not. Set a pace for yourself and keep on keeping on. Keep on expecting even when things look worse than when you started. Hold on! Keep believing! Keep looking! After Abraham patiently endured, he received the promise. He was waiting for the city which has foundations, whose builder and maker is God (Heb. 11:10). Abraham was looking for something because of what God said. What are you looking for? Faith won't stop looking for the fulfillment of what God said no matter how long it takes and no matter how contrary it looks. How will you find what God has promised? You look for it. Patience keeps looking and doesn't stop looking. The good news is that Jesus promises that if you look for the promise with cheerful endurance, you will find it. He said in Luke 11:9,10, "And I say to you, ask, and it will be given to you; seek and you will find; knock, and it will be opened." Keep looking and keep expecting and you will be perfect and complete, wanting and lacking nothing. Indeed, you will live a good life.

| 20 |

"THE GRATITUDE OF FAITH"

In every fight there is a winner and a loser, and in the good fight of faith "we are more than conquerors through Him Who loved us" (Rom. 8:37). Paul writes in 2 Cor. 2:14-16, "Now thanks be to God who always leads us in triumph in Christ, and through us manifests the fragrance of His knowledge in every place. For we are to God the fragrance of Christ among those who are being saved and among those who are perishing. To one we are the aroma of death to death, and to the other the aroma of life to life." God leads you to victory and the steps you take are steps of thankfulness. Giving thanks is the most powerful expression of faith there is and it increases your capacity to receive from God. The Message Bible states, "In the Messiah, in Christ, God leads us from place to place in one perpetual victory parade. Through us, He brings knowledge of Christ. Everywhere we go, people breath in the exquisite fragrance. Because of Christ, we give off a sweet scent rising to God, which is recognized by those on the way to salvation - an aroma redolent with life. But those on the way to destruction treat us more like the stench from a rotting corpse."

Throughout the Old Testament priests were commanded to burn incense that would become a sweet fragrance in the nostrils of the Lord. This is what you will become when you develop a lifestyle of giving thanks unto His holy Name. Victory has a smell to it. You can smell the fragrance of victory. Spiritual things have a smell to them and so often people miss out on these vital truths because they're so caught up in the natural, physical world. You need to realize that God intends for His people to be fragrant, to have a heavenly odor radiating out of them, a sweet aroma that is pleasing to the Lord. You are to smell like life, like victory. Giving thanks will cause a heavenly fragrance to radiate out of you. You can't smell this spiritual fragrance with your natural senses like you would perfume or cologne. No, this is a spiritual smell and it is not imaginary. It is real in the same way that God is spiritual and He is real. How you smell can affect how well you feel and perform in life. You can smell like depression and defeat, or you can smell like victory and newness of life.

It all begins with having a grateful heart that is forever giving thanks unto God. Saying "thank you" is more than a polite response. It's a powerful, spiritual force that will lead you to victory in the good fight of faith. Giving thanks to God before the manifestation comes is an expression of faith that releases the power and grace of God into your life. Jesus set the example when He fed the multitude with five barley loaves and two small fish. John 6:11 states, "And Jesus took the loaves, and when He had given thanks He distributed them to the disciples, and the disciples to those sitting down; and likewise of the wish, as much as they wanted." Jesus also gave thanks to the Father at the tomb of His dear friend Lazarus. "And Jesus lifted up His eyes and said, 'Father, I thank You that You have heard Me. And I know that You always hear Me, but because of the people who are standing by I said this, that they may believe that You sent Me'" (John 11:41,42). When Jesus encountered these problems the first thing He did was give thanks to the Heavenly Father. This reveals that there is a divine connection between thanksgiving and victory.

Faith will always thank God for things that haven't manifested yet. When faith is expressed, God will pour out His grace into your situation to bring to pass that which you are believing for. You gain access to God's grace through words of thanksgiving. Developing a lifestyle of giving thanks won't happen by itself. You must work at it, you must do it day and night, at work, at home, and at play. Make it a habit to say several times a day, "Thank You, Lord!" Being thankful will keep you focused and connected to God. It's not faith if you wait until your prayer is manifested to thank God. No, thank Him before the manifestation. Let every problem and need you have be a reminder to thank Him more. The devil is forever roaming around like a roaring lion seeking whom he may devour (1 Peter 5:8). He performs his evil schemes by offering to the weak and uninformed alternate choices and lifestyles that are contrary to the will of God. The Lord offers blessings and prosperity whereas the devil brings curses and poverty.

The opposite of divine health is sickness and disease, and the great enemy of faith is doubt and unbelief. There is also an alternate lifestyle to thanksgiving and that is the devilish act of murmuring and complaining. The root of these "profane and vain babblings and contradictions of what is falsely called knowledge" (1 Tim. 6:20) is self-pity. 1 Samuel tells the story of a woman drenched in this sometimes suicidal act of desperation and what she had to do to receive from God. This book of the Old Testament describes the transition of leadership in Israel from judges to kings. Samuel was the last judge and first prophet and would be used by God to anoint Saul as the first king of Israel and later David as the king-elect. Chapter one describes the events leading up to his birth. His father's name was Elkanah "and he had two wives: the name of one was Hannah, and the name of the other Peninnah. Peninnah had children, but Hannah had no children" (vs. 2). Elkanah loved Hannah more but this brought no comfort to his grieving wife.

"And her rival also provoked her severely, to make her miserable because the Lord had closed her womb. So it was, year by year, when she went up to the house of the Lord, that she provoked her; therefore, she wept and did not eat" (vs. 6,7). Hannah cried night and day and was almost suicidal. This is not right. There is no excuse to be this way. The Bible says to come boldly to the throne of grace, not sobbing. God wants to hear words of faith coming out of your mouth, not words of desperation. Hannah was feeling sorry for herself until finally her husband had enough of it. "Then Elkanah her husband said to her, 'Hannah, why do you weep? Why do you not eat? And why is your heart grieved? Am I not better to you than ten sons?'" (vs. 8). Essentially what Elkanah was saying is that if you don't thank God for what you already have, you can lose it all and not receive from Him in the future. At no time did words of thanksgiving escape out of Hannah's lips and her tears of un-belief "limited the Holy One of Israel" (Ps. 78:41).

If you're not thankful you will have no gratitude and waiting to give thanks is an act of unbelief. "So Hannah arose after they had finished eating and drinking in Shiloh. Now Eli the priest was sitting on the seat by the doorpost of the tabernacle of the Lord. And she was in bitterness of soul, and prayed to the Lord and wept in anguish" (vs. 9,10). Silently Hannah made a vow unto the Lord that if He would give her a male child, she would give him back to the Lord to be His servant all the days of his life. Still no comfort came to her heart and so sorrowful was she when the vow was made that the priest who watched her thought she was drunk. "And Hannah answered and said, 'No, my lord, I am a woman of sorrowful spirit. I have drunk nei-ther wine nor intoxication drink, but have poured out my soul before the Lord'" (vs. 15). Upon hearing Hannah's explanation Eli, the priest, sent her away and said the Lord would grant her petition.

Hannah heard from the Lord and vs. 18-20 shows the Biblical way to receive from Him. "So the woman went her way and ate, and her face was no longer sad. Then they rose early in the morning and worshipped before the Lord, and returned and came to their house at Ramah. And Elkanah knew Hannah his wife, and the Lord remembered her. So, it came to pass in the process of time that Hannah conceived and bore a son, and called his name Samuel." As long as Hannah wept and was sor-rowful, she did not receive the answer to her prayer. But when the wailing stopped and, along with her husband, she began to worship and thank the Lord, then and only then was she able to conceive the son she so desperately wanted. Samuel grew up to be one of the greatest prophets in all the Bible but he may not have even been born had his mother not stopped feeling sorry for herself.

Jesus was once encouraged to bask in self-pity and His stern rebuke when this happened should be a wake-up call to those desirous to walk by faith. Matt. 16:21-23 says, "From that time Jesus began to show to His disciples that He must go to Jerusalem, and suffer many things from the elders and chief priests and scribes, and be killed, and be raised again the third day. Then Peter took Him aside and began to rebuke Him, saying, 'Far be it from You, Lord; this shall not happen to You.' But He turned and said to Peter, 'Get behind Me, Satan! You are an offense to Me, for you are not mindful of the things of God, but the things of men.'" The phrase "far be it from You" literally means 'pity yourself' and Satan was using Peter to get Jesus to think about Himself and fall into the snare of self-pity. The timing of Peter's rebuke could not have come at a worse time. It happened shortly prior to the Lord's trial in the Garden of Gethsemane where He fought the temptation to have self-pity and quit.

The soul of Jesus was exceedingly sorrowful, even to the point of death, and He fell on His face, and prayed, saying, "O My Father, if it is possible, let this cup pass from Me; nevertheless, not as I will, but as You will" (Matt. 26: 38,39). Because of the sin of mankind that He was about to carry to the cross, Jesus knew He would be separated from and forsaken by the

Father and this is what made the struggle so severe. The temptation Jesus faced was whether or not to be led by His feelings, and this is precisely what Peter wanted Him to do. The salvation of sinful man was dependent on the Lord winning this battle, thus the harshness of the Lord's rebuke to Peter. Never feel sorry for yourself. One of the most destructive things you could do is submit to self-pity. This is pride, selfishness, and unbelief and will cause you to be cut off from the grace of God. A person who feels sorry for themself is never thankful because they feel they deserve whatever is due them. Grace is given to the humble and not to those who think they deserve it.

The main characteristic of a humble person is they are always giving thanks unto God. God "gives us richly all things to enjoy" (1 Tim. 6:17) and the humble receive this grace as a personal gift from God. Thanksgiving and grace go hand in hand so never say that you deserve anything. Instead, cultivate a lifestyle of thanksgiving and experience victory every day of your life. The more thankful you are, the more the grace will flow. There is a story in the Bible about a wealthy man who thought he deserved everything, even to the exclusion of others. King Ahab was the husband of the wicked Queen Jezebel and 1 Kings 21 tells the story of how he wanted to own a personal vineyard next to his palace that belonged to Naboth the Jezreelite. This particular vineyard was Naboth's inheritance from his forefathers and he refused to sell it to the king. "So Ahab went into his house sullen and displeased because of the word which Naboth the Jezreeite had spoken to him; for he had said, 'I will not give you the inheritance of my fathers.' And he lay down on his bed, and turned away his face, and would eat no food" (vs. 4).

Ahab was the king and had everything a person could possibly want. He had great wealth and an abundance of land. He had soldiers to fight for him and servants to grant his every wish. Still, he was not thankful for the things he did have and thought he deserved more. Proverbs 27:20 states, "Hell and Destruction are never full; So the eyes of man are never satisfied." If a person is not thankful for what they already have, the more they'll want. They falsely believe they deserve more and will not be satisfied until they obtain even that which belongs to another. Eccl. 5:10 says, "He who loves silver will not be satisfied with silver; Nor he who loves abundance, with increase. This also is vanity." Self-pity is a dangerous thing and before long an evil plot was made to bring false charges against Naboth for which he would be stoned to death. This plot was devised by Jezebel when she went into her husband's chamber and fed his self-pity. "But there was no one like Ahab who sold himself to do wickedness in the sight of the Lord, because Jezebel his wife stirred him up" (vs. 25).

Vs. 12-16 tell the details of this evil plot, "They proclaimed a fast, and seated Naboth with high honor among the people. And two men, scoundrels, came in and sat before him; and the scoundrels witnessed against him, against Naboth, in the presence of the people, saying, 'Naboth has blasphemed God and the king!' Then they took him outside the city and stoned him with stones, so that he died. Then they sent to Jezebel, saying, 'Naboth has been stoned and is dead.' And it came to pass, when Jezebel heard that Naboth had been stoned and was dead, that Jezebel said to Ahab, 'Arise, take possession of the vineyard of Naboth the Jezreelite, which he refused to give you for money; for Naboth is not alive, but dead.' So it was, when Ahab heard that Naboth was dead, that Ahab got up and went down to take possession of the vineyard of Naboth the Jezreelite." An innocent man died because Jezebel fed Ahab's self-pity. The only thought in the mind of her self-centered husband was that he deserved what belonged to another man.

The favorite subject of the carnal mind is one's self and Rom. 8:5 states, "For those who live according to the flesh set their minds on the things of the flesh." The difference between carnal people and spiritual people is what's on their mind. The Message Bible says in vs. 8,9, "Obsession with self in these matters is a dead end; attention to God leads us out into the open, into a spacious, free life. Focusing on the self is the opposite of focusing on God. Anyone completely absorbed in self ignores God, ends up thinking more about self than God. That person ignores Who God is and what He is doing. And God isn't pleased at being ignored." So what should Hannah and Ahab have done instead? They should have realized that faith works through love and so also does thanksgiving. Peninnah had her children and Naboth had his vineyard so words of praise and thanksgiving should have flowed out of their innermost being. Love cares about the other person and spiritual maturity comes when you can be thankful when another person is blessed.

Rom. 12:15 says to "Rejoice with those who rejoice" and vs. 14 says "bless and do not curse." How you treat other people reveals how thankful you are for what the Lord has already done for you. Therefore, never be envious or jealous but forever strive to obey the words of the apostle Paul recorded in Eph. 5:20, "Giving thanks always for all things to God the Father in the name of our Lord Jesus Christ." When evil thoughts cloud your mind and prevent you from giving thanks unto God, special attention must then be given to the words of the apostle Paul recorded in 2 Cor. 10:3-5, "For though we walk in the flesh, we do not war according to the flesh. For the weapons of our warfare are not carnal but mighty in God for pulling down strongholds, casting down arguments and every high thing that exalts itself against the knowledge of God, bringing every thought into captivity to the obedience of Christ." This is what Jesus was doing when He rebuked Peter. Peter was trying to put an image on the inside of Jesus and He sternly cast it down. This is also what Adam and Eve should have done to the serpent in the Garden of Eden.

You don't receive from God according to His power or what His will is. You receive by faith and faith is expressed with praise and thanksgiving. When you are not thankful there is a void inside of you and something bad will fill it. Thoughts of jealousy, envy, hatred, and self-pity will try to enter in whose only objective is to destroy your life. Joseph's brothers were envious and it led to bitterness and hatred. They didn't know that love envies not and if another member is honored then all the members should rejoice with him. Always give thanks unto God both for what He is doing in your life and in the lives of others. This will give you access to God's grace and Col. 1:12 states, "Giving thanks to the Father Who qualified us to be partakers of the inheritance of the saints in the light." To be "thankful" means 'to be grateful, to acknowledge, to remember.' David wrote in Ps. 103:2, "Bless the Lord, O my soul, and forget not all His benefits."

A story recorded in Luke 17 reveals the Lord's attitude on the subject of thanksgiving. "Now it happened as He went to Jerusalem that He passed through the midst of Samaria and Galilee. Then as He entered a certain village, there met Him ten men who were lepers, who stood afar off. And they lifted their voices and said, 'Jesus, Master, have mercy on us!' So, when He saw them, He said to them, 'Go, show yourselves to the priests.' And so it was that as they went, they were cleansed" (vs. 11-14). According to Old Testament law, you go and present yourself to the priest after you're healed, not before. When these lepers left to go to the priest, they were not yet clean. They acted in faith and as they went, they were cleansed. "Now one of them, when he saw that he was healed, returned, and with a loud voice glorified God, and fell down on his face at His feet, giving Him thanks. And he was a Samaritan. So Jesus answered and said, 'Were there not ten cleansed? But where are the nine? Were there not any found who returned to give glory to God except this foreigner?' And He said to him. 'Arise, go your way. Your faith has made you whole'" (vs. 15-19).

It is commonly taught that a leper who is cleansed means that the disease has stopped growing and no longer eats away the skin of the person. However, the dead skin is still there. A leper who is made whole, however, means that the skin that has rotted away gets restored to its original condition. This is what happened to the man who returned to glorify Jesus and give Him thanks. Thanksgiving qualified this man for greater grace. The message to be learned here is that you can thank your way out of darkness into the light, out of defeat and into victory. When you give thanks, your bondage will be turned into liberty, your poverty into plenty, and your sickness into health. Thanksgiving is giving glory to God and magnifying His holy Name. David wrote in Ps. 69:30, "I will praise the name of God with a song and will magnify Him with thanksgiving." You can thank your way out of any problem you have, or you can bask in self-pity and murmur and complain your way into a life of defeat and victory. The choice is yours. Never let the Lord say of you, "Where are the other nine?"

| 21 |

"THE COMPASSION OF FAITH"

The time drew near for Jesus to fulfill His calling and purpose for coming to planet earth in human form. Within a few short hours He would be beaten, ridiculed, spat upon, and shamefully hung naked on a cross between two thieves. For what reason did He come to die? In the upper room during the last supper Jesus prayed, "I do not pray for these alone, but also for those who will believe in Me through their word; that they all may be one as You, Father, are in Me, and I in You, that they also may be one in Us." (John 17:20,21). The Message Bible says, "The goal is for all of them to become one heart and mind - just as you, Father, are in Me and I in You, so they might be one heart and mind with Us." Jesus came to bridge the gap of sin between man and the Father and to bring unity among the brethren. Jesus came to make all believers into one big, happy family and unity in the body of Christ begins when people realize that they are all individual members of God's household.

Believers are one family in Christ. He is the vine, His children are the branches (John 15:5). Together as joint heirs with Christ, you are to become "like-minded, having the same love, being of one accord, of one mind" (Phil. 2:2). This is called the "law of unity" and is so vital today in the body of Christ. Jesus himself said, "Every kingdom divided against itself is brought to desolation, and every city or house divided against itself will not stand" (Matt. 12:25). The family of God is joined together in a covenant relationship with one another because of the shed blood of Jesus, and the bonding element that holds and binds us together is love, the "bond of perfection" (Col. 3:14). Jesus came to make all believers a family, and Paul says that as a member of the family of God you need to be "rooted and grounded in love" (Eph. 3:17). This is the foundation of your walk with Christ and will cause you to be filled with the fullness of God. If you are rooted in love, you are rooted in God, for God is love (1 John 4:8).

The love of God is no ordinary love. It is a love that continues loving no matter what. The love of God will always focus on the one loved with thought of self-second. Jude 21 says to "keep yourself in the love of God." If everybody would do that then the body of Christ would be undivided because the love of God always seeks and desires unity. Ps. 133:1 says, "Behold, how good and how pleasant it is for brethren to dwell together in unity." Dwelling together in unity means to have a continual courtship with one another. When you are courting somebody in the natural you are always on your best behavior and will do anything to win the affection of the other person. Likewise, you need to delight to be in the presence of other believers and strive to promote and further their welfare and calling in life. Paul says, "Let each of you look out not only for his own interests, but also for the interests of others" (Phil. 2:4). It is God's desire that all believers dwell together as a holy family having one heart, one soul, and one interest.

1 John 4:7 says, "Beloved, let us love one another, for love is of God; and everyone who loves is born of God and knows God." Love is a spiritual force that takes residence in the hearts of every believer. Love is a commandment and it must be foremost in the center of your will. As a believer your first responsibility is to draw close to God and develop a love relationship with Him. You will quickly realize that the love you have for others will always be in direct proportion to your love for God. The way you love God is the same way you will love others. You can always tell where a person is at in their walk with the Lord by the way they love and treat others. Do you want to know the love of God more? Then practice loving one another more. This will help you to build up a greater degree and measure of love for God which in turn helps you to love others more. It is a continuous cycle of love. God is love and His greatest desire is for you to love Him with all your heart and in turn love one another. This is how unity comes to the body of Christ.

People who love are a blessed people and it brings constant delight and comfort to those who are living in harmony and unity with one another. Ps. 133:2 says dwelling together in unity "is like the precious oil upon the head, running down the beard, the beard of Aaron, running down on the edge of his garments." Believers are taught by God to love one another (1 Thess. 4:9) and it is His grace working through us. It is like the precious oil running down the beard of Aaron. This ointment was holy and was not made for common use. So must your brotherly love be. In order to dwell together in unity, you must love with a pure heart that is solely devoted to God and the fulfillment of His will. As with the anointing oil, holy love is also of great price and is precious indeed. It is like ointment and perfume which will rejoice the heart. It is the "oil of gladness" that brings celebration, exaltation, and exceeding joy. If you will take the time to develop a love relationship with other believers, then dwelling together in unity will be "like the dew of Hermon, descending upon the mountains of Zion" (Ps. 133:3).

The morning dew represents fertility and growth. 1 John 4:12 says, "If we love one another, God abides in us and His love has been perfected in us." God's love is perfected by practicing love and hospitality on one another. This causes love to grow. Love is not selfish and you are to manifest the love of God and His nature to others. Peter says, "Above all things have intense and unfailing love for one another" (1 Peter 4:8). Jesus said in John 13:34,35, "A new commandment I give to you, that you love one another; as I have loved you, that you also love one another. By this all will know that you are My disciples, if you have love for one another." Jesus is talking to His disciples here and He is talking about the relationship of believers to one another. Certainly, you are to love the unsaved people of the world because John 3:16 says, "For God so loved the world that He gave His only begotten Son." However, this commandment that Jesus is talking about here is not a command to love the world, it is a command for Christians to love one another.

Loving one another is a sign of true discipleship. You are to be so happy, and so excited, and treat other believers with a true, genuine love that those outside the family of God will want to become Christians also. People of the world don't get drawn to the Lord by you quoting scriptures to them all the time. No, what draws them in is when they observe how Christians treat each other with a brotherly love that surpasses anything they've ever experienced before. Some believers push God on people so hard that it causes bitterness and strife. Don't do that. God never forces himself on anybody and neither should you. If you want to draw an unbeliever in then let them see you do something nice to another believer. It doesn't matter how right you are or how much they need to hear what you have to say. The bottom line is that if they're not ready to hear what you have to say, your forceful words will do more harm than good. Sometimes it's better to be quiet and walk away.

Jesus said in Matt. 7:6, "Do not give what is holy to the dogs; nor cast your pearls before swine, lest they trample them under their feet, and turn and tear you to pieces." Talking to the wrong person at the wrong time can push them away indefinitely and possibly terminate their desire to ever come to the Lord. So what should you do? Love one another. This is your primary witness to the unsaved world. Your actions toward other believers will speak louder to the unsaved than all the preaching you do to them. The love you have is a love the world does not have. Rom. 5:5 says the love of God has been poured out in your heart by the Holy Spirit who was given to you. The only love the world has is based on feelings but you can love in faith even when the feelings are not there. People get in trouble when they're dominated by their feelings and you must rise above that. Feelings are temporary, they're always changing. God is love and He never changes. Jer. 31:3 says God loves you with an everlasting love.

1 John 4:11 says, "Beloved, if God so loved us, we also ought to love one another." Your love for others is not based on if they deserve it or not. God loved you when you didn't deserve it, and it's with this same type of love that you are to reach out and love others. If the feelings aren't there, so what? Love them anyway. "Therefore be followers of God as dear children. And walk in love, as Christ also has loved us and given Himself for us, an offering and a sacrifice to God for a sweet-smelling aroma" (Eph. 5:1,2). As a born-again believer you are to be an imitator of God as dear children imitate their parents. Jesus came to lay down His life for you and you ought to do the same. John 15:13 says, "Greater love has no one than this, than to lay down one's life for his friends." Become to others "a friend who sticks closer than a brother" (Prov. 18:24). Become "zealous for good works" (Titus 2:14). The entire Bible is a book of love and throughout its pages are recorded several principles of covenant love that should govern the thoughts, words, and actions of every born-again child of God.

One of the first things to learn about the love of God is that it always gives. In Acts 20:35 the apostle Paul quoted the Lord Jesus and said, "It is more blessed to give than to receive."

The word "blessed" means 'happy' and several translations say, "There is more happiness in giving than receiving." Jesus said this so it must be true. God is a giving God and there is no better indicator of His presence in your heart than in the attitude you develop about giving. Love always gives and you need to make a quality decision to become a quality giver. 1 Tim. 6:18 says, "Let them do good that they may be rich in good works, ready to give, willing to share." Giving should be the lifestyle of every born-again believer. Giving is what believers do. Jesus said, "Give to him who asks you, and from him who wants to borrow from you do not turn away" (Matt. 5:42). 2 Cor. 9:7 says that "God loves, cherishes above all things, a cheerful giver." Even though this verse is referring to money, the principle is the same in all areas of giving.

Before money can be given you need to first be willing to cheerfully give of yourself. You need to get involved in the lives of other people. When you do that, you'll quickly realize that there is always something you can give to promote the lives of others. Love always gives. And what precisely does love give? Whatever is needed. Money is only a small part of giving. You can give people your love, time, fellowship, counsel, prayers, and any natural resource you have at your disposal. Also, you need to be consistent in your giving. Daily look for ways to give and enrich those around you. You were born to love and can develop in your life the ministry of being nice to other people. Buy a coworker a cup of coffee or bake a dozen cookies and give them to a neighbor. Give somebody you know a phone call and tell them how blessed you are to have them as a friend. Offer to baby sit for a mother of six children who never gets a chance to be by herself and do the things she likes to do. Take an elderly person to the shopping mall with you or a fatherless child to a ball game.

If nothing else, you can always give somebody a smile and a friendly "hello." Let people see the joy that is within you. And who knows? These acts of kindness may birth in them the desire to know the same God you know. What more can a person offer another than the opportunity to receive eternal life? Covenant love treats people as God treats you. Rom. 5:8 says, "But God demonstrates His own love toward us, in that while we were still sinners, Christ died for us." 1 John 3:16 says, "By this we know love, because He laid down His life for us. And we also ought to lay down our lives for the brethren." Love is not selfish and you also need to die to yourself so you can have the freedom to love and bless others. You need to engage your time and effort into what others like to do and get involved in what interests them. If you are willing, God will see to it that you will always have the resources from which to give. He will also provide the opportunities to do so. Daily look for those opportunities. Surely, they are there.

In the world there are two types of people, givers and takers. Takers believe the more they get, the happier they will be. They base their happiness on how big their house is, what type of car they drive, and how much money they have in the bank. They don't believe what Jesus said and, if the truth be told, rich people who don't know Jesus are the poorest people on the planet. If you are sad and depressed, become a cheerful giver and watch your joy increase. Jesus said it would. There is no greater joy in all the world than to be at the right place, at the right time, and having God use you to be an answer to somebody's prayer. There is more joy and happiness in doing this than in receiving something for yourself. Jesus never said receiving was a bad thing. He said in Luke 11:10, "For everyone who asks receives." It is a good thing to receive something, especially if you have a need and that need gets met. For sure, that will make you happy, but being able to give will make you even more happy.

Eph. 4:28 says, "Let him who stole steal no longer, but rather let him labor, working with his hands what is good, that he may have something to give him who has need." It is ingrained in the minds of most people that you are to work for a living, but Paul says here you are to work for a giving. Yes, you are supposed to work but the Bible says you are to live by faith. That is different than living off your paycheck each week. According to Paul, you work so that you can have something to give to those who are in need. There is a difference between a person who is in need and a person who won't work. It goes against scripture to help a lazy person, and that includes members of your own family. 2 Thess. 3:10 says, "If anyone will not work, neither shall he eat." If you feed a lazy person you are only prolonging their pain. There are times when the Lord will let a person go hungry but their friends and relatives won't. What this person needs is tough love. If a person goes hungry long enough, they'll eventually call out to God and repent from a lifestyle of being lazy all the time.

When you give, you override the selfish nature of your flesh and you yield to the love of God that is shed abroad in your heart. Don't concern yourself with the amount you give because God will use you right where you are. Even a small amount can help a certain individual on any given day. It's like taking a thorn out of the paw of a lion. A thorn is a small thing but it made a big difference to that lion. Daily look for ways to be a blessing to another person. Ask the Lord to lead you to a person who could use a word of encouragement, a compliment that can pull them out of the pit of gloom and despair. Everybody likes praise. God likes praise, people like praise, cats and dogs like praise. Praise is a sign of acceptance. Is not acceptance the primary need of all people? People have a craving to be received willingly and favorably. They want to be approved of and believed in. You need to learn to accept people not based on your preference or their performance but because God has accepted them (Rom. 14:3).

Paul says in Rom. 15:7, "Therefore receive one another, just as Christ also received us, to the glory of God." As you praise and worship God for His worthiness, so must you also compliment and lift up one another. Eph. 4:29 says, "Let no corrupt communication proceed out of your mouth, but what is good for necessary edification that it may impart grace to the hearers." Compliments make a person feel good about themselves and births in them the desire to respond back to the person giving the compliment. This leads to unity. A compliment spoken from the heart can "break the ice" between strangers and can open up the doorway to a life of love, fellowship, and faithful service to the Heavenly Father. The Bible in Phil. 4:8 even tells you what types of compliments you are to give people, "Finally, brethren, whatever things are true, whatever things are noble, whatever things are just, whatever things are pure, whatever things are lovely, whatever things are of good report, if there is any virtue and if there is anything praiseworthy - meditate on these things."

If you will meditate on these types of things concerning other people, it will eventually get down into your heart and Jesus said, "For out of the abundance of the heart the mouth speaks" (Matt. 12:34). If you will take the time and make the effort, you will always be able to find something good in the lives of other people to compliment them about. And, by all means, be sincere in your praise giving. Nobody likes false praise. Nobody likes to be lied to. Covenant love means you will be real and sincere in your relationships. Let your compliments come from a conviction in your heart that you really believe what you're saying. And if you will remain honest and sincere, you also will be blessed as you heap praises upon those around you. "A man has joy by the answer of his mouth, and a word spoken in due season, how good it is" (Prov. 15:23). Blessing and ministering to one another is what "loving thy neighbor" is all about. But if you are to please God in your quest for unity, then you will have to get your faith involved for "without faith it is impossible to please Him" (Heb. 11:6).

Gal. 5:6 (NLT) says, "For when we place our faith in Christ Jesus, there is no benefit in being circumcised or being uncircumcised. What is important is faith expressing itself in love." This love is the love of God working in you and through you to reveal His righteousness. Since God is love, and faith comes by hearing the Word of God, then faith must be all about expressing the love of God. The Amplified Bible says "faith activated and energized and expressed and working through love." The Greek word for "working" is 'energeo' and is where the word "energy" comes from. Faith is activated and energized through love. The word "energized" means 'to give energy to; rouse into activity.' Love is what makes faith work. 1 Cor. 13:2 says, "And though I have all faith, so that I could move mountains, but have not love, I am nothing." Without love your faith will not work. Just like a dead battery can be recharged and become useful again, you can recharge your faith by plugging it into love. It is love that energizes faith.

The way you treat other people will affect your faith. 1 Peter 3:7 tells how husbands should be considerate of their wives and treat them with honor and respect so "that your prayers may not be hindered." You can make faith confessions all day long, and you can fast and pray, but it won't do you any good if you don't walk in love. Losing your temper all the time and gossiping about other people will keep your faith from operating at full capacity. Love seeks not its own and is more interested in the well-being of others than in itself. When you stay busy helping others unselfishly, you will in time find honor, success, and promotion for yourself. Not only will you reap spiritual blessings but you'll also reap natural blessings and benefits that you never thought possible. Promotions will come, your body will be healed, and your relationships will be restored. When you walk in love you don't have to work to make good things happen to you, they'll happen automatically. What you make happen for others, God will make happen for you.

Faith is not about seeing how much money you can believe for, it's about allowing the love of Jesus to flow through you at all times. You love people when you stop using them to meet your needs, but instead you rejoice that God would use you to help supply their needs. Faith produces this love and takes away the barriers of greed and self-centeredness. It creates in you a new appetite for the thrill of allowing God to show His mercy in and through you. This appetite propels you into a love walk that God himself would find admirable. Because faith expresses itself through love, you can check your love for others as a way to monitor your faith. The concept of faith working by love is a continual cycle of growth and maturity. As your faith grows, it will prompt you to do good things for other people, and as love becomes a lifestyle for you, the very works you do will produce a stronger faith. The more you practice loving others, the deeper your faith becomes. The deeper your faith becomes, the more you will endeavor to work to love others. One response affects the outcome of the other.

"And now abide faith, hope, love, these three; but the greatest of these is love" (1 Cor.13:13). Love is the answer to every problem and faith works by the same love that has been shed abroad in your heart. Love is not selfish, it does not seek its own (1 Cor. 13:5). Likewise, God did not give you faith to consume it all on yourself. All too often people use their faith to get their own needs met with no regard for the needs of others. If a problem or an obstacle arises in your life, you immediately put your faith to work on it. But if this is all you do with your faith, then you have missed the heartbeat of God. Faith always used on oneself is called immature faith. You need to grow beyond that and use your faith to help others. Gal. 6:2 says, "Bear one another's burdens and so fulfill the law of Christ" which is the law of love. "And let us not grow weary while doing good, for in due season we shall reap if we do not lose heart. Therefore, as we have opportunity, let us do good to all, especially to those who are in the household of faith" (Gal.6:9,10).

Faith always proves itself by works. James 2:26 says that "faith without works is dead." You need to believe and confess the Word of God concerning the needs of others and also provide works and actions to help meet those needs. John the Baptist, the forerunner of Christ, said, "He who has two tunics, let him give to him who has none; and he who has food, let him do likewise" (Luke 3:11). James 2:14-17 asks what does it profit if a brother or sister who is naked and destitute of daily food comes to you and all you do is pray for them and send them on their way? The answer is obvious. It profits nothing! 1 John 3: 17,18 says, "But whoever has this world's goods, and sees his brother in need, and shuts up his heart from him, how does the love of God abide in him? My little children, let us not love in word or in tongue, but indeed and in truth." True Biblical faith and Godly love will feed and clothe those in need and will find shelter for them and help them find a job. This is faith and love in action. Yes, you were born to love but you were also called to serve.

Jesus taught that the kingdom of God is like a mustard seed that is planted in the ground. After it is sown "it grows up and becomes greater than all the herbs, and shoots out large branches, so that the birds of the air may nest under it's shade" (Mark 4:32). As the mustard seed of faith grows up, it will reach out beyond itself and help provide shelter for the birds of the air. Likewise, your faith should be used to help sustain life in others. If your faith is not being used to help other people, then it has not yet grown up to maturity. As with the birds of the air, the ultimate goal of your faith should be to help produce positive results in the lives of other people. One example is when you give by faith. You don't give of your resources to get your own needs met. No, you give to help other people get their needs met. Rom. 15:1,2 says, "We then who are strong ought to bear with the failings of the weak, and not to please ourselves. Let each of us please his neighbor for his good, leading to edification." Doing this on a consistent basis will bring great joy to the body of Christ and unity among those in the household of faith.

| 22 |

"THE JOY OF FAITH"

Your entire life, both in the here and now and in the age to come, will be the result of your response to the Word of God. If you receive the gospel message, you will be saved. If you reject it, you'll be judged and condemned. The choice of what you believe is yours and yours alone. In Acts 13 Paul preached the gospel to the Jews who rejected the message and opposed the things told to them. Paul then turned to preach to the Gentiles and vs. 47,48 says, "For so the Lord has commanded us: 'I have sent you to be a light to the Gentiles, that you should be for salvation to the ends of the earth.' Now when the Gentiles heard this, they were glad and glorified the word of the Lord. And as many as had been appointed to eternal life believed." The Jews rejected the word spoken to them but the Gentiles received it with joy and gladness. Paul later wrote in Rom. 15:13, "Now may the God of hope fill you with all joy and peace in believing, that you may abound in hope by the power of the Holy Spirit." There is no excuse for going a single day where you're not excited about God and what you are believing to receive.

Real faith brings with it joy and peace in believing. If you are depressed and not excited then you have chosen to yield to depression and unbelief. If you are truly believing then you will have hope and this will give you joy and peace. If you don't have joy and peace then you're not expecting something good to happen to you which means you are not walking in faith. If you're not excited then you're not expecting, and if you're not expecting you're not believing. Concerning Jesus 1 Peter 1:8 says, "Though now you do not see Him, yet believing, you rejoice with joy inexpressible and full of glory." This is joy that is so strong and potent you can't express it with words. It is joy unspeakable and full of glory. If you're not rejoicing then you're not believing. But when you do believe, joy will bubble up and overflow from within you. Phil. 1:25 says, "And being confident of this, I know that I shall remain and continue with you all for your progress and joy of faith." There is no such thing as a believer in faith who is depressed about it. If you are depressed, you are not in faith.

Faith pleases God. It pleases Him more when you believe for something than when you actually receive it. 1 Peter 1:7 says, "That the genuineness of your faith, being much more precious than gold that perishes, though it is tested by fire, may be found to praise, honor, and glory at the revelation of Jesus Christ." What this verse is saying is that God will one day praise you for walking in faith. He is giving you honor when He says to you in the presence of others, "Well done, good and faithful servant." The Message Bible says, "When Jesus wraps this all up, it's your faith, not your gold, that God will have on display as evidence of His victory." When you walk in faith and do what

He tells you to do, God says He will reveal Himself to you. He'll make Himself to be clearly seen and known by you and when that happens you rejoice with joy unspeakable and full of glory. If you're not rejoicing it's because you're not walking in faith. When you believe, you rejoice. When you believe a lot, you rejoice with joy unspeakable.

It pleases God when you walk in faith because this is how He created the universe. He believed it before it existed. He spoke it before it happened. He said it and then it was. You are a faith child of a faith God and He is training you in this life to rule and reign with Him in the next life. You will rule and reign by faith so it should be a normal thing for you to operate in before you leave this life. The just shall live by faith. You call things that be not as though they were. It is a wonderful thing that God gives you the means to change what you see and what you don't see. To show you what to do and how to do it, He sent His only begotten Son to be your guide and example. Jesus pleased the Father in everything He did because He was a man of great faith. He walked by faith and not by sight. He then said in John 14:12, "Most assuredly, I say to you, he who believes in Me, the works that I do he will do also; and greater works than these he will do, because I go to My Father."

Walking by sight keeps you in the present, faith puts you in the future. Jesus endured the cross for the joy that was set before Him (Heb. 12:2). By faith He looked into the future and saw how everything was going to turn out and this brought Him great joy. You can do the same thing. If you are having a hard time today then get in faith and go back to the future. Looking at the end result of your faith will give you the strength to endure the unpleasant circumstances you are currently going through. When you walk in faith, you're expecting something good to happen. You're expecting all your needs to be met and for your body to be healed. In faith you've always got something to be excited about no matter what is happening around you. Matt. 5:11,12 says, "Blessed are you when they revile and persecute you, and say all kinds of evil against you falsely for My sake. Rejoice and be exceedingly glad, for great is your reward in heaven, for so they persecuted the prophets who were before you." Luke 6:23 says, "Rejoice in that day and leap for joy!"

Do you know what a trial is? It's a distraction. That's all it is, plain and simple. A trial is the devil's attempt to distract you from doing what God has called you to do. How can a person focus on fulfilling their dreams if all they do is sit around all the time and worry about their problems? The answer is they can't. This is why many are called but few are chosen. The hardest part of faith is the final half hour and the closer a person gets to the fulfillment of their dream the bigger and more consistent the distractions will be. This is why the servants of God so desperately need to learn to cast all their care onto the Lord. It is so easy to get distracted. You're trying so hard to serve the Lord when you hear that a major layoff is about to happen at your job. Your children get sick, your spouse is mad at you, the in-laws come for a visit, your car breaks down. These are all distractions. Nothing more, nothing less. What should you do? Press on! Remain focused on the call. Do what you can in the natural and leave the rest in God's very capable hands. Let Him lead you beside the still waters.

As you rest and lay down in green pastures, you'll sense a song rising up from the inside of you. It's a song of praise and worship and thanksgiving. It's a new song. It's a song of joy. All during David's reign over Israel the Philistines were continually a thorn in his flesh. 2 Sam. 21:15 says, "When the Philistines were at war again with Israel, David and his servants with him went down and fought against the Philistines; and David grew faint." David is now old and he had been a man of war for his entire life. Almost non-stop he had been in battle after battle after battle. At this time in his life his nation was in famine, his son had been killed, and once again he was at war with the Philistines. The Bible says David grew faint. He became weary and exhausted. Does this passage describe you? Do you need a miracle right now? If so, then consider what David did in 2 Sam. 22:1, "Then David spoke to the Lord the words of this song..." David sang a new song to the Lord and when you read and study the entire chapter you will see that it is indeed a song of joy. It was a psalm of thanksgiving.

Vs. 2-4 says, "The Lord is my rock, my fortress, and my deliverer; The God of my strength, in Him I will trust, my shield and the horn of my salvation, my stronghold and my refuge; My Savior, You save me from violence. I will call upon the Lord, who is worthy to be praised; So shall I be saved from my enemies." When you sing a new song to the Lord, a song of joy, you also shall be saved from your enemies. In Ps. 144:9,10 David wrote, "I will sing a new song to You, O God; on a harp of ten strings I will sing praises to You, the One Who gives salvation to kings, who delivers David His servant from the deadly sword." David was a man after God's own heart and often he labeled himself the Lord's servant. He knew that his God was a covenant-keeping God and this is why he was able to rise up and sing a song of joy during times of peril. Ps. 89:34,37 says, "My covenant I will not break, nor alter the word that has gone out of My lips. Once I have sworn by My holiness; I will not lie to David; His seed shall endure forever, and his throne as the sun before Me; It shall be established forever like the moon, even like the faithful witness in the sky."

David knew that God is not a man that He should lie (Num. 23:19) so he was able to stand firm on what God had said to him. Over and over again God had delivered David from his enemies and he remembered these victories often. Before he faced Goliath, he told Saul how the Lord had delivered him from the lion and the bear (1 Sam. 17:34-37). He was saying that he had seen God work before. If He delivered him once, He can do it again. And again. And again. The devil wants you to have tunnel vision and see only the problem but like David you need to broaden the horizon of your vision and see the God who is more than enough. Habakkuk put his trust in the same God David served when he wrote, "Though the fig tree may not blossom, nor fruit be on the vine; Though the labor of the olive may fail, and the fields yield no food; Though the flock be cut off from the fold, and there be no herd in the stalls - Yet I will rejoice in the Lord, I will joy in the God of my salvation. The Lord God is my strength; He will make my feet like deer's feet, and He will make me walk on my high hills" (Hab. 3:17-19).

This was Habakkuk's song of joy. You need to sing a song of joy during times of trial and not only when things are going good. You can have the confidence that God will never leave you or forsake you. He is always there. He is the great "I AM"! He does not take His children out on a limb and leave them there. No, He is an ever-present help in time of need. David wrote in Ps. 27:9,10, "Do not hide Your face from me; Do not turn Your servant away in anger; You have been my help; Do not leave me nor forsake me, O God of my salvation. When my father and my mother forsake me, then the Lord will take care of me." This was why David was always singing songs of joy unto His Lord. We ought to also do the same. Paul wrote, "Rejoice in the Lord always. Again, I will say, rejoice!" (Phil. 4:4). James said, "My brethren, count it all joy when you fall into various trials." (James 1:2). Even Jesus said, "These things I have spoken to you, that in Me you will have peace. In the world you will have tribulation; but be of good cheer, I have overcome the world" (John 16:33).

During times of trial, you need to lie down beside the still waters and sing unto the Lord a song of joy. In other words, calm down and cheer up! Rest assured, it is not the will of God for His servants to suffer defeat. Just as He leads you beside the still waters, you can sing a song of joy because He "always leads us in triumph in Christ" (2 Cor. 2:14). Ps. 23:3 says, "He restores my soul; He leads me in the paths of righteousness for His Name's sake." Yes, David grew faint but he was able to sing a song of joy because the words he wrote in Ps. 37:23,24 were burning in his heart, "The steps of a good man are ordered by the Lord, and He delights in his way. Though he fall, he shall not be utterly cast down; For the Lord upholds him with His hand." This is why David could write in Ps. 40:1-3, "I waited patiently for the Lord; And He inclined to me, and heard my cry. He also brought me up out of a horrible pit, out of the miry clay, and sit my feet upon a rock, and established my steps. He has put a new song in my mouth - Praise to our God; Many will see it and fear, and will trust in the Lord."

Never forget that Satan is a thief and like a roaring lion he roams about seeking whom he may devour. He's after the Word in your heart, your joy and power, your peace, courage, and comfort, your physical belongings and, more than anything else, the call of God that is on your life. This is why when the Philistines heard that David was anointed king over all Israel they rose up in battle against him (1 Chron. 14:8). The devil is trying to discourage you and if he can't defeat you in the spiritual realm, he'll attack you in the natural realm. Read what the writer of Hebrews says in Heb. 10:32-35, "But recall the former days in which, after you were illuminated, you endured a great struggle with sufferings: partly while you were made a spectacle both by reproaches and tribulations, and partly while you became companions of those who were so treated; for you had compassion on me in my chains, and joyfully accepted the plundering of your goods, knowing that you have a better and an enduring possession for yourselves in heaven."

The Message Bible bears even more light on what the writer is saying, "Remember those early days after you first saw the light? Those were the hard times! Kicked around in public, targets of every kind of abuse - some days it was you, other days your friends. If some friends went to prison you stuck by them. If some enemies broke in and seized your goods, you let them go with a smile, knowing they couldn't touch your real treasure. Nothing they did bothered you, nothing set you back. So don't throw it all away now. You were sure of yourselves then. It's still a sure thing! But you need to stick it out, staying with God's plan so you'll be there for the promised completion." In the midst of this long passage of scriptures is the key to having victory in your life. Vs. 34 says they "joyfully accepted the plundering" of their goods. When the enemy broke into their homes and took everything they had, a song of joy rose up on the inside of them. The only way Satan can defeat you and stop you from going forward is to prevent you from singing your song of joy.

Neh. 8:10 says, "Do not sorrow, for the joy of the Lord is your strength." The devil can't beat a believer who is joyful. He wants you weak and powerless so he attacks your joy because there is no power without it. Jesus spoke to the Heavenly Father in John 17:13,14, "But now I come to You, and these things I speak in the world, that they may have My joy fulfilled in themselves. I have given them Your Word." Jesus also said in John 15:11, "These things I have spoken to you, that My joy may remain in you, and that your joy may be full." The Word of God produces joy. His Word is good news and good news produces joy. When you've been robbed of your joy you've been robbed of the Word because it's the Word that produces joy. So be of good cheer. The Word of God and the joy of the Lord gives you the strength to secure for yourself victory every time the devil attacks you. Jesus came from the tribe of Judah and this word means "praise." You are joint-heirs with Jesus so every day you should shout praises unto your God and sing to Him a song of joy. For sure, God can work in the lives of those who praise Him. The game's not over as long as you're still praising Him.

The Message Bible says in 1 Thess. 1:5,6, "When the Message we preached came to you, it wasn't just words. Something happened in you. The Holy Spirit put steel in your convictions. You paid careful attention to the way we lived among you, and determined to live that way yourselves. In imitating us, you imitated the Master. Although great trouble accompanied the Word you were able to take great joy from the Holy Spirit! - taking the trouble with the joy, the joy with the trouble." Paul went on to say in 2:1,2, "So, friends, it's obvious that our visit to you was no waste of time. We had just been given rough treatment in Philippi, as you know, but that didn't slow us down. We were sure of ourselves in God, and went right ahead and said our piece, presenting God's message to you, defiant of the opposition." How is it that Paul was able to write these words? Because he continually had a song of joy in his heart.

Acts 16:25 says, "But at midnight Paul and Silas were praying and singing hymns to God, and the prisoners were listening to them." Joy has a voice. It can't be kept quiet. Jer.33:11 talks about "the voice of joy and the voice of gladness, the voice of the bridegroom and the voice of the bride, the voice of those who will say: 'Praise the Lord of hosts, for the Lord is good, for His mercy endures forever' - and of those who will bring the sacrifice of praise into the house of the Lord." David wrote in Ps. 16:11, "In Your presence is fullness of joy." Joy must be expressed! Paul and Silas sang praises at the midnight hour. In 2 Sam. 6 David brought the ark to Jerusalem and vs. 14,15 says, "Then David danced before the Lord with all his might; and David was wearing a linen ephod. So David and all the house of Israel brought up the ark of the Lord with shouting and with the sound of the trumpet." Vs. 16 says David was "leaping and whirling before the Lord."

Ps. 33:1-3 says, "Rejoice in the Lord, O you righteous! For praise from the upright is beautiful. Praise the Lord with the harp; Make melody to Him with an instrument of ten strings. Sing to Him a new song; Play skillfully with a shout of joy." A crippled man received a healing miracle and Acts 3:8,9 says, "So he, leaping up, stood and walked and entered the temple with them - walking, leaping, and praising God. And all the people saw him walking and praising God." These are all expressions of joy. Even Jesus said in the Beatitudes, "Blessed are you who weep now, for you shall laugh. Blessed are you when men hate you, and when they exclude you, and revile you, and cast out your name as evil, for the Son of Man's sake. Rejoice in that day and leap for joy! For indeed your reward is great in heaven." (Luke 6:21-23). If you will follow these examples and give expressions to your joy, there is no way the devil or anybody else can defeat you. That is good news.

Ps. 2:11 says, "Serve the Lord with fear, and rejoice with trembling." The Amplified Bible adds, "lest you displease Him." God does not want you down and depressed. He's the glory and the lifter of your head and it displeases Him when you don't give expression to joy. So be happy on purpose because you can't have strength without rejoicing. Joy has nothing to do with how you feel so don't wait for some emotion to bring you goosebumps. Paul said in Rom. 5:3 that we are to "glory in tribulations" and the Amplified Bible says to do it "NOW!" The Message Bible says, "We continue to shout our praise even when we're hemmed in with troubles." Be joyful at all times! From a jail cell filled with raw sewage Paul wrote, "Rejoice in the Lord always. Again I say rejoice!" (Phil. 4:4). You must keep your joy, or you won't win your battle. You don't win being depressed or negative-minded. No, you win by being filled with the joy of the Lord. Job 5:22 says, "You shall laugh at destruction and famine, and you shall not be afraid of the beasts of the earth."

You laugh so you don't lose your joy. Laughter releases joy and joy is a spiritual force that makes you unafraid of what the enemy can do to you. It gives you the courage to run through a troop and leap over a wall. God shows up with power and might when you give expression to joy. And when God shows up, problems leave. Is. 64:5 says, "For since the beginning of the world men have not heard or perceived by the ear, nor has the eye seen any God besides You, Who acts for the one who waits for Him. You meet him who rejoices and does righteousness." God will meet you where you're at when you rejoice and sing unto Him a song of joy. 1 Cor. 4:20 says "For the kingdom of God is not in word, but in power." Joy is a major spiritual force, and the joy of the Lord is your strength. Joy causes you to be "strengthened with might through His Spirit in the inner man" (Eph. 3:16) and this translates into having the ability to do anything. Phil. 1:25 talks about the "joy of faith." Trusting God should make you happy and full of good cheer. Faith is the dynamite that defeats the enemy, but joy is the fuse. Joy comes from having the confidence that your faith is working and this confidence comes from knowing God.

Paul wrote in 2 Tim. 1:12, "For I know whom I have believed and am persuaded that He is able to keep what I have committed to Him until that day." Paul was fully persuaded because he knew God. Knowing God comes from fellowship with Him on a daily basis and fellowship in turn produces fullness of joy. A wealth of spiritual might and power to overcome the enemy is available to you through the joy of the Lord. Understand that joy is not the same thing as happiness. Happiness is a state of well-being and contentment. It is dependent upon the condition of the circumstances that surround you. If things are going good for you, you're happy. If they're not, you're not happy. Joy, on the other hand, has very little to do with how happy you are. You can be joyful in the midst of the most adverse circumstances. The joy of the Lord is one of the fruits of the Spirit (Gal. 5:22,23) and is the one fruit from which you get your strength. Joy is not a state of mind. It is a force that gives strength to all the other fruit. It is the strength of peace, long-suffering, gentleness, goodness, faith, meekness, and of temperance.

Your breakthrough doesn't come when the storm clouds pass from over your head. No, it comes when you learn to sing and dance in the rain. Joy will cause you to have a proper attitude when trials come your way. It will keep you out of self-pity so you can be strong in the Lord and the power of His might. Whatever circumstances you face, you can always be full of the joy of the Lord. Be confident knowing that the devil can't oppose you with anything powerful enough to defeat you when you are walking in the joy of the Lord. Remember always that Jesus is everything! He's the origin of life, the essence of life, the aim of life, and the reward of life. In His presence is fullness of joy. And it is Jesus who will bless you every day of the week. In Him you'll have a happy Monday, a blessed Tuesday, a joyful Wednesday, a delightful Thursday, a good Friday, a glorious Saturday, and a heavenly Sunday. This is what your life will be like when you sing to the Lord a new song, a song of joy.

| 23 |

"THE EVIDENCE OF FAITH"

The only thing required of the church today is faith. Everything you will ever want or need was purchased for you
by Jesus on the cross, but it takes faith to receive those provi-
sions and blessings. Nothing in or of yourself allows you to
earn God's grace and favor, it's all based on what you believe.
Is. 53:1 says, "Who has believed our report? And to whom has
the arm of the Lord been revealed?" To believe the report of
what Jesus did for you is to have the grace of God revealed in
your life. It matters not how good you are, what matters is
whether or not you believe the report. Do you believe that all
the promises of God are Yes and in Him Amen? Do you believe
that by Jesus' stripes you are healed? God will not force you to
believe Him, you must believe Him willingly. You need to trust
Him with all your heart and soul and then take your life and all
your needs and concerns and place them in the nail-scarred
hands of Jesus. 1 Peter 5:7 says "casting all your cares upon Him,
for He cares for you."

You need to spend quality time alone with God every day. When you are in the presence of Jesus, His love rubs off on you and His faith rubs off on you as well. When trials come you will know what to do because you are in the presence of the source of every blessing. Jesus will never leave you or forsake you and to be in His presence is faith itself. The power of the Lion of Judah is in you and when you walk in faith the chains of bondage will be broken. His love never fails and neither does His faith. When the Bible says you need the God-kind of faith, it's talking about the faith God uses to heal all your diseases and solve all your problems. If God is going to heal you, then He must have faith that He can do it. He has faith for every miracle you need and when you base your faith on His faith, all things will be possible for you. You are now to rest in His faith for when you do that, the life and faith that is in the Vine will flow to the branches.

Without Jesus you can do nothing. He is the author and fin-isher of your faith (Heb. 12:2). The NLT Bible says Jesus is "the champion who initiates and perfects our faith." This means that He will breathe His faith into you. His faith becomes your faith and since nothing is impossible to Him, nothing will be impossible to you. Matt. 9:27-31 tells the story of two blind men who came to Jesus wanting to be healed. The Lord asked them, "Do you believe that I am able to do this?" Everything Jesus did was by faith so this question could also be asked, "Do you believe that I have faith to do this?" When they said "Yes, Lord" Jesus touched their eyes and said, "According to your faith let it be to you." According to their faith in what? Ac-cording to their faith in His faith. The faith of Jesus is what they based their faith on and this is what got their sight restored. Jesus said in John 15:5 (NLT), "For apart from Me you can do nothing." Like these two blind men, you must learn to base your faith on His faith and when you do that the struggle is over.

The disciples had once fished all night and caught nothing but when Jesus told them to cast their net on the right side of the boat they obeyed and caught a great multitude of fish (John 21:6). Jesus later said to them, "Bring some of the fish which you have just caught" (vs. 10). Jesus performed the miracle but He gave the disciples credit for catching the fish. What this means is that your faith is connected to His miracle-working faith. This is why He says "According to your faith be it done unto you." You must have faith that He is able to do what you ask Him to do. It is the power of His faith that makes Him able and this is what you base your faith on. It's His faith but He gives you the credit by saying "According to your faith." In His eyes your faith and His faith are one and the same. This is all well and good but never get puffed up thinking you have great faith to move mountains. It's not your faith, it's His faith working in you. If He didn't give you the faith, you wouldn't have any faith to use. And when you do use the faith He gives you, He will reward you by giving you everything you ask for. How wonderful is that?

After Jesus fed the multitude people came to Him and asked, "What shall we do that we may work the works of God?" Jesus answered and said, "This is the work of God, that you believe in Him whom He sent" (John 6:28,29). In other words, the

Lord and His faith must be involved in everything you do. Vs. 66 then says, "From that time many of His disciples went back and walked with Him no more." Why did this happen? They wanted to do the works of God on their own, independent of Him. This is foolishness to the highest degree. God will not give you something of such great value so you can go off and be independent of Him. To be cut off from the way, the truth, and the life is to fall into the snare of the evil one. Works of the flesh is when people try to do God's job with their own power and ability and it is impossible to accomplish anything worthwhile this way. No, you need God involved in everything you do. You must rest in His faith that never wavers and never fails. You will know when your faith is in Him because there will be a rest that you will enter into.

Gal. 3:29 says, "And if you are Christ's, then you are Abraham's seed, and heirs according to the promise." If you are born again, the same blessings God gave to Abraham are yours because you are Abraham's seed. You are heirs according to the same promise. Rom. 4:13 says, "For the promise that he would be the heir of the world was not to Abraham or to his seed through the law, but through the righteousness of faith." God will make you healthy because you can't be the heir of the world if you get sick and die an early death. God will make you prosperous because if you're not rich you also can't be heir of the world. These blessings are through the righteousness of faith. It's called that because the only way you can know you're righteous is by faith. You don't need faith to know you're sinful because you already know that. In spite of what your conscience tells you, or your spouse or anybody else, you can know in your heart that you are righteous in God's eyes. It is the just and righteous who live by faith (Heb. 10:38).

God demands righteousness from spiritually bankrupt people who can't become righteous on their own. It is for this reason that His grace was poured out on you when you got born again. You are saved by grace (Eph. 2:5) and it is by faith in what Jesus did that you become the righteousness of God in Christ Jesus (2 Cor. 5:21). God says that you are the heir of the world and this promise is to be received by faith and not human effort. You do not receive this promise by keeping the ten commandments but rather by the righteousness of faith which is described in Rom. 4;20-22, "He did not waver at the promise of God through unbelief, but was strengthened in faith, giving glory to God, and being fully convinced that what He had promised He was also able to perform. And therefore 'it was accounted to him for righteousness.'" If you are required to work for the blessings of God then He will give it as a debt He owes to you. God is God and He will be in debt to no man. This is why all the promises of God are yours to freely receive through Christ's finished work on the cross.

People miss the mark when they try to please God with good behavior and by keeping the ten commandments. Heb. 11:6 says "without faith it is impossible to please God." When Jesus walked the earth there were only two people in whom He said was great faith, the Roman centurion and the Shulamite woman. What these two people had in common was that they were both Gentiles. They did not know the ten commandments and were not conscious of sin. They were Jesus conscious and this is why they had great faith. In Holland an experiment was done in a small city where they removed all the street signs. The drivers were no longer told what to do and what not to do. The only thing they relied on was common sense and in two years time not a single accident occurred. This is what grace does for you. It removes sin consciousness and magnifies the favor and goodness of God. People speed and break the rules of the road because they are rebellious and walk in the flesh. But where there is no law, there is no transgression (Rom. 4:15).

You are to cease from your own labor and rest in the knowledge that you are the apple of His eye and that He cares for you. God's grace is on you, in you, and will work through you. When you see God in His grace, He will see you in your faith. It is then that you will be well pleasing in His eyes and this is when He will do exceedingly, abundantly above all you could ask or think. The woman with the issue of blood did not think about how much faith she had but instead focused on the grace of Jesus. She thought about how good and wonderful He is and how powerful He is. She thought about how willing He was to use that power on her behalf. Her comprehension of Him was so large that she believed all she had to do was touch the very hem of His garment and she would be healed. It happened just as she believed it would and Jesus turned around and said, "Be of good cheer, daughter; your faith has made you well" (Matt. 9:22). In all the gospels this is the only person Jesus called "daughter." She saw His grace; He saw her faith.

It is of vital importance that you understand how faith works. Just before the Passover, God told the people to kill a lamb without blemish and put its blood "on the two doorposts and on the lintel of the houses where they eat at" (Ex. 12:7). This blood was on the outside of the house. It wasn't there for the people to see, it was there for God to see (vs. 13). Likewise, your faith is not for you to see, your faith is for Him to see. Your part is to see His grace, His part is to see your faith. This is God's pattern for you to receive. If you are born-again, God does not see you, He sees your faith in the blood of Jesus. Acts 17:28 says "for in Him we live and move and have our being." God does not deal with you based on who you are, He deals with you based on your Savior and on the merit of His perfect work. If you want to know how rich you are, find out how rich Jesus is. If you want to know how healthy you are, find out how healthy Jesus is. Whatever He is, so are you in the eyes of God.

You receive your miracle when you rest and believe. This is the kind of faith God is pleased with. It brought health and wealth to Abraham and it will do the same to you. Rom. 4:16 says, "Therefore it is of faith that it might be according to grace, so that the promise might be sure to all the seed, not only to those who are of the law, but also to those who are of the faith of Abraham, who is the father of us all." In order for God's blessings to "be sure" in your life it must be by grace through faith. It is not based on how good you are, it is based on how good He is. Most people are not living like they're the heir of the world because they're trying to obtain the blessings through human effort and good behavior. Yes, a holy lifestyle is important. Jesus did say in Matt. 5:16, "Let your light so shine before men, that they may see your good works and glorify your Father in heaven." Just remember that you are justified by faith and good behavior is the fruit of right believing. You can take heart knowing that you never have to struggle or strive to make good things happen to you.

The pastor of a large church told how one day the burdens of life and the ministry were bearing down on him so he decided to go jogging to help relieve some of the stress. It was the fall season and the route he was on brought him to a park where all the trees were dropping their colorful leaves in majestic splendor. It was a sight to behold so the pastor stopped running so he could take it all in. He then decided to try to catch one of the falling leaves so he jumped and stretched and did everything he could but the light breeze kept blowing them out of his reach. Becoming more determined he tried harder and harder to catch one to no avail and frustration began to set in. He stopped his efforts and stood still for a moment when something on the inside of him told him to stick out his hand with his palm upward. He obeyed and in almost no time at all a single leaf fell and landed dead center in the palm of his hand. He stood there amazed and down in his heart he heard God say, "Be still, and know that I am God" (Ps. 46:1).

God's grace is supernatural power that comes to you free of charge when you believe and it enables you to do with ease what you could never do with struggle and effort. You can't work hard enough to earn God's grace and favor. The first place where grace is mentioned in the Bible is Gen. 6:8, "But Noah found grace in the eyes of the Lord." The name "Noah" means 'rest' and to say that Noah found grace is to say that rest found grace. If you are working then there can be no grace. Luke 2:40 says about Jesus, "And the Child grew and became strong in spirit, filled with wisdom; and the grace of God was upon Him." Jesus lived a life of rest and this is why He said in John 5:19, "Most assuredly, I say to you, the Son can do nothing of Himself, but what He sees the Father do; for whatever He does, the Son also does in like manner." Jesus was busy all the time but He lived a life of rest. He was never rushed and was never in a hurry. He was relaxed in everything He did because He had a faith that rests and a faith that believes.

Resting in God does not mean you get lazy and do nothing for the kingdom. On the contrary, resting in God will make you more vibrant and energetic than you've even been before. What it means is that you are trusting Him to do the work through you. No longer do you rely on human effort but in the living God who created the heavens and the earth. Jesus said in Matt. 11:28, "Come to Me, all you who labor and are heavy laden, and I will give you rest." In other words, enjoy the journey of life. Relax, lighten up and don't be so rigid. Receive grace and mercy to help in time of need. The Message Bible says, "Are you tired? Worn out? Burned out on religion? Come to Me. Get away with Me and you'll recover your life. I'll show you how to take a real rest. Walk with Me and work with Me - watch how I do it. Learn the unforced rhythms of grace. I won't lay anything heavy or ill-fitting on you. Keep company with Me and you'll learn to live freely and lightly." That is an offer you can't refuse.

Jesus said if you'll only but come to Him, He will lead you out of frustration and doubt and into the land of rest and belief. Of all the things He could have said He would give you, Jesus chose to say He will give you rest. The children of Israel angered God in the wilderness with all their murmuring and complaining. They refused to find rest in Him so God said, "So I swore in My wrath, 'They shall not enter My rest'" (Heb. 3:11). There was rest in the promised land, a land that flowed with milk and honey. God described this rest in Josh. 24:13 when He said, "I have given you a land for which you did not labor, and cities which you did not build, and you dwell in them; you eat of the vineyards and olive groves which you did not plant." The promised land for the believer today is rest. It's a land of health and prosperity but God doesn't call it that. He calls it a land of rest. It's a land where you cease from all your labor brought about by human effort.

Do not seek after health and prosperity, seek after rest. This does not mean you take a nap all day but rather is a rest given by God. Jesus said, "I will give you rest." His presence will rest you. Knowing that He loves you and cares for you will give you rest. The Hebrew word for "healing" means 'relax' so if you want to get well then seek His rest. God said in Is. 30:15, "In returning and rest you shall be saved; In quietness and confidence shall be your strength." The same Hebrew word for "strength" is found in Ps. 90:10, "The days of our lives are seventy years; And if by reason of strength they are eighty years." The more you rest in God, the more you will prolong your life. The average lifespan of a lion in the wild is ten years but in a zoo the average lifespan is twenty years. It goes through much stress to hunt down its prey in the wild and this shortens its lifespan. But in a zoo its food is provided for him. The stress is gone, he rests more, and he prolongs his life.

Scientific studies show that stress causes premature aging and if you use up the strength allotted to you too fast and too soon, you will die an early death. Women live an average five to eight years longer than men because they're not as stressed out as men are. Men carry their burdens on their shoulders whereas women find relief from stress by walking the dog and going shopping. God wants to satisfy you with a long life (Ps. 91:16) and this is why He wants you to slow down and enter His rest. He said in Is. 28:16, "Behold, I lay in Zion a stone for a foundation, a tried stone, a precious cornerstone, a sure foundation; Whoever believes will not act hastily." Paul quoted from this verse in Rom. 9:33 and said, "And whoever believes on Him will not be put to shame." When you don't make haste, you will not be put to shame. Faith rests and when you believe in God you won't set a frantic pace for yourself. Fast food is bad for you but meat cooked slowly on a grill is better for you. Stop being in such a hurry all the time. Slow down. Be still and know He is God.

David wrote in Ps. 23:2, "He makes me to lie down in green pastures; He leads me beside the still waters." He later wrote in vs. 4, "Yea, though I walk through the valley of the shadow of death, I will fear no evil for You are with me." This verse is a source of great comfort but it only applies when you dwell beside the still waters. It is when you are in a peaceful calm that you come under the protection of God and receive from Him divine direction. Jesus is called the "Prince of Peace" (Is. 9:6) and the word "peace" means 'a deep, inner silence.' The rest of God is spiritual warfare and if you're peaceful on the inside you can be peaceful on the outside. 1 Peter 3:4 says that a quiet spirit is very precious in the sight of God. To remain calm and not panic in times of adversity is a sign that you are wholly trusting God for your breakthrough. You are not walking in faith unless you come to a place where there is no anxiety, no worry, no frets, no looking at circumstances, and no feeling of being overwhelmed by the impossibilities of life. Is. 26:3 says, "You will keep him in perfect peace whose mind is stayed on You, because He trusts in You."

Resting in God is the evidence of faith and it is faith alone that will see you through the trial. You enter into rest because you're no longer struggling, murmuring, and complaining. You are committed to God, your soul is at rest, and you are no longer trying to figure everything out. There is a quiet assurance on the inside of you, a spiritual peace. A heavenly tranquility gives you relief and freedom from anything that worries, troubles and disturbs you. If you're going to walk by faith you have to forever remove from your vocabulary the questions "Why?" and "When?" You have to trust God completely and resist the temptation to tell God how to fix your problem. A powerful life is one that can face and deal with whatever happens in life and still remain the same. A calm spirit destroys evil. It's how you win the battle. It's how you have breakthrough in your life. The prophet Isaiah knew something about entering into the rest of God. Is. 7:4 says, "Take heed, and be quiet; do not fear or be fainthearted."

No matter what's going on, always stay calm during your storm. Don't let the devil scare you. Paul says in Phil. 1:28 that we are to be "not in any way terrified by your adversaries, which is to them a proof of perdition, but to you of salvation, and that from God." The Message Bible says we are "not flinching or dodging in the slightest before the opposition. Your courage and unity will show them what they're up against: defeat for them, victory for you - and both because of God." Staying calm is a sign that the devil is defeated. This is why you need to be addicted to peace. It is part of the armor of God (Eph. 6:15) and Phil. 4:7 says "the peace of God, which passes all understanding, will guard your hearts and minds through Christ Jesus." The Message Bible says, "Don't fret or worry. Instead of worrying, pray. Let petitions and praises shape your worries into prayers, letting God know your concerns. Before you know it, a sense of God's wholeness, everything coming together for good, will come and settle you down. It's wonderful what happens when Christ displaces worry at the center of your life."

God is called "the God of peace" (Phil. 4:9) and Is. 41:10 says, "Fear not, for I am with you; Be not dismayed, for I am your God. I will strengthen you, yes, I will help you, I will uphold you with My righteous right hand." Col. 3:15 says, "And let the peace of God rule in your heart." Satan sets you up to try to get you upset. When you're upset you are not able to walk and flow in the anointing that is necessary to fulfill your call. Thankfully, the God of peace gives you peace that passes all understanding. He leads you beside the still waters. It is there that He'll speak to you and give you divine direction. God told Elijah, "'Go out, and stand on the mountain before the Lord.' And behold, the Lord passed by, and a great and strong wind tore into the mountains and broke the rocks in pieces before the Lord, but the Lord was not in the wind; and after the wind an earthquake, but the Lord was not in the earthquake; and after the earthquake a fire, but the Lord was not in the fire; and after the fire a still small voice" (1 Kings 19:11-13).

God speaks in a soft, delicate whisper and you must be peaceful and still in order to hear it. When you get still, He speaks, and what He says will reveal to you that He indeed is God. If you don't follow God as He leads you beside the still waters, you'll never go any further in your walk with the Lord. So many people want God to listen to them but they don't want to slow down to the point where they can listen to Him. This is sad because the secret things belong to God (Deut. 29:29) and He reveals them to you in a whisper, a gentle stillness. 1 Thess. 4:11 says to study to lead a quiet life. Why does Paul say this? So you can hear from God! Prov. 4:20 says, "My sons, give attention to my words; Incline your ear to my sayings." You are to incline your ear and not engage your mouth. It is hard to listen if you're always talking. Yes, God reveals secrets but in order to hear what they are you must first get quiet. Be still, calm down, have peace, keep quiet and know that He is God. David wrote in Ps. 29:11, "The Lord will give strength to His people; The Lord will bless His people with peace."

There is strength to be found when you dwell beside the still waters. Ps. 119:165 says, "Great peace have those who love Your law, and nothing causes them to stumble." Peace is a place of protection. If you will remain peaceful in the time of adversity the devil can't touch you. It renders him ineffective. Ps. 94:12,13 says, "Blessed is the man whom You instruct, O Lord, and teach out of Your law, that You may give him rest from the days of adversity, until the pit is dug for the wicked." Stop looking for solutions all the time. Be still and let God work on your problem. Stay cool, calm, and collected. Before you do anything wait on God and give Him an opportunity to lead you beside the still waters. Waiting on God means you're expecting Him to do something. Expect Him to move at any minute. Look for and long for Him to provide for you the victory that only He can give. Get excited and stay excited for what God has planned for your life. Get out of bed and say, "Something good is going to happen to me today." If you remain hopeful, and get still before the Lord, then you can be sure that He will do something special for you.

God is waiting, looking, and longing to show favor to those who are waiting, looking, and longing for Him. Ps. 25:1-3 records these words of David, a man who was led beside the still waters, "To You, O Lord, I lift up my soul. O my God, I trust in You; Let me not be ashamed; Let not my enemies triumph over me. Indeed, let no one who waits on You be ashamed; Let those be ashamed who deal treacherously without cause." It is important to understand that having the peace of God in your heart does not mean that all your problems will instantly go away. No, peace is not the absence of conflict but instead is the presence of God in your life. Jesus said in John 14:27, "Peace I leave with you, My peace I give to you; not as the world gives do I give to you. Let not your heart be troubled, neither let it be afraid." Why does Jesus want you to dwell in His peace? Because peace precedes power!! Jesus was sleeping peacefully in the boat while the storm raged around Him. When awakened by the fearful disciples He had the power to calm the storm. He said, "Peace! Be still!" (Mark 4:39). Jesus had authority over the storm because He had peace in the storm.

Everything you do should be centered around peace. Matt. 10:1 says, "And when He had called His twelve disciples to Him, He gave them power over unclean spirits, to cast them out, and to heal all kinds of sickness and all kinds of disease." Jesus gave them power to perform mighty miracles but notice what He said in vs. 11,12, "And when you go into a household, greet it. If the household is worthy, let your peace come upon it. But if it is not worthy, let your peace return to you." In other words, peace precedes power! This is why God wants you to have peace in the midst of the storm. It is wonderful to have a problem and not have to care or worry about it. So learn to enter into the rest of God. For sure, there is not a more wonderful place to be. Moses knew that peace precedes power. When the Egyptian army was closing in on the children of Israel he said, "Do not be afraid. Stand still, and see the salvation of the Lord, which He will accomplish for you today. For the Egyptians whom you see today, you shall see again no more forever. The Lord will fight for you, and you shall hold your peace" (Ex. 14:13,14).

Moses was saying to be still, firm, confident, and not dismayed. He said to hold your peace and remain at rest. This tells God that you're trusting Him. The battle is the Lord's and Rom.

16:20 says, "And the God of peace will crush Satan under your feet." Ps. 34:14 says, "Seek peace, and pursue it." Stop trying to figure everything out. Instead, "Trust in the Lord with all your heart, and lean not on your own understanding; In all your ways acknowledge Him, and He shall direct your paths" (Prov. 3:5,6). At the Red Sea God told Moses, "Why do you cry to Me? Tell the children of Israel to go forward." Direction came when they got still and held their peace. God can do in a single moment what you can't do in fifty years. So why try? Instead, lie down in green pastures and rest beside the still waters. Be peaceful on purpose. Seek, pursue, and crave peace as a vital necessity to your well-being. Is. 40:31 says, "But those who wait on the Lord shall renew their strength; They shall mount up with wings as eagles, they shall run and not be weary, they shall walk and not faint."

Consider also what David said in Ps. 62:1,2, "Truly my soul silently waits for God; From Him comes my salvation. He only is my rock and my salvation; He is my defense; I shall not be greatly moved." Strength comes when you silently wait on God beside the still waters. Ps. 33:20-22 says, "Our soul waits for the Lord; He is our help and our shield. For our heart shall rejoice in Him, because we have trusted in His holy name. Let Your mercy, O Lord, be upon us, just as we hope in You." Wait hopefully and put your trust in God. Get passionate once again with your faith. Let a holy fervor rise up on the inside of you. Refuse to live without passion and enthusiasm. Get white hot for God. Fan your flame and don't let the fire go out. Rest beside the still waters and give God everything you've got and do it with passion. God put a need and a desire in your heart for freshness, so don't let the things of God in your life get dull and stale. Instead, stir yourself up and get out of the boat. Take a risk and watch what God will do.

| 24 |

"THE DIRECTION OF FAITH"

E verything about God and your walk with Him is progres-
sive. What looks big to you today should not look big to
you next year. In the process of time, what now looks huge will
one day look normal. Every day that you're with the Lord you
are consistently moving forward. Your faith is increasing and
your joy is increasing and your peace is increasing. Never are
you to reach a point where you want to set up camp and go
forward no more. Every day you should be moving and getting
closer to God and being even more led by the Holy Spirit.
Never be satisfied where you're currently at. Always be content
but never be satisfied. There are huge clusters of grapes waiting for you in the promised land and you want to eat each and
every one of them. For that to happen, you must keep going
forward and cross over to the other side. Don't settle for second best but keep striving to receive everything Jesus died to
give you. You need to forget the past and keep your eyes focused on the glorious future that awaits you.

In life you never stay stationary. You're either moving forward or you're moving backward. Prov. 14:14 says, "The backslider in heart will be filled with his own way." Doing your own thing and operating in your own ways will cause you to go backward in life. True believers don't wake up in the morning and decide to openly rebel against God. No, it's subtle. Little by little they do things and make decisions on their own without seeking the Lord's counsel. They know they shouldn't watch a certain television program but they watch it anyway. They know they should go pray but decide to go have fun with their friends instead. They let this slide and that slide when, suddenly, they realize they're not as spiritual as they were the month before. This doesn't mean they hate God and that they're bad people. It's just that for a certain season in their life they wanted to do things their own way. They trusted in themselves more than they trusted in God and this caused them to backslide in their relationship with Him and in their effectiveness in His kingdom.

David wrote in Ps. 20:7,8, "Some trust in chariots, and some in horses; But we will remember the name of the Lord our God. They have bowed down and fallen; But we have risen and stand upright." Who is your source? You find out by seeing who you run to during a time of need. Will you look to the arm of the flesh for help or the hand of God? Is. 31:1 says, "Woe to those who go down to Egypt for help, and rely on horses, who trust in chariots because they are many, and in horsemen because they are strong, but who do not look to the Holy One of Israel, nor seek the Lord!" It's important what you put your trust in and who you look to. God said in Jer. 17:5,6, "Cursed is the man who trusts in man and makes flesh his strength, whose heart departs from the Lord. For he shall be like a shrub in the desert, and shall not see when good comes." He then said in vs. 7,8, "Blessed is the man who trusts in the Lord, and whose hope is the Lord. For he shall be like a tree planted by the waters, which spreads out its roots by the river, and will not fear when heat comes."

You need to reach a point where if you can't believe for something by faith, then you don't want it in your life. Yes, God's will is for you to be rich and prosperous but never use money as a substitute for faith. 1 Tim. 6:17 says, "Command those who are rich in this present age not to be haughty, nor to trust in uncertain riches but in the living God, who gives us richly all things to enjoy." Faith needs to be exercised and if you are in a position where you can buy everything you need then your faith will lie dormant and eventually fade away. You need to lay your finances aside and use your faith even if you have the money to buy what you want with cash. You need to know that there are many things that money can't buy. It can buy you a new car but it won't do you much good if the medical report says you have cancer or if your spouse asks for a divorce. There will come a time when faith in God will be the only solution to your problem and, if it hasn't been used and exercised on a continual basis, it won't be there when you need it the most.

It is not wrong to have horses and chariots, to have tanks and fighter jets. And for sure it is a good thing to have a bank account that is full and overflowing. God will bless you with all these things but your trust is not to be in the possessions He graciously gives you, your faith is to be in Him and Him alone. Trusting in things other than God causes you to go backward but operating in God's ways causes you to go forward. Problems arise when you stop walking in faith and start walking by sight. This is truly a matter of life and death. God is faithful and is forever endeavoring to get people to go down the right path. The problem is that people are not listening to His voice because they're trying to do things their own way. God is telling people everywhere to not go back but to go forward in their walk with Him. God is doing a new thing and He doesn't want you to go back to the way you used to do things. He wants you to do things His way and not your own. Walk in the light you have and put your hand to the plow and don't look back.

God is a God of increase which means His plan and will for your life is on the increase as well. Prov. 4:18 says, "But the path of the just is like the shining sun, that shines ever brighter unto the perfect day." Jesus is the light of the world and, if you're not progressing in your walk with Him, you're not on the path you should be on. It is His will for your love for Him and others to increase. It is His will for your faith to grow exceedingly. It is His will for you to have more influence in the world than you've ever had before. Increase is the evidence that God is blessing your life. Ps. 115:14,15 says, "May the Lord give you increase more and more, you and your children. May you be blessed by the Lord, Who made heaven and earth." Increase in every good thing is always the will of God. He wants you to go forward and not backward in everything you do. This is not automatic and it will not happen on its own. It will take a deep-seated commitment from you to submit to God's plan for your life and to always do what He tells you to do.

Not everybody obeys God and not everybody is blessed by Him. Jer. 7:24 says, "Yet they did not obey nor incline their ear, but walked in the counsels and in the imagination of their evil heart, and went backward and not forward." You must highly esteem the things of God and consider them of great value. If you don't, you will begin to look back at the things of the world and go in the opposite direction of where you should be going. God wants you to go forward, not backward. Jesus said in Luke 9:62, "No one, having put his hand to the plow, and looking back, is fit for the kingdom of God." The Message Bible says, "No procrastination. No backward looks. You can't put God's kingdom off till tomorrow. Seize the day." In the kingdom of God and the walk of faith there is no turning back. There is a price to pay to go forward in the things of God and, if you're not willing to pay that price, Jesus says you're not fit for the kingdom of God. You've got to be willing to make some sacrifices. The value of something is based on the sacrifices you're willing to make to get it. Jesus died for you. Are you willing to do the same for Him?

Your future with God is better than your past in the world. Going forward in God's plan is better than where you are right now and better than where you've been. To go where you've never been before takes a willingness to put one foot in front of the other and never look back. It takes faith to do this but you can have the assurance that as you move forward God will direct your steps. To receive your miracle and fulfill your destiny there is only one direction you can go and that's forward. Joshua and Caleb wanted to go forward into the promised land while the rest of the children of Israel wanted to go back to Egypt. They preferred slavery along with its fish and melons above the land flowing with milk and honey. They weren't looking at the light in front of them that gets brighter and brighter. No, they looked at the darkness behind them and, the farther back they looked, the darker it became. Their minds were clouded and wrong decisions were made. Eventually they all died in the wilderness and never did enter in.

One of the worst things in life you could ever do is look back. When the angels rescued Lot and his family from Sodom and Gomorrah, they took them outside the city and said, "Escape for your life! Do not look behind you nor stay anywhere in the plain. Escape to the mountain, lest you be destroyed" (Gen. 19:17). The angels told them to leave and not look back. Lot should have obeyed immediately with no hesitation but he didn't. He reasoned with his rescuers, asking permission to go to a smaller city that was nearby instead of going all the way to the mountains. In his heart he had an unholy attachment to these evil cities. He didn't want to let go of them. He knew the place was evil but at the same time there were some things he liked about it. Little did he know that "a little leaven leavens the whole lump" (Gal. 5:9). 1 Cor. 15:33 says, "Do not be deceived: 'Evil company corrupts good habits.'" Sodom and Gomorrah were not a good place to be but still the angelic messengers gave Lot permission to go to the nearby city of Zoar. Not long after he arrived the two cities were destroyed with fire and brimstone.

This should have been the end of the story but it isn't. Gen. 19:26 says, "But his wife looked back behind him, and became a pillar of salt." Deut. 29:23 (NIV) tells how fire and brimstone includes the ingredients of salt and sulfur. Lot's wife became what she was longing for. The cities were becoming salt and sulfur and she became the same thing. She became what she looked at. Luke 17:32,33 says, "Remember Lot's wife. Whoever seeks to save his life will lose it, and whoever loses his life will preserve it." Jesus is telling you to remember Lot's wife so you won't do what she did. There will be times when He will tell you to turn loose of some things and not look back. It is God's will for you to move forward for that is the direction faith moves in. Lot's wife didn't look back because she was curious and wanted to see what was happening. No, she looked back because that's where her heart was and it was tearing her apart on the inside to leave. She wouldn't lose herself from the snare of the city and, the same thing that happened to it, happened to her.

Matt. 6:21 says, "For where your treasure is, there your heart will be also." The heart of Lot's wife was in Sodom and Gomorrah even as the cities were being destroyed. There was nothing to go back to even if she could. Still, she wouldn't turn loose of what was in her heart and she paid for it with her life. 1 John 2:15 says, "Do not love the world or the things in the world. If anyone loves the world, the love of the Father is not in him." It is wrong to love anything that is ungodly and does not line up with the Word of God. 1 Peter 3:3 says, "Do not let your beauty be that outward adorning and arranging the hair, of wearing gold, or of putting on fine apparel." The

Greek word for "adorning" is the same Greek word for "world" and, while there is nothing wrong with looking nice, you can't get caught up in the glitz and glamour of the unsaved world. This is what happened to Lot's wife. She loved the city and the life that was there. She loved the looseness and the absence of moral restraints that allowed people to do as they pleased. This is how she wanted to live.

James 4:4 says, "Adulterers and adulteresses! Do you not know that friendship with the world is enmity with God? Whoever therefore wants to be a friend of the world makes himself an enemy of God." The Message Bible says, "You're cheating on God. If all you want is your own way, flirting with the world every chance you get, you end up enemies of God and His way." You can't love and value the things of the ungodly world and love God at the same time. The two don't mix. You can't serve two masters. 1 John 2:16,17 says, "For all that is in the world - the lust of the flesh, the lust of the eyes, and the pride of life - is not of the Father but is of the world. And the world is passing away, and the lust of it; but he who does the will of God abides forever." Don't sacrifice your eternal security for the longings of this temporary world. The sinful pleasures the world enjoys today will be gone tomorrow but the things of God are eternal. Don't be like Lot's wife who looked back longing for the ways of the world, loving it more than loving God.

The Bible says that you are in the world but not of the world (John 17:16). You live a different life with higher standards than other people. You are a light in a dark world and you're supposed to stand out in a crowd, not blend in. Jesus is coming soon and "the form of this world is passing away" (1 Cor. 7:31). Time is of the essence so don't complicate your life unnecessarily. You may have some dealings in the world with people who are unsaved but don't get too engrossed in it. Don't get involved in the ungodliness of what's going on. If you close on a business deal, don't go out with your associates and get drunk to celebrate what happened. James 1:27 says you are to keep yourself "unspotted from the world." Keep things simple even in the ordinary daily routines of life. Deal as sparingly as possible with the things the world thrusts on you. Lot's wife didn't do this. She got engrossed by it all and it became a part of who she was. She loved the very things that God hates and became friends with His enemies. She embraced the spirit that was in Sodom and Gomorrah and it cost her dearly.

You have been justified by your faith in Jesus and the path you are on only gets brighter and brighter. As you move forward you are to experience more light and more glory and have more victories in your life. If you don't look back, things will keep getting better and better for you which is all part of the fulfillment of your destiny. Faith always looks forward and never draws back. It will help you beyond measure if you would grasp the reality of why you're here in the first place. You are here to reveal to God what you love and what you're willing to pursue with all your heart and soul. This life shows who you are and what you're made of, what's important to you and what isn't. The life you now live is your proving ground and it is preparing you for the next life. One of the most evil and diabolical things a person could ever say is "let's eat, drink, and be merry for tomorrow we die." They think this life is all there is but they are wrong, dead wrong. For sure, there is an afterlife and what you do in the here and now determines what happens to you when you cross over to the other side.

You have an entire lifetime to show God what He means to you. Still, there are millions of people who don't want God in their lives. They are "lovers of pleasure rather than lovers of God" (2 Tim. 3:4). They have no time for Him yet each day they stand on the very planet He made. Ps. 19:1 says, "The heavens declare the glory of God." Those stars are talking but people aren't listening. God makes it so easy to believe in Him yet millions have decided they don't want to believe. This is the only logical explanation for all the doubt and unbelief that is in the world. People can believe but have decided they don't want to. Yes, they'll believe the neighbor who gossips all the time but won't believe the words of the Bible. They'll believe some silly theory about how the universe was created but not the great God who spoke it into existence. The bottom line is that people believe only what they choose to believe and will not believe what they choose not to believe. The only reason they don't believe God is because they don't want to believe Him. How sad is that?

Daily you are given the opportunity to show God that you trust Him. In the Garden of Eden, Adam and Eve had such an opportunity but they failed the test. Gen. 3:6 says, "So when the woman saw that the tree was good for food, that it was pleasant to the eye, and a tree desirable to make one wise, she took of its fruit and ate. She also gave to her husband with her and he ate." The problem began because Eve was looking at the wrong thing. People think there's no harm in looking but it sure hurt Adam and Eve. It matters what you look at. Lot's wife looked back and it ended her life. Eve enjoyed what she looked at. It was appealing to her and pleasant to her eyes. She saw that it was a tree desirable to make one wise. Looking fuels desire which is the greatest motivational force in all the world. Desire is a force that moves you to obtain what you're looking at and longing for. The Bible says "seek and you shall find" whether it be good or evil. The sad news is that evil desires have replaced the righteous desires that all believers should have.

Eve looked at the fruit on the tree, and the more she looked at it, the more she wanted it. That desire moved her to obtain it and moments later both she and her husband committed a sin that has affected all of humanity ever since. Their actions proved they wanted to satisfy their fleshly desires more than they wanted to please God. They were willing to believe the lies of the cunning serpent more than the good God whom they had fellowship with on a regular basis. Believers today are not immune from these same temptations and this is why you need to get your priorities in order. Only desire the things God says you can have and look to Him and the glorious future He has planned for your life. If you are always looking at Him then you won't look at the wrong things. Jesus said in Matt. 5:6, "Blessed are those who hunger and thirst for righteousness, for they shall be filled." The Message Bible says, "You're blessed when you've worked up a good appetite for God. He's food and drink in the best meal you'll ever eat."

Don't look back. Stop longing for "the good ole days." When you do that you are walking in unbelief. Unbelief can't see good in the future and causes a person to believe their best days are behind them. Faith believes that the best is yet to come. Job 8:7 says, "Though your beginning was small, yet your latter end would increase abundantly." The path of the just gets brighter and brighter. In Christ, you have been promised a glorious future. Because of the finished work of Jesus, you don't have to be burdened by the mistakes of the past or the challenges you are currently facing. Jesus forgives every sin and overcomes every obstacle and, because of Him, your future is brighter than you could ever imagine. If you don't look back your future can be as bright as the morning sun. You can look forward to a life of freedom for days of abundant blessings and glorious hope await you. Jesus has provided everything you will ever need so get excited about all the good things He is going to do in your life as you move forward in faith.

You can't stay where you are. You're either increasing or decreasing, going forward or going back. God wants you to be bigger and stronger in Him than you've ever been before. This will happen when you put your flesh down and do things His way. God has a plan and a purpose for your life but a lot of what happens in your future depends on you. God told Abram to look around him and said in Gen. 13:15, "For all the land which you see I give to you and your descendants forever." He then said in vs 17, "Arise, walk in the land through its length and its width, for I give it to you." The Lord's guidelines for a bright future is that you've got to see something, then you've got to go get it. It's a good thing to dream big dreams, it's even better to live it out and walk in it. It takes courage to go after your dreams and a knowing that faith always goes forward. You have a divine destiny, an assignment from on high, but it won't happen on its own. You've got to rise up and go after it.

What does your future look like? What do you see? Jer. 1:11 says, "Moreover the word of the Lord came to me saying, 'Jeremiah, what do you see?' And I said, 'I see a branch of an almond tree.'" The Amplified Bible says this is "the emblem of alertness, activity, blossoming in late winter." Many people feel like they're living in the winter years of their life. It's cold outside, the trees are bare, and not much is happening. People feel they're past the point of doing much with their lives, much less serving the Lord. In the midst of all this God asked Jeremiah, "What do you see?" to which he responded, "I see new life. I see activity. I see growth." Change comes when you see the fresh blossoms of spring in the midst of your winter season. What do you see yourself doing at this same time next year? How about five years from now? Ten years? Jeremiah saw activity and alertness and vs. 12 says, "Then the Lord said to me. 'You have seen well, for I am ready to perform My word.'" The Message Bible says, "Good eyes! I'm sticking with you. I'll make every word I give you come true."

Prov. 29:18 says people perish and cast-off restraint when there is no vision. The Message Bible says, "If people can't see what God is doing, they stumble all over themselves; But when they attend to what He reveals, they are most blessed." When people have no vision for their future they get destroyed and ruined. Their lives begin to deteriorate and many die an early death.

Don't let this happen to you. Spend quality time with God, find out what He wants you to do with your life, and then go after it with everything you've got. Don't stop when trials come your way. Keep on keeping on. You must fight the good fight of faith and stand strong in the storm. You must face the wind and the cold and the darkness. When the storm blows you need to not run away but realize that God is teaching you to be strong. When you're strong you'll take one more step toward the top of the hill, toward the fulfillment of your destiny. When you walk forward in faith, the smallest step you take is stronger than the fiercest storm. Keep going no matter what's going on around you.

A good life is when you've always got something good to look forward to. Get excited about all the wonderful things God has planned for your future. Don't look back, look forward. Rom. 4:17 says God "gives life to the dead and calls those things which do not exist as though they did." As you press on in life and move forward God will take that barren winter season and fill it with all the wonderful sights and sounds of springtime. What was once dead is now alive. What was once barren is now fruitful. You've got a lot of living to do and God is going to use you in a powerful way. You serve a God who gives life to the dead. All things are possible with Him. God looks at your barren life and sees an abundance of fruit being produced. He sees you as an ambassador for Him. He sees you as the head and not the tail, above and not beneath. He sees the lives of other people being blessed beyond measure because they've been around you for just a little while. He sees you fulfilling your destiny. The question is, what do you see?

SUMMARY

The fight of faith is not for the timid or the easily shaken. It is for those who have made up their minds to stand firm on the promises of God no matter what comes against them. Life's storms are not meant to break you — they are meant to build you. Every gust of wind, every crashing wave, every dark cloud is an opportunity for your faith to prove its strength and your God to show His power.

When the enemy comes in, like a flood you must rise up like a warrior. When fear whispers, *"It's over,"* faith must thunder back, *"It's already won."* The Word of God must become your weapon, your defense, your foundation. You cannot fight this battle with feelings or emotions — you fight it with truth, with perseverance, and with unshakable confidence in the God who cannot fail.

To fight the good fight of faith means refusing to let go of your confession, no matter how fierce the storm becomes. It means standing when others fall, believing when others doubt, and pressing forward when everything in you wants to quit. It is not about comfort — it is about commitment. It is not about what you see — it is about what you *know*: that God is faithful, that His Word is true, and that His victory is certain.

So rise up, soldier of the cross. Strengthen your stance. Lift your shield of faith high and fix your eyes on the Author and Finisher of your faith. The storm may roar, but the Spirit within you roars louder. The darkness may press in, but the light of Christ within you cannot be extinguished.

You were not created to be tossed by the waves — you were created to command them. You were not called to run from the fight — you were called to win it. The same Spirit that raised Jesus from the dead lives inside you, and with Him, you are unstoppable.

This is your charge: Stand your ground. Speak the Word. Refuse to bow to fear. Endure the storm and fight until the victory manifests.

Because when the dust settles and the storm passes, it will not be the strength of the storm that is remembered — it will be the steadfastness of your faith. And through it all, Christ will be glorified in your endurance, your obedience, and your unwavering trust in Him.

So, take up your armor. Set your face like flint. Fight the good fight of faith — and never back down. The storm cannot take what God has already secured. The victory is yours. Stand firm and fight on.